Expanding Opportunities
and Building Competencies
for Young People
A New Agenda
for Secondary Education

THE WORLD BANK
Washington, D.C.

Contents

Figures

Tables

Foreword

Today, knowledge and skills increasingly hold the key to a gainful and productive future. But in many quarters young people languish without jobs, assailed by HIV/AIDS, drug abuse, and other predatory conditions of poverty. In our rapidly changing world the case for expanding the reach of secondary education in developing countries is beyond question. As this report makes clear, we must move from elitism, where a lucky few get the chance to go to secondary school and realize the dreams and rewards of higher education, to inclusiveness, where everyone gets the same chance to cross the bridge from primary education into a new realm of secondary learning, with university and the job market beckoning as distinct possibilities.

Secondary education is back on the agenda of developing countries, after a period of historical neglect. Far from being the weakest link in education systems, it is now emerging as the cornerstone of the transformational process of education. We in the World Bank have to acknowledge that over the past two decades our education strategy has given less attention to secondary education than to primary and tertiary education, and we are focusing anew on the important links between all levels of education.

Secondary education was long considered a priority only in middle-income countries, and only if they had already achieved universal access to primary education. A substantial turn in this long-standing trend came in 1995, when the strategic focus shifted from primary to basic education, a concept that encompasses the lower secondary school grades. In low-income and some middle-income countries this shift was accompanied by efforts to achieve Education for All (EFA) as part of the Millennium Development Goals (MDGs) for 2015. This has brought about a major change in the approach to secondary education: it is now viewed more as a necessary extension and upgrading of basic primary education than as the preparation of an elite for higher education.

Consequently, secondary education has taken on a mission of its own. Given its transformational ability to change lives for the better, it is little wonder that for young people all over the world, primary education is no longer enough. They need secondary education to give them the technical ability and the academic and life skills to make the most of their schooling and to contribute to their societies.

Secondary education is the highway between primary schooling, tertiary education, and the labor market. Its ability to connect the different destinations and to take young people where they want to go in life is crucial. Secondary education can act as a bottleneck, constricting the expansion of educational attainment and opportunity—or it can open up pathways for students' advancement.

Secondary education can also make a difference in improving the personal health of students and helping to protect them against HIV infection. There is now convincing evidence that young people in Africa who complete basic education are at reduced risk of HIV/AIDS, and this effect is even stronger for those who complete secondary education. Paradoxically, the secondary education system, which is the source of this "social vaccine," is itself being destroyed by HIV/AIDS in many African countries, through the increased mortality and absenteeism of teachers. Ensuring the supply of education therefore implies a need for special efforts to protect both teachers and the young people now in secondary school who are the teachers of the future.

Providing quality secondary education to young people not only opens up more opportunities and aspirations; it can also build tolerance and trust among a group of people whose informed citizenship is crucial to the formation and maintenance of cohesive, open societies. In addition to fostering the qualities of engaged citizenship in today's young people, secondary education can reduce the likelihood that youngsters will engage in risky or asocial behaviors. This effect has important benefits for society.

In a global development community where gains and successes are always hard-won, providing youngsters with a dynamic education that takes them from basic through secondary to tertiary education and beyond and that helps spur economic growth is surely one of the best investments a country can make, especially when it applies equally to girls and boys. The challenges are twofold: to increase access to secondary schooling for all young people and, at the same time, to improve the quality and relevance of secondary education.

Although governments are expected to finance the compulsory phase of secondary education, families and communities should play a more active role in financing the postcompulsory phase. In addition, public-private partnerships, complemented by the collaborative endeavors of multilateral and bilateral partners, can contribute in an important way to making mass secondary education affordable.

This report, *Expanding Opportunities and Building Competencies for Young People: A New Agenda for Secondary Education*, sets forth evidence-based, "tried and true" policy options for decision makers. The findings and suggestions presented are intended to help developing countries and transition economies adapt their secondary education systems to the demands arising from the successful expansion of primary education, the social and economic challenges presented by globalization, and the dizzying pace of the knowledge-based economy.

Jean-Louis Sarbib
Senior Vice President
Human Development Network
The World Bank

Acknowledgments

This report was prepared by a team led by Ernesto Cuadra and Juan Manuel Moreno and including Luis Crouch, author of chapter 7, Yidan Wang, Dina Abu-Ghaida, and Shobhana Sosale. Additional contributions were made by Thomas Welsh, Gwang-Jo Kim, Irene Psifidou, Yoko Nagashima, Yoshiko Koda, Donald Bundy, and Phillip Hay. The team was assisted by Fahma Nur and Ines Kudo. Special thanks are due to Inosha Wickramasekera for her assistance in the production of the final version of the document and to Veronica Grigera of Education Advisory Services and Lianqin Wang and Saida Mamedova of Education Statistics (EdStats) for their timely and indispensable support. The work was carried out under the general direction of Jean-Louis Sarbib, senior vice president of the World Bank's Human Development Network, and under the immediate supervision of Ruth Kagia, director of education, and Jamil Salmi, interim director of education.

An external advisory group provided initial guidance and contributed valuable comments that assisted in shaping the messages of the report. Its members were Paulo Renato Souza, former minister of education, Brazil; Francoise Caillods, deputy director, International Institute for Educational Planning–United Nations Educational, Scientific, and Cultural Organization (IIEP–UNESCO); Ulf Lundgren, professor of education, Uppsala University, Sweden; Pai Obanya, former assistant director-general, UNESCO; Kai-ming Cheng, pro-vice chancellor, University of Hong Kong; Chong Jae Lee, president, Korean Education Development Institute (KEDI); and Cristian Cox, director of curriculum, Ministry of Education, Chile. The team was also advised by an internal peer review panel consisting of Christopher Thomas, Jacob Bregman, Michel Welmond, Alberto Rodriguez, Norbert Schady, Susan Hirshberg, and Toby Linden, who provided invaluable comments and insights at review meetings throughout the preparation of the report.

The team is grateful for comments and contributions received from World Bank staff members, including Jamil Salmi, Birger Fredriksen, Maureen McLaughlin, Dzingai Mutumbuka, Myriam Waiser, Eduardo

Velez, Michelle Riboud, Regina Bendokat, Martha Ainsworth, Emmanuel Jimenez, James Socknat, Viviana Mangiaterra, Vincent Greaney, Gillian Perkins, Kin Bing Wu, Deepa Sankar, David Fretwell, Jon Lauglo, Pasi Sahlberg, Martha Laverde, Juan Prawda, Adriana Jaramillo, Emiliana Vegas, Suhas Parandekar, Robert Hawkins, Richard Hopper, Carolina Sánchez-Páramo, Carolyn Winter, Adrian Verspoor, Peter Buckland, and Manorama Gotur.

The team benefited from comments, suggestions, and contributions provided by colleagues from other international agencies and institutions: Peter de Rooij and Vincent McBride of the European Training Foundation; Stephen Tournas and Gregory Loos of the U.S. Agency for International Development (USAID); Yumiko Yokozeki of the Japan International Cooperation Agency (JICA); Aaron Benavot of UNESCO; Alejandro Tiana of the Organization of Ibero-American States for Education, Science and Culture (OEI); Wout Ottevange of the Center for International Cooperation, Vrije University, Amsterdam; and Mark Bray of the Comparative Education Research Center, University of Hong Kong. The contributions of authors who prepared background papers for the report are listed in the bibliography.

Book design, editing, and production were coordinated by the Production Services Unit of the World Bank's Office of the Publisher under the supervision of Rick Ludwick, Monika Lynde, and Paola Scalabrin. We are especially grateful to the copy editor, Nancy Levine, whose work added enormous value to the text.

The team thanks all those colleagues, within and outside the World Bank, who contributed their insights and suggestions. The team bears the ultimate responsibility for any shortcomings, errors, or misinterpretations.

Executive Summary

Demand for secondary education is soaring worldwide owing to the confluence of at least three factors. First, as more countries achieve universal primary schooling, demand for education is moving to higher levels of the education system, and the world is witnessing an explosion of individual and family aspirations for secondary education. Second, the largest-ever cohort of young people is clearly going to make a difference for the future of many countries, especially in the developing world. The way to turn what many perceive as a global risk into a global opportunity is by building and harnessing the values, attitudes, and skills of young people through quality secondary education, thus ensuring that they will become active and productive citizens of their communities. Third, economies increasingly need a more sophisticated labor force equipped with competencies, knowledge, and workplace skills that cannot be developed only in primary school or in low-quality secondary school programs. In short, provision of secondary education of good quality is seen as a crucial tool for generating the opportunities and benefits of social and economic development.

For all these reasons, secondary education is a focus of increasing policy debate and analysis worldwide. This debate is framed by the need to respond to the twin challenges of increasing access to secondary education and, at the same time, improving its quality and relevance. For several decades now, most of the education reforms proposed and implemented throughout the world have focused on the compulsory and postcompulsory levels of secondary education. This centrality of secondary education will persist in the foreseeable future and will certainly be reinforced.

One outcome of the past decades of reform is that secondary education has evolved in such a way that one could speak of a change of partners within the overall structure of education systems. Secondary education was born fully attached to and coupled with higher education: curriculum, pedagogical practice, and legal framework; teacher recruitment, selection, and status; and student background were the same as in higher education. In the past 40 years, however, significant changes have taken place:

- Secondary education has become more and more coupled with primary and basic education.
- The curriculum is less specialized and evolves toward arrangements closer to those in primary schools.
- Teachers in secondary education tend to be trained and recruited in the same way as primary school teachers; and pedagogical practices are converging as participation rates in secondary education increase.

All this has been a direct result of the democratization of education. In the poorest countries of Africa, the Middle East and North Africa, Latin America, and Asia, secondary education reform is becoming an integral part of Education for All (EFA) efforts. This increases pressure on the public budget in an already constrained public financial environment.

Globalization, the increased importance of knowledge as a driving force in economic development, and the consequent skill-biased nature of technological changes in the workplace are putting additional pressure on national governments to modernize and revamp their secondary education systems in order to produce graduates who are well prepared for work and for further learning. At the same time, the realization of democracy demands citizens who are equipped with the values, attitudes, and skills that will enable them to participate actively in their communities. Secondary education plays a central role in preparing students to become active citizens.

In addition to its contribution to economic growth and to formation of social capital, secondary education makes a crucial contribution to primary and tertiary education. It is the articulation node between those levels of formal education and between education and the labor market. In playing that articulating role, secondary education may serve as a pathway for students' advancement, or it may be the main bottleneck preventing the equitable expansion of educational opportunities. Indeed, the particular shape of the articulation between primary and secondary education and between secondary and tertiary defines the overall role, features, and priorities of the school system of any given country. Whereas EFA policies de facto place lower secondary education within the realm of basic and compulsory education, emphasis on increasing the number of secondary graduates qualified for entry into tertiary education restores and indeed heightens the value of the traditional preparatory function of upper secondary school. Thus, the policy choices for secondary education are quite different for the lower and upper secondary levels, particularly in low-income countries. The double face of secondary education, and its political ambiguity and complexity, become more visible as education systems expand.

Challenges in secondary education vary among countries. Despite all the efforts made in recent decades in the developing world, secondary education remains a bottleneck for the expansion of educational attainment. In most countries inequity in access to quality secondary education is a major barrier to human development, economic growth, and poverty reduction. Whereas the primary school completion gap between rich and poor countries has diminished, the gap in the proportion of the population with secondary education has widened in the past 40 years.

Sub-Saharan African countries, along with other low-income countries, face the greatest challenge. Those countries have to contend with a growing population that puts pressure on basic educational services, and many of them are likely to have to struggle to meet the goal of providing quality basic education to all school-age children by 2015. In addition, the AIDS pandemic is devastating the teaching force and undermining the entire educational fabric. In South Asia the relative success that countries have had in expanding primary school enrollment, combined with the fact that most of these countries are still in the midst of a population explosion, is generating considerable demand for expansion of secondary education. An additional source of pressure in the region is the large proportion of girls and of the very poor who are not yet enrolled in secondary education.

Middle-income and transition countries, in particular those in Eastern Europe, Latin America, and East Asia, have already achieved high enrollment levels in secondary education. Their main challenge is to improve quality, relevance, and efficiency to better align their education systems with those in open democracies and to respond to the rapidly changing demands of increasingly globalized economies.

Purpose and Messages of This Report

The purpose of this report is to set forth policy options for supporting developing countries and transition economies in adapting their secondary education systems to demands arising from the successful expansion of primary education and the socioeconomic challenges presented by globalization and the knowledge-based economy.

Despite the importance of these matters, the World Bank has not until now issued a policy statement on secondary education. The need for more analytical work in secondary education has been felt for a long time. After the substantial emphasis that had been placed on primary and tertiary education, the time and the opportunity has arrived to address the missing link of secondary education. The 1999 World Bank Education Sector Strategy already reflected a more holistic conception of education, including the need to tackle many of the issues specific to the secondary level. The 2005 update of the strategy confirmed the need to take a sector-wide approach and to integrate education into the country context.

Preparation of this report involved an extensive consultative process that began with the creation of an external advisory panel made up of six high-level international experts on secondary education. World Bank staff working in all regions of the world, colleagues from other international organizations, and counterparts from ministries of education contributed in ad hoc meetings and through exchanges of written communications. This consultation process was complemented by an extensive literature review and the commission of background papers, all of which resulted in a rich information base for the preparation of the report.

The report analyzes the key issues facing secondary education in the 21st century and, on the basis of global experience, presents a policy framework to guide decision makers in their efforts to transform and expand secondary education systems. It focuses on six main messages, as outlined next.

1. **Secondary education has taken on a mission of its own, one that has the policy peculiarities of being at the same time terminal and preparatory, compulsory and postcompulsory, uniform and diverse** (chapters 1 and 2).

   - For young people all over the world, primary education is no longer enough. Secondary education provides a specific set of competencies and skills that enable students to participate in the knowledge society. It can also contribute decisively to social cohesion and civic participation by increasing individual propensity to trust and be tolerant, thus enabling youngsters to become active members of society.
   - The United Nations Millennium Development Goals (MDGs) for education can only be achieved through systematic policies for postbasic or postcompulsory secondary education. In fact, expansion of secondary education creates a powerful incentive for students to complete primary education. Longer schooling carries significant social benefits; for example, increased female participation in secondary education is positively associated with significant reductions in infant mortality rates.
   - Secondary education has a special part to play in HIV/AIDS prevention in affected countries because of its role in equipping youths with greater ability to process information and in bringing about long-term behavioral change.
   - Demand for quality secondary education is increasing in all countries. Political consensus concerning secondary education reform is, however, particularly difficult to build up, as the constituencies and champions for the subsector appear to be weak or nonexistent.

2. **Expanding equitable access and improving quality to ensure relevance are the twin challenges of secondary education worldwide** (chapters 3 and 4).

- Developing countries are investing more today in secondary education than their counterparts in industrial countries did when they had similar levels of income. Yet the gap between rich and poor nations, in coverage and in quality, continues to widen.
- The formula used in the past to expand access to primary education is not necessarily applicable to secondary education today. Access to secondary education cannot increase without major changes in service delivery and without addressing simultaneously the quality and relevance dimensions. Moreover, expansion of access can only happen if significant inefficiencies such as high repetition and dropout rates at the primary and lower secondary levels are drastically reduced.
- There is no single best formula for expanding secondary education; multiple and simultaneous strategies are needed to target an increasingly heterogeneous school population.
- In countries that have achieved rapid and sustainable expansion of secondary education, investment in democratization of secondary education has gone hand in hand with "extra-support" policies to reach the adult population with only primary education.
- Rapid and significant expansion of secondary education is generally perceived as having a cost in terms of quality. Implementation planning must therefore take quality issues explicitly into account. Quality, grounded in diverse institutional responses to a growing range of individual demands, emerges as the most important long-term challenge for secondary education in all countries.
- Evidence on the linkage between education and economic growth points to the importance of balanced expansion of access to quality education. Ensuring universal basic primary education coverage and quality should come first, but this requires a simultaneous and cumulative effort to expand secondary and tertiary education.
- Unchecked and unbalanced expansion of secondary education can lead to increased social, gender, and ethnic inequality. A key policy objective is to ensure that access to quality secondary education is enhanced for those strata of society that have been excluded because of poverty, ethnicity, gender, and other related factors.

3. **In the context of the knowledge society, changing work patterns are leading to radically new approaches in the way curricular knowledge is selected, organized, and sequenced** (chapter 5).

- Although countries exhibit different trends in the relative supply and wages of workers who are secondary education graduates, there is evidence of increased demand for skilled workers, reflecting skill-biased technological change.

- Curriculum-based reform of secondary education in the 21st century is prioritizing skills and competencies that go beyond and cut across the traditional general-vocational divide. The frontier between general and vocational curricula is shifting and fading, and the heretofore hard-to-strike balance between vocational and general education at the secondary level is becoming increasingly irrelevant.

- There is a gap between what is currently being taught in secondary schools and the knowledge and skills required if countries, firms, and individuals are to be competitive. New subject matters and types of knowledge have become socially and economically meaningful and compete to occupy a place in the secondary curriculum. The challenge is to determine the best alternatives for enriching the curriculum without worsening the prevailing overload of the secondary education curriculum.

- Information and communication technologies (ICTs) offer new avenues for expanding access to quality secondary education and can be used as levers for curriculum reform and innovation. They can, however, trigger new forms of inequity, as is evident in the significant digital divide within many countries and among countries.

4. **Qualified and motivated secondary school teachers are critical to the success of reforms of secondary education** (chapter 6).

- There is a profound mismatch between learning needs, competencies, and skills demanded from students in the knowledge society and the teaching skills of secondary teachers after their passage through teacher training colleges and in-service training programs.

- There are no low-cost shortcuts to training high-quality teachers. Preservice academic training of secondary school teachers continues to be vital, but school-based training and mentoring for novice teachers have proved more effective and less costly than traditional preservice training for developing core teaching and professional skills. Experimentation with new ways of balancing preservice and school-based in-service training could yield positive results in teacher education policy.

- Teacher shortages negatively affect the quality of secondary education and create a barrier to expansion of access to secondary education. This challenge is severely compounded in AIDS-affected countries, which are suffering from the loss of massive numbers of teachers.

- Comprehensive incentive policies to attract and retain high-quality teachers should be devised, especially in countries that are losing their most experienced teachers to richer nations. Such policies should factor in professional development issues, teacher deployment and class size policies, and accountability systems.

5. **Multiple sources of funding and efficiency-enhancing measures should be considered to cover the significant financial investments required to expand access and improve the quality of secondary education** (chapter 7).

- Many developing countries will have serious problems bearing the full financial burden of expanding access and improving quality in secondary education. These countries need to put in place cost-sharing strategies and to complement supply-side interventions with demand-side financing mechanisms.
- Although governments are expected to make substantial contributions to financing the compulsory phase of secondary education, families and communities should play a more active role in financing the postcompulsory phase. Public-private partnerships can contribute in an important way to making mass secondary education affordable.
- Demand-side financing mechanisms such as stipends or scholarships are sometimes the best and only means of attracting and retaining in secondary education children from poor families and minority communities. This approach has proved successful in promoting girls' education.
- The countries that have succeeded in expanding secondary enrollment in the past two decades are characterized by balanced ratios of per-student public spending across the three levels of the education system. Spending per secondary student is, on average, only 1.4 times higher than spending per primary student, and spending per tertiary student is only about 3 times the expenditure per secondary student. In contrast, in less successful countries the respective ratios are 2.6 and about 9.
- Public and private sector resource mobilization efforts in developing countries will need to be complemented by substantial financial contributions from multilateral and bilateral partners. Countries can also profit from multilateral funding for HIV/AIDS education because of the potential impact of secondary education on AIDS prevention.

6. **Traditional modes of state intervention and public management strategies need to be reformed in order to promote delivery of high-quality secondary education services** (chapter 8).

- To produce good educational outcomes, secondary schools need to move away from the "factory model of producing education," in which young adolescents are put on a conveyor belt and moved from one individual teacher to the next, to be doused with unconnected course material administered in six or more lessons a day. Creating a teaching and learning environment that breaks away from this pattern is the real mission of secondary school management.

- Significant changes in the economic and political conditions that once framed government action have cleared the way for new forms of interaction between the state, communities, and markets in the provision of secondary education. The changes have not made the state's presence in secondary education less significant. On the contrary, governments are increasingly being required to play a leading role in steering, monitoring, and supporting service delivery to ensure equity and quality in the provision of secondary education.
- Clear, achievable goals and a transparent system of incentives and accountability mechanisms help improve delivery of secondary education services. Unlike the prescriptive mechanisms of the past, the new ones, rather, set goals and provide guidance.

World Bank Involvement in and Support for Secondary Education

Over the past two decades, the World Bank's strategy for the education sector has given less attention to secondary education than to primary and tertiary education. If anything, secondary education was considered a priority only in middle-income countries, provided that they had already achieved universal access to primary education. An important turn in this long-standing trend came in 1995, when the strategic focus moved from primary to basic education, which in many cases included the lower secondary school grades. In low-income and some middle-income countries this change was accompanied by efforts to achieve Education for All as part of the Millennium Development Goals. The shift in emphasis entailed a major change in the approach to secondary education in terms of lending priorities and practices: it was seen more as an extension and upgrading of basic primary education than as the preparation of an elite for higher education.

Since the mid-1990s, several factors have prompted a rapid increase in the share of lending for general secondary education. One has been the growing demand for secondary education places resulting from rising graduation rates in primary education. Another factor, especially in low-income countries, has been the challenge to provide equitable and sustainable financing of secondary education, which entails the design of new structures and regulations that can cope with the growing demand for lower and upper secondary education. A third is the reassessment of the role of secondary education in economic and social development, in a context defined by new labor market demands stemming from mounting pressure to increase competitiveness and by changes in the workplace driven by rapid shifts in technology. A final factor is the effort to enhance the potential response of secondary education to HIV/AIDS prevention through both education lending and the Multi-Country AIDS Program (MAP).

The main areas of World Bank support to secondary education projects can be grouped in six categories (World Bank 2004b): (a) expanding access and absorbing the rising demand that is being experienced as a result of progress on the education MDGs and on EFA policies; (b) alleviating poverty and promoting equity; (c) supporting gender equality in access; (d) focusing on qualitative improvements; (e) rehabilitating physical facilities; and (f) improving efficiency and management in secondary education.

World Bank supported secondary education projects (listed in table J.1 in appendix J) have performed relatively poorly in low-income countries. Evaluations have attributed this outcome to factors such as excessive complexity of projects in relation to capacity for implementation and insufficient attention to social and labor market demand and to rising recurrent costs. These shortcomings reflect the need for more country-level analytical work to match strategies closely to specific country conditions. Lessons from secondary education projects in the 1990s suggest that greater attention is needed to implementation capacity and to realistic phasing and sequencing of interventions (World Bank 2004b).

Directions for Future World Bank Support

Future World Bank support for secondary education should consist of intertwined and complementary activities that include lending, financial assistance to pilot programs, analytical work, promotion of global partnerships, and systematic evaluation of programs and projects. Together with continuing support for universal provision of high-quality primary and basic education, the World Bank should increase its support for the expansion and democratization of high-quality secondary education. Future lending must be based on in-depth analysis of country situations and systematic consultative processes that enable a good understanding of the direction in which the country's economy and social institutions are moving.

An example of the kind of work needed can be seen in Africa, where the World Bank is partnering with African countries and other donors in the Secondary Education in Africa (SEIA) initiative. This multiyear (2002–06) study is designed to contribute to the debate on secondary education in Africa and to assist countries in developing sustainable national strategies for increased access and improved quality. (See the SEIA Web site, www.worldbank.org/afr/seia.)

Some key areas for analysis and research that deserve further attention
are

- institutional linkages between labor market institutions and secondary
  schools, with special emphasis on school-to-work transition issues and
  youth employment
- the impact of expansion and quality improvement of secondary education in a given country on productivity and the introduction of new
  technologies
- the nature of bottlenecks in secondary education and how they affect the
  provision and completion of education in many developing countries
- benchmarking of secondary education systems along dimensions related
  to efficiency, effectiveness, organization, and management
- the educational aspirations and demands of young people, with a view
  to making secondary education more relevant to their needs and motivating them to continue in and graduate from secondary education.

Organization of the Report

The report begins, in chapter 1, by outlining the historical background
of secondary education, examining how particular sociocultural and
economic conditions shape its definition and structure, and highlighting
the secondary education policy paradox. Chapter 2 then examines the
direct benefits and externalities of secondary education; chapter 3
describes the magnitude of the challenges developing countries face as
they seek to upgrade the quality and relevance of secondary education;
and chapter 4 proposes an analytical framework to help identify the main
socioeconomic factors that shape specific country responses to the
challenges. Chapter 5 addresses the response to the twin challenges of
expanding access and improving the quality of secondary education by
presenting the new ways in which curriculum knowledge is being
selected, organized, and sequenced and the changing role of monitoring
and evaluation policies. Chapter 6 looks at the response from the perspective of the teaching profession, including issues related to teachers'
education and professional development, recruitment, and deployment.
It also discusses the potential perils and promises linked to the use of
information and communication technologies (ICTs) in secondary
schools. Chapter 7 explores options for increased and more sustainable
financing of secondary education, concentrating on features that make
funding at this level a somewhat different problem from financing
primary or tertiary education. Chapter 8 examines governance issues,
analyzing how relationships between the center (national and provincial
government) and the local level (local authorities and schools) are being
redefined in order to respond to the twin challenges and exploring the

key organizational characteristics of effective secondary schools. Finally, the epilogue argues that the task of expanding access and improving the quality of secondary education demands a radical transformation of policies and of institutional practice; doing more of the same is definitely not the way to deal effectively with the twin challenges. The appendixes present additional data on secondary education, discuss selected topics in greater detail, and review the World Bank's involvement in support for secondary education.

Abbreviations, Acronyms, and Data Notes

AIDS	Acquired immune deficiency syndrome
CEL	Compulsory Education Law (China)
EdStats	Education Statistics
EFA	Education for All
EMIS	Education Management Information Systems
FIDE	Full investment-driven economy
FTI	Fast Track Initiative
GDP	Gross domestic product
GER	Gross enrollment rate
GPI	Gender parity index
HIV	Human immunodeficiency virus
HSEP	High school equalization policy
IAEP	International Assessment of Education Progress
IALS	International Assessment of Literacy Study
IBE	International Bureau of Education
ICT	Information and communication technology
IIEP	International Institute for Educational Planning
IRI	Interactive radio instruction
LEP	Local Education Partnership
MDGs	Millennium Development Goals
NAEP	National Assessment of Education Progress
NGO	Nongovernmental organization
NRC	National Research Council (United States)
OECD	Organisation for Economic Co-operation and Development
OED	Operations Evaluation Department (of the World Bank)
PCK	Pedagogical content knowledge
PIDE	Partial investment-driven economy
PISA	Programme for International Student Assessment
SBM	School-based management

SGB   School governing body
SMC   School management committee
TIMSS   Trends in International Mathematics and Science Study
TVET   Technical and vocational education and training
UIS   UNESCO Institute for Statistics
UNESCO   United Nations Educational, Scientific, and Cultural
              Organization

Throughout this book, the generally accepted OECD definitions for education are used. Basic education consists of six years of primary and three to four years of lower secondary school. Secondary education is normally divided into two cycles: lower secondary (generally three to four years in duration) and upper secondary (generally, two to four years). Chapter 2 presents a more detailed account of alternative structural models of secondary education.

All dollar amounts are current U.S. dollars unless otherwise indicated. A billion is 1,000 million.

1

Secondary Education: From Weakest Link to Cornerstone

Secondary educational systems differ more by world time and because of their historical traditions—especially the legacy of colonialism—than by development levels or educational expansion per se . . . Broad curricular outlines . . . are less affected by economic development, political forces and the degree of educational expansion at the national level than by the broader currents of world history and a nation's location in that history.

—D. Kamens, J. Meyer, and A. Benavot (1996), 138

One of the main challenges countries around the world face is to equip their young people to become active citizens, to find employment in constantly changing workplace environments, and to cope with and respond to change throughout their lives. Countries need to respond to this challenge with approaches that are appropriate to their capacities and long-term development objectives. In this context, secondary education takes on special significance. This chapter describes the historical development of secondary education, examines how countries' sociocultural and economic realities lead to differences in the definition and structural organization of the secondary level, and highlights the policy paradox posed by secondary education.

Historical Background

The historical background of secondary education is highly relevant for the analytical framework of this document. Historical patterns, more than any other factor, account for worldwide variance in secondary school curricula (Kamens, Meyer, and Benavot 1996). The influence of historical forces continues to shape secondary education models, institutional structures, and curricula.

Historically, in the developed countries secondary education was subsidiary to higher education, and this relationship has influenced policy, choice of providers, curriculum decisions, teacher recruitment and training, evaluation, accreditation, and certification. In the developing world secondary schooling has been the forgotten sector in the education realm. In many countries the power of wealthy elites has ensured that tertiary education receives a good share of funding and attention. Similarly, the interest of the international development community in the expansion of primary education since the 1970s has persuaded developing-country governments to direct substantial resources to the initial stages of schooling. Secondary education, meanwhile, despite its potential role as a link between primary and tertiary education, has slipped through the cracks (Bloom 2003).

At the risk of oversimplification, it could be said that in the developed world and in some of its oldest colonies, public education systems were constructed from roof to floor. That is, first came the foundation of universities, beginning in the 12th century; then, from the 15th and 16th centuries on, the establishment of secondary schools; and finally, well into the 19th century, the creation of public primary schools. Historically, secondary education was at the service of universities and had the mission of preparing students for higher studies. Accordingly, the secondary school curriculum was built around the teaching of Latin—the language of instruction in the universities. This accounts for earlier denominations of secondary schools in many countries, such as *grammar school, Gymnasium* (still used in Germany, Austria, and some countries of Central and Eastern Europe), and *escuela de latinidad*. Later, secondary education began to emerge as a distinct sector, being seen as a fundamental means of training the administrative class of the new nation-states. The new secondary school started to take shape with the French Revolution and, internationally, with the bourgeois revolutions of the first half of the 19th century. (The experience in the United Kingdom was somewhat different, but there too, the schools were linked to the training of the emerging industrial bourgeoisie.) By the end of the 19th century it is already possible to talk about a modern secondary school, partly of a terminal nature and featuring a process of segmentation into alternative tracks—academic, vocational, and general.

In the 20th century both U.S. and Soviet education policies led to secondary education models aimed at the creation of massive systems that emphasized open access and universal coverage. After 1945, what were later called comprehensive secondary schools began to spread from northern to southern Europe. In comprehensive schools all students receive secondary education in a single institution, based on a common curriculum, and may be streamed through elective subjects. This is in contrast to students being tracked and grouped either by academic ability or by choice on entering secondary education. Meanwhile, the vocational approach to secondary schooling developed rapidly in Eastern Europe.

By the 1960s and 1970s secondary education was de facto linked more to primary than to tertiary education. The extension of compulsory education had entirely changed the concept, as well as the duration, of basic education, to the point that basic education usually included lower secondary schooling.[1] A rising average level of schooling was seen as an important objective and as a measure of the success of education reforms. Many other countries have embraced the goal of extending and expanding the notion of basic education to encompass much of what used to be restricted-access, elitist secondary schooling.

The U.S. Template for Expansion of Secondary Education

The advent of a new economy in the early 20th century increased the demand for a small cadre of scientists and engineers, for a larger workforce of bureaucrats and public administrators, and, most significantly, for skilled and educated labor. In 1900 there emerged in the United States the notion that schooling could make ordinary office clerks, shop floor workers, and even farmers more productive (Goldin 2001). This prompted a change in education policy to acknowledge the shift from physical to human capital.

Goldin (2001) argues that the spectacular expansion of secondary education in the United States, which took place 40–50 years (two full generations) before the corresponding expansion in European countries, has to do with a template that entailed a sharp departure from the European tradition of secondary schooling. This U.S. template encompassed a number of virtues: public funding and provision; an open and forgiving system (nonselective, with no early specialization or academic segregation); an academic yet practical curriculum; numerous small, fiscally independent school districts; and secular control of schools and school funds.

Critics assert that those virtues have come to constrain rather than advance education. This assessment is at the core of the ongoing debate. Public funding and provision are judged insufficient, and so vouchers and public funding of private providers are being introduced. An open and forgiving system with no tracking at early ages had been deemed egalitarian and nonelitist, but some now see it as lacking in standards and accountability. And although a general and academic education for all may enhance flexibility, it may in practice have left many behind and may have worsened rising inequality from the 1980s on. Finally, although a decentralized system of small, fiscally independent districts competing for residents may once have fostered investments in education, the system is now seen as producing serious funding inequities.

European Patterns of Expansion of Secondary Education

In sharp contrast with the United States, in European countries nearly half a century elapsed between when primary education was generalized and made free and compulsory and when access to secondary education was opened to all. In 1945 countries such as France, Ireland, and Spain enrolled a fairly low proportion of the relevant age group in secondary education. Although participation rates were somewhat higher in, for example, Sweden and the United Kingdom, they were still less than 50 percent. Secondary education was elitist and was perceived as high quality. Employability of graduates was not an issue, given the system's exclusive function of preparing graduates for university and then for careers as high-ranking civil servants.

Immediately following World War II European countries began to realize that they were lagging behind the United States in development of human capital. The reinforced leading role of the United States in the global arena further increased the influence of its education policies. Selection measures, such as the legendary 11+ examinations, were seriously questioned. The credibility of the system, and public confidence in it, began to wane. Labor market needs, combined with strong social demand for democratization, made it evident that restricted and elitist secondary schools entailed losses of talent that no country could sustain. This realization led to radical secondary education reform along comprehensive lines, first in Nordic countries, then in France and the United Kingdom, and later in Italy, Portugal, and Spain.

In the 1980s widespread criticism of the comprehensive model led to political devaluation of comprehensive schools in the United States and in Europe. Comprehensive reforms began to be seen as purely ideological and as leading to excessive intervention of the state in education. The forgiving aspect of comprehensive schools would, it was thought, bring about an overall decline in academic standards, loss of elite control over universities, and a breach in the exclusiveness of the deeply entrenched academic establishment. Progressives criticized comprehensive schools for creating an internal system of selection through the elective system, which tended to reproduce inequality. In several European countries, it was felt that elite private alternatives to public secondary schooling were being reinforced, especially when they became eligible for public funding. And there was a perceived high risk that secondary schools were creating among young people expectations about their educational and employment prospects that could not be fulfilled. Proponents of this view were handed a good argument when, in the late 1980s, youth unemployment skyrocketed in most European countries. In addition, the critics blamed comprehensive schools for sharp segmentation and stratification of higher education and for restrictions on admission to particular courses of study.

Asian Patterns of Expansion of Secondary Education

From 1945 on, primary and secondary education received great attention in East Asia, and significant public investments were made in these levels. Mundle (1998) discusses the policies that the advanced economies of Japan, the Republic of Korea, Singapore, and Taiwan (China) adopted to increase access to education and improve its quality. One path was to concentrate on vocational education in upper secondary school until per capita incomes reached about $8,000 (at the 1992 exchange rate) and then to shift to a more general curriculum. In some East Asian countries, however, even at lower incomes the share of vocational education in secondary education enrollments never reached 50 percent (Gill, Fluitman, and Dar 2000).

The East Asian countries that took an early lead in expanding secondary education through high public investment reaped rich dividends (McMahon 1998). A broad human capital base was critically important to vigorous economic growth in the high-performing Asian economies, led by Japan. Rapid accumulation of human capital reduced income inequality by increasing the relative abundance of educated workers, thereby lowering the scarcity rents associated with cognitive skills (World Bank 1993, 349). Basic education in these economies is highly oriented toward the acquisition of general skills, while postsecondary education tends to emphasize vocational skills.

Despite remarkable achievements, the general public in East Asia, just as in Europe and the United States, has become increasingly discontented with the secondary education system. In Korea and Japan, for example, questions have been raised about school quality; it is felt that schools are not producing such noncognitive skills as creativity, spontaneity, flexibility, and entrepreneurship, which are in great demand in the productive sector (Cave 2001). Concern about rote learning associated with high-stakes college entrance examinations was one of the main reasons behind education reform in many East Asian countries; in China in recent years more than 10 provinces have revised their college entrance examinations.

Definition and Organizational Structures of Secondary Education

The most common terms used to label the main phases of (nonuniversity) education are primary, lower secondary, and upper secondary. Primary schooling starts between ages 5 and 7 and is compulsory, lower secondary starts between ages 10 and 14 and is compulsory in most countries, and upper secondary starts between ages 14 and 16 and generally falls outside the boundaries of compulsory education.[2] A broad definition of secondary education includes general secondary education (lower and upper levels) and vocational education, starting at the upper secondary level, which provides opportunities for specialization. In some countries the lower secondary level is categorized as basic and compulsory and is grouped for policy purposes with primary education. Although the difference between general secondary education and vocational education is fading in some countries, in many developing countries the bifurcation is entrenched.

Lower secondary education may be further divided into a comprehensive phase and a selective phase, when students are placed in specialized schools on the basis of perceived ability or aptitude. Upper secondary education in most countries is noncompulsory and, by and large, is shaped as a dual system in which a comprehensive structure coexists with a specialized tracking structure. (See table 1.1 for country examples.)

Table 1.1 Organizational Models in Secondary Education

Level	Examples
Lower secondary	
1. Basic education, with no distinction between primary and lower secondary education.	Angola, Botswana, Burkina Faso, Cambodia, Chile, China, Comoros, Cyprus, Denmark, Ecuador, Finland, Ghana, Grenada, India, Indonesia, Kazakhstan, Republic of Korea, Moldova, Nepal, Slovakia, South Africa, Sweden, Ukraine, Republic of Yemen
2. Distinct primary and lower secondary education. Students in lower secondary school are not separated into specialized tracks.	Canada, Colombia, England, France, Greece, Italy, Portugal, Scotland, Spain, Turkey, United States, Wales
3. Two-cycle system in which a distinct primary cycle is followed by a secondary education cycle, with no distinction between lower and upper secondary education. Secondary education does not offer specialized tracks.	Brazil
4. Distinct primary and lower (general) secondary education, with a proportion of lower secondary students selected for differentiated tracks.	Austria, Belgium, Bulgaria, Croatia, Germany, Ireland, Luxembourg, Netherlands, Peru, Poland
Upper secondary	
5. General secondary education and specialized tracks within the same institution.	Canada, Chile, England, Ireland, New Zealand, Spain, Sweden, United States
6. General secondary education and specialized tracks in separate institutions.	Australia, Bulgaria, Finland, France, Germany, Hungary, India, Italy, Japan, Republic of Korea, Netherlands, Poland, Singapore, Switzerland, Republic of Yemen

Sources: Adapted from Green, Wolf, and Leney (1999); Le Métais (2002); see also appendix A.

As for the duration of the cycles, there are three main structural models:

- two cycles—primary education, with 4, 5, or 6 grades, and secondary education, with 9, 7, or 6 grades
- two cycles—a long first cycle, with 8, 9, or 10 grades, and a shorter second cycle, with 2, 3, or 4 grades
- three separate cycles of 5 + 4 + 3 or 6 + 3 + 3 grades

Differential Traits of Secondary Education

Secondary education has specific features and peculiarities, compared with primary and tertiary education, that create a differential context for policy making. The list below highlights the key differences between secondary and primary education. (Differences between secondary and tertiary education can be derived by generalization.) Some of the characteristics are related but are treated separately for emphasis, and some may be self-evident but are included for completeness.

Secondary education differs from primary education in the following respects:

- Greater need for heterogeneity of curricular offerings to clients, both among and within schools, in response to (a) the greater likelihood that secondary students will go on to work from school, and (b) the need to maintain student interest, as adolescents in general have more choices and are more likely to be emotionally disaffected than children or older youths.
- Greater need for responsiveness of curricular offerings to changes in demand over time.
- A smaller number of larger schools with greater heterogeneity among clients.
- Greater need and greater scope for professional management and managerial autonomy. Managers and teachers in secondary schools are more highly trained than those in primary schools because of requirements or because of competition and self-selection.
- Less of a collective, local-community base because the geographic extent of the student and parent base makes "the community" harder to define.
- Less political commitment to universal access, particularly at the upper secondary level. Most compulsory and many "free" education laws do not cover upper secondary education.
- The creation of externalities for primary schools in their catchment areas— for example, through pressure (or lack of pressure) for quality of primary school graduates and through incentives for children to stay in and complete primary school, even if there is no direct quality pressure from secondary on primary schools.
- A greater labor market filtering or screening function. Even though the benefits of secondary education itself could perhaps be seen as having a

larger private component, the labor market screening function is more of a public good.

- Possibly higher ratio of private to social returns, regardless of whether the private or social returns are higher or lower than for primary schooling.
- Within social returns, higher rate of return to the national and regional society and economy than to the local society and economy because graduates from secondary education are more mobile than those with only primary schooling.
- Higher opportunity cost for students, many of whom can work for wages, are forced by parents to help in the home or home business, or become pregnant.
- Students who are more mature and often politically active and are more likely than not to perceive that they have interests in common with tertiary students. As societies develop, and as happened in the developed world starting in the 1950s, secondary students are more likely to have their own culture, which may include alienation from parents and from the prevailing culture, gang culture, disaffection with schooling, and other characteristics that, again, might undermine the notion of community and hence the options for community-based finance.
- Less parental ability to judge quality of schools, choose between schools, or advise schools, resulting in fewer options for "voice" and "choice" as mechanisms for accountability. There may be fewer voice options because the divergence between parental education and student, teacher, and principal education is much greater than in primary school. There may be fewer choice options because secondary schools, which in any country are much less numerous than primary schools, are more regionally monopolistic.
- Greater potential for the individual student's identification with and loyalty to school to be character defining; more student self-interest in quality of schooling, insofar as it provides identity and collective identification (school pride). The "community" the schools serve is not so much an exogenous geographic entity as one created by the school itself.

In assessing secondary education policy issues, many of the characteristics listed above require careful consideration. For example, international agencies lobby for primary schooling, and university students and elite parents lobby for universities, but secondary education in most countries is said to be bereft of lobbies. The tendency of secondary students to be politically active could plausibly be seen as a remedy for the relative absence of lobbies for this level of education. Yet the likelihood that secondary students might protest excessive allocations to the university level is at least doubtful, as in politicized situations secondary students often take the lead from university students and express solidarity with them over the total education budget rather than press for resource reallocation.

Duration of Study .

The duration of study—the average length of time it takes to progress from lower to upper secondary education and, more generally, from one educational level to the next—varies across countries. It depends on the prevailing education policies and labor market conditions, on the quality and relevance of the educational experience provided, and on the flexibility offered by different pathways, which is particularly germane at the upper secondary level. It has been observed that in countries where upper secondary pathways are not sufficiently flexible (that is, where students cannot combine general and vocational schooling), students tend to take longer to graduate in order to acquire qualifications in both kinds of education. As demand for upper secondary education increases, a main policy challenge is to develop pathways that can accommodate growing and diverse student needs, interests, and capacities, as well as content that is responsive and relevant to labor market demands. From a systemic perspective, the secondary education curriculum needs to be well integrated into an articulated system of lifelong learning.[3]

In developed countries a high proportion of the school-age population is currently enrolled in school for at least 12 years (see table 1.2), and a

Table 1.2 Model of Instructional Organization, Kindergarten through Grade 12 (K–12)

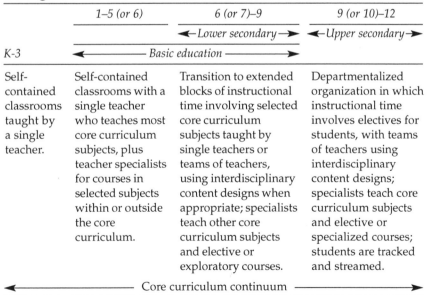

	1–5 (or 6)	6 (or 7)–9	9 (or 10)–12
		◄—Lower secondary—►	◄—Upper secondary—►
K-3	◄————— Basic education —————►		
Self-contained classrooms taught by a single teacher.	Self-contained classrooms with a single teacher who teaches most core curriculum subjects, plus teacher specialists for courses in selected subjects within or outside the core curriculum.	Transition to extended blocks of instructional time involving selected core curriculum subjects taught by single teachers or teams of teachers, using interdisciplinary content designs when appropriate; specialists teach other core curriculum subjects and elective or exploratory courses.	Departmentalized organization in which instructional time involves electives for students, with teams of teachers using interdisciplinary content designs; specialists teach core curriculum subjects and elective or specialized courses; students are tracked and streamed.
◄————————— Core curriculum continuum —————————►			

Source: Adapted from California State Department of Education (1987).

Table 1.3 Duration of Secondary Education Cycle by Region

Region	Min	Max	Mode
Africa	4	8	7
East Asia and the Pacific	4	8	6
Eastern Europe and Central Asia	5	9	7
Latin America and the Caribbean	4	7	5
Middle East and North Africa	6	8	6
South Asia	5	8	5
European Union and United States	5	8	6

Source: Benavot (2004).

compulsory or mandatory duration of schooling that sets minimum standards for educational attainment no longer represents a boundary defining participation in education. In developing countries the obligatory period is still an important boundary for the social contract that defines expectations with respect to the role of the state in providing and funding education and the obligation of families to keep their children in school.

Benavot's (2004) study of curriculum trends in 185 countries shows that the mean duration of secondary education around the world is 6.09 years, with significant variations (ranging from 4 to 9 years) between and within regions (table 1.3). These findings should be interpreted cautiously, since in many countries lower secondary education constitutes part of the cycle of basic education, for a duration of up to 9 years altogether.

Ages at entry and exit for compulsory education vary between and within regions (figure 1.1). The lowest age at entry is age 3, in the Netherlands, and the highest is in Mongolia, where children are not required to enroll until age 8. Worldwide, the median age at entry into basic education is about 5 or 6. The duration of primary education is typically 5 to 8 years, and that of secondary education is between 4 and 9 years. Consequently, children between ages 11 and 19 can be expected to be in secondary school.

Differences in the structure of the education cycle, combined with differences in age at entry and length of compulsory education, affect the expected age of graduation from schooling. For example, in Africa, which has the highest age of entry and the lowest average age requirement for exit of any region, children are expected to stay in school, on average, until age 13; in the United States and Europe they are expected to stay until age 16. Differences in age requirements among individual countries are even more significant. In Myanmar 10-year-olds are no longer required to be in school, while in Poland and the Russian Federation students are expected to stay in the system until they are 19. These differences in expectations and requirements result in wide disparities in educational attainment around the globe.

Figure 1.1 Ages of Entry to and Exit from Compulsory Education by Region, circa 2000

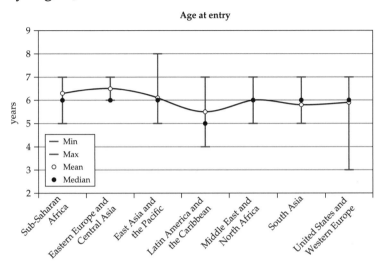

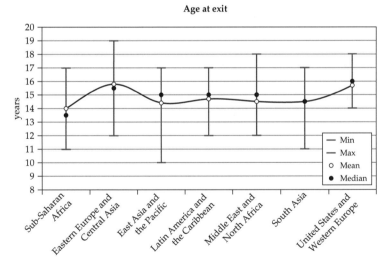

Source: Authors' compilation.

School-to-Work Transition

A guiding principle for policy decisions in secondary education is to align the secondary education curriculum with labor market needs in order to facilitate the school-to-work transition. Accordingly, a central policy

value = price in market, but not necessarily pay off to employer

question for decision makers and educators is the extent to which the skills and qualifications acquired in secondary education should be responsive to changing labor market requirements. How this question is answered accounts for different approaches toward structuring and organizing secondary education, especially upper secondary education.

assumption Labor markets signal the value of certified skills for successful entry into the workplace. There are important variations among countries. In countries where labor markets are organized by occupation and where jobs and qualification profiles are matched or designed according to corresponding skill requirements, the secondary education system tends to offer coherent vocational education pathways leading to widely agreed-on and recognized occupational qualifications (OECD 1998). Job classification becomes important in defining skill requirements and directly influences curriculum content and rules for certification and diplomas. Policy makers seek industry input in designing curriculum and qualification systems and in providing hands-on training opportunities for students. Stakeholder inputs are facilitated by the active participation of strong employer organizations and trade unions. Austria and Germany are good examples of this approach.

Countries with relatively open labor markets where skill requirements are more likely to be spelled out at the enterprise level and where jobs are less defined tend to value generic employability attributes (OECD 1998). Policy makers aim to provide more general and less occupationally specific programs in secondary education by focusing on transversal core skills such as adaptability, problem solving, and communication skills. Vocational education at the upper secondary level is not as well developed, signifying the blurring of the distinction between general secondary education and vocational education (see box 1.1). Specific skills tend to be acquired through on-the-job learning and career development within enterprises. Australia, Brazil, Canada, and the United States follow this approach.

Some countries where labor markets are not tightly organized around occupations (the Nordic countries, for example) combine the above approaches. Systems are designed with some pathways that are more vocationally oriented.

Many European countries with specialized lower secondary education tracks enroll students in comprehensive or polyvalent schools that offer more than one track within the same institution and allow students to move between tracks. From a practical perspective, this arrangement has relaxed the rigid differentiation into tracks, and it is forcing curriculum differentiation to take place at a later stage. Another trend in Europe is that because the option for secondary students to specialize is delayed, tracking is occurring at an older age. This has helped students and parents become better informed about options and about the consequences of early specialization.

Box 1.1 Country Responses to the Changing Status of Secondary Vocational Education

Over the past two decades, developed countries have been experimenting with more flexible educational pathways in upper secondary education in order to respond to the falling status of this level of schooling, to the demands being generated by a growing and diverse student population, and to changes in work organization. The main challenge is to put in place a system that allows students completing the general education pathway to acquire recognized labor market qualifications and that also permits students completing the vocationally oriented pathway to gain entrance into tertiary education institutions. A significant constraint on attempts to combine general and vocational education has been the lack of specialized equipment and related resources in schools, which limits choices of modules and subjects and renders earned diplomas or certifications of little value. Employers' expectations and tertiary education institutions' entry requirements are often more demanding than what schools are able to deliver.

A study conducted in several European countries, Australia, Canada, and the United States (OECD 1994b) identified the following four common elements in this trend:

1. Reducing the number of vocational education fields or programs by broadening vocational areas and qualifications
2. Creating linkages between general and vocational education
3. Developing combinations of school- and work-based learning
4. Building bridges between secondary vocational education/training and tertiary education

The study highlighted two fundamental dilemmas that policy makers face in their efforts to reform secondary vocational education:

1. Increasing the share of general education content in upper secondary education would enhance the value of such programs as preparation for tertiary education, but the programs may become more selective than intended, as less successful students would tend to avoid them. Yet tailoring upper secondary vocational programs too exclusively to the needs of less successful students would make them unattractive to successful students, which could devalue upper secondary vocational education altogether as a desirable option.
2. Attempts to broaden the content of upper secondary vocational programs and make them more generic to a significant number of related occupations could limit the programs' appeal for employers who demand more specialized skills. In addition, these attempts

(Continued)

Box 1.1 Continued

might flounder because of limited equipment and physical facilities and poorly trained teachers.

The study yielded some important recommendations for policy makers:

1. Avoid making upper secondary vocational education programs a residual and dead-end pathway linked to poor-quality jobs and directed at the lowest achievers.
2. Provide institutionalized bridges between secondary vocational education and tertiary education and ensure that significant proportions of students take this pathway.
3. Design vocational education and training programs for less successful young people as an element of safety nets rather than as ordinary vocational programs; make sure that safety net programs prepare young people for later participation in mainstream vocational education and training.

Source: OECD 1994b.

The Policy Paradox of Secondary Education

There appears to be a policy vacuum around secondary education. Most countries have experienced less difficulty in building political consensus and in designing and implementing policies for primary and tertiary education than for secondary education. Secondary education policy choices are more ambiguous and complex because of the intrinsic duality of secondary education, which is at once

- terminal and preparatory
- compulsory and postcompulsory
- uniform and diverse
- meritocratic and compensatory
- geared to serving both individual needs and interests and societal and labor market needs
- involved in integrating students and offsetting disadvantages but also, within the same institution, in selecting and screening students according to academic ability
- charged with offering a common curriculum for all students and a specialized curriculum for some.

Secondary education thus features a double discourse. To give just one example, secondary schooling is called on to integrate youngsters in order to prevent social exclusion and achieve greater social equality and, at the same time, to stream, track, and label them, sometimes at an early age, thus introducing a powerful source of inequality and irreversibly determining their future life chances.

Secondary education reflects all the major contradictions and dilemmas of core policy choices in education. The issues are therefore highly politicized. They generate parental anxiety and even give rise to corruption and fraud when it comes to high-stakes examinations and other screening devices. Paradoxically, despite the centrality of secondary education in the contemporary political arena and the increasing demand for secondary education worldwide, the constituency and lobbying—the champions—for the subsector tend to be weak or even absent, especially when compared with the strong national and international lobbies that support and foster primary and tertiary education agendas.

Conclusion

Despite the significant overlap in general objectives from country to country, structures and practices in secondary education vary considerably. The differences are reflected not only in the terminology used to describe each phase of education but also in the structure and length of the compulsory education cycle.

Yet in every country, quality secondary education is indispensable for individual and national development alike. Today, well into the process of universalization of basic education, secondary education is taking on a mission of its own—one that combines the policy peculiarities of being at the same time terminal and preparatory, compulsory and postcompulsory, uniform and diverse, general and vocational. The duality, complexity, and ambiguity of this level of schooling pose challenges for its provision. In the context of the soaring demand for secondary education, it is the responsibility of policy makers to tackle the inevitable duality and formulate secondary education policies designed to provide pathways and alternatives that will enable students to achieve their full potential.

Secondary education is a bridge between primary or basic education, the labor market, and tertiary education. The bridge can have many lanes and pathways, so that everybody fits, or, it may act as a bottleneck, squeezing a minority of privileged students from primary through to tertiary education and heavily conditioning participation rates and the quality of both primary and tertiary education. In making education policy, decision makers face a basic choice: whether secondary education is to be the weakest link of the education system—or its cornerstone.

Notes

1. Basic education in many countries encompasses primary and lower secondary education. The duration of basic education varies anywhere from five to nine years.

2. Upper secondary schools are also called high schools; lower secondary schools are sometimes called middle schools or junior secondary schools.

3. A lifelong learning framework encompasses learning throughout the life cycle, from early childhood through retirement. It includes formal learning (schools, training institutions, and universities), nonformal learning (structured on-the-job training), and informal learning (skills learned from family members or people in the community). It allows people to access learning opportunities as needed rather than because they have reached a certain age (World Bank 2003c).

2

The Importance of Investing in Secondary Education

A powerful case can be made for the expansion of secondary education in developing countries on the grounds of growth, poverty reduction, equity, and social cohesion. The argument is particularly germane for countries that have achieved high levels of primary education coverage but still have low enrollments at the secondary level. This chapter examines the evidence for the growing importance of secondary education by describing its direct benefits and externalities and documenting the increasing demand for this level of schooling.

Direct Benefits and Externalities

Investment in education is beneficial in a multiplicity of ways, both for individuals and for society as a whole. Secondary education, the focus of this report, has been shown to contribute to individual earnings and economic growth. It is associated with improved health, equity, and social conditions. It buttresses democratic institutions and civic engagement. And the quality of secondary education affects the levels above and below it—primary and tertiary education. This section looks at each of these interactions in detail.

Contribution to Growth and Poverty Reduction

Secondary education and growth. Education increases individual productivity, as measured by the well-documented link between educational attainment and personal earnings. At the national level education plays an important role in fostering economic growth. Today's rapidly growing economies depend on the creation, acquisition, distribution, and use of knowledge, and this requires an educated and skilled population. In addition, there is growing evidence that perhaps half or even more of aggregate economic growth is driven by increases in factor productivity rather than by factor accumulation in either capital or labor (Easterly and Levine 2002).

17

Secondary education plays a particularly important role in this regard. In many countries the increased demand for workers with secondary schooling (discussed more fully later in this chapter) has been associated with skill-biased technological change. Barro (1999), analyzing a panel of about 100 countries observed between 1960 and 1995, finds that economic growth is positively related to the (1960) starting level of average years of adult male school attainment at secondary and higher levels but is insignificantly related to years of primary attainment. His interpretation is that there is a strong effect of secondary and higher schooling on the diffusion of technology.

In an increasingly globalized economy, developing countries may be able to achieve increases in factor productivity through technology transfer from global "leaders." Such technology transfer may take place through trade, foreign direct investment, and learning across international supplier-producer chains. Much of the technology developed in the leader countries, however, is very skills-intensive and therefore "inappropriate" for developing countries without a minimum threshold level of skills (Acemoglu and Zilibotti 2001).

Secondary education is a vital part of a virtuous circle of economic growth within the context of a globalized knowledge economy. Many studies have documented that a large pool of workers with secondary education is indispensable for knowledge spillover to take place and for attracting imports of technologically advanced goods and foreign direct investment (Borensztein, de Gregorio, and Lee 1998; Caselli and Coleman 2001; Xu 2000). In a study on education and technology gaps in Latin America, de Ferranti et al. (2003) found that the bulk of the difference in computer penetration between Latin America and the East Asian "tigers," with their significantly wider computer coverage, can be explained not only by differences in the share of trade with countries of the Organisation for Economic Co-operation and Development (OECD) but also, and most important, by the proportion of the workforce with secondary schooling. The authors further speculate that this explains why the demand for skilled workers has not increased in Brazil, which has much lower schooling levels than other countries in Latin America.

The importance of balanced development of education.[1] A case for expanding secondary education can also be made on the grounds of economic growth, even where the rate of return to secondary education is low in comparison with that to tertiary education (as is the case in many Latin American countries; see de Ferranti et al. 2003) and where expansion of secondary education might have a smaller short-term effect than would expansion of the coverage of the university system. Historically, the countries that have experienced the most rapid and sustainable increases in educational attainment, as well as outstanding economic performance, have pursued balanced upgrading of the primary, secondary, and tertiary levels of education.

Goldin (1999) demonstrates the importance of the extension of secondary schools in the United States between 1910 and 1940—a transformation that gave the United States a half-century lead over European countries. De Ferranti et al. (2003) stress the importance of balanced upgrading of an education system after analyzing the examples of Korea, Singapore, Taiwan (China), and other East Asian "tigers," which make a stark contrast with the "unbalanced" transitions observed in many Latin American countries.

Secondary education and inequality. Although a central goal of education is to allow all individuals to develop to their full potential, the realization of this goal does not imply the elimination of individual differences in educational achievement and the associated benefits, nor does it necessarily mean access for all to the same educational experiences. It does, however, imply full access to intellectual and skill development opportunities that will enable each individual to develop his or her full potential. Thus, consideration of equity in education must address issues related to outcomes, as well as to access. The question is not whether outcomes vary but whether they vary to an unreasonable extent and whether the distribution of outcomes is equivalent in groups among which it is not reasonable to expect differences—for example, between the genders (Blondal, Field, and Girouard 2002).

A significant challenge for public policy is to provide learning opportunities for all students irrespective of their home backgrounds. International evidence from the Programme for International Student Assessment (PISA) provides encouraging evidence in this regard (OECD 2001b). While the results for all participating countries show a clear positive relationship between home background and educational outcomes, experience in some countries demonstrates that high average quality and equity in educational outcomes can go together. One of the most important findings of PISA is that students' home background explains only part of the story of socioeconomic disparities in education, and in most countries it is the smaller part. The combined impact of the school's socioeconomic intake can have an appreciable effect on the student's performance, and it generally has a greater effect on predicted student scores than do the characteristics of students' families. Thus, the message from PISA findings is that national education policy and practice can mitigate the influence of social and economic privilege on educational achievement without sacrificing the overall level of achievement.

Public policy affects the distribution of the costs and benefits of secondary education most directly through the arrangements for public funding. Analysis of the shares of public resources allocated to various social sector interventions going to poor and nonpoor households (the average incidence of public expenditures) often finds investments in secondary schooling to be of intermediate incidence. These expenditures are not as regressive as spending on university (which is often captured by rich elites) but are not as progressive as spending on primary schools (because of the greater coverage of primary education and because poor families tend to have more children). It is obvious, however, that such analyses of average incidence could be misleading as a guide for government policy, as the average and marginal incidence of expenditures can be quite different. A simple example will illustrate this point. If all children from rich families are already in secondary school and no children from poor families are, the average incidence of expenditures on secondary school would be highly regressive, but the marginal incidence (a measure of who benefits from one additional unit of funding spent) may be highly progressive. This kind of analysis may show that the poor stand to benefit a great deal from expansion of the coverage of secondary education in some countries.

Investments in secondary school can also be justified on the basis of distributional arguments, although the case here is somewhat speculative. Further research is needed to better establish the likely distributional implications of secondary school expansion. Children who receive more education now may have higher earnings in the future, and investments in schooling can therefore influence the future distribution of per capita income or of consumption. "Simple" simulations of the effect of educational expansion on the Gini coefficient are feasible; an example is the work done by Bourguignon, Ferreira, and Leite (2003). Such simulations essentially compare the current distribution of earnings with the distribution of earnings if an additional number of workers in the future have more education and therefore earn higher wages, where these wages are imputed on the basis of the present-day rate of return to schooling. Unfortunately, these simulations yield only very rough measures of the impact of school expansion on distributional parameters because the rate of return to education is itself endogenous, a function of the supply of and demand for workers with different amounts of schooling.

Expanding the coverage of secondary school, other things being equal, will depress the earnings of workers with secondary education relative to those with only primary education, as well as relative to those with university education. The extent to which changes in supply would change the returns to a particular level of education depends on the degree to which workers with secondary education are substitutes in production for those with primary or university education. This is intimately related to the elasticity of substitution among different kinds of worker. The exact value of these elasticities of secondary-to-primary and secondary-to-tertiary workers in developing countries is largely unknown, and there is therefore little agreement on the likely effect of expansion of secondary coverage on the future distribution of earnings. A simulation exercise with "reasonable" elasticity values (perhaps between 1 and 3) and "reasonable" assumptions on changes in relative demand (perhaps an extrapolation from current trends) would provide policy makers with upper- and lower-bound estimates of the effects of secondary school expansion on aggregate measures of inequality in individual countries.

Millennium Development Goals (MDGs). Investing in secondary education can have a direct impact on the effort to reach Millennium Development Goal 2—achieving universal primary education. Increasing the provision and coverage of secondary education can boost completion rates in primary education. If a student has a realistic opportunity to continue with studies in (lower) secondary school, this can increase motivation (and the family's perceived incentives) for graduation from primary school. An analysis of global education trends by the United Nations Educational, Scientific, and Cultural Organization (UNESCO) shows that developing countries need "some critical mass of secondary participation" (UNESCO 2004b, 9) in order to meet the goal of universal primary education. Clemens (2004, 19) observes that "no country today has achieved over 90% primary net enrollment without having at least roughly 35% secondary net enrollment."

In Ghana, Lavy (1996) found that improving access to secondary education facilities not only improved enrollment at the secondary level but also served as an incentive for primary school completion. If transition rates from primary to secondary education fall, it is likely that primary completion will decline as well and that dropout rates in the final years of primary education might not be easily reduced. In addition, gender equality cannot be achieved without expanded and balanced access to secondary education.

Education for All (EFA) policies tend to position lower secondary education within the realm of basic (and compulsory) education. Lower secondary education is therefore being increasingly identified with primary or basic education, and the emphasis is more on a general than on a specialized curriculum. For example, in many African countries junior (that is, lower) secondary education is now being incorporated as the last stage of basic education, which many governments are defining, when possible, as free and compulsory (Bregman and Bryner 2003). Curriculum, teacher training and recruitment, and even school organizational arrangements are increasingly converging at the primary and lower secondary levels. In addition to appropriate basic (and compulsory) education policies, the achievement of the MDGs and of the EFA goals set in the Dakar Framework for Action in 2000 call for a systematic policy for postbasic or postcompulsory education in developing countries.

Contribution to Improvements in Health, Gender Equality, and Living Conditions

Health. An important private benefit of increased education is its positive impact on personal health. In both developed and developing countries, a strong correlation exists between schooling and good health, whether measured by mortality rates, morbidity rates, or self-reported health status (Cave 2001; Mahy 2003). Indeed, education has an effect on health independent of income, race, or social background (OECD 2001a).

Education has been proven to provide protection against HIV infection (World Bank 1999a). There is now convincing evidence that young people in Africa who complete basic education are at reduced risk of HIV/AIDS, and this effect is even stronger for those who complete secondary education.[2] A longitudinal study in Uganda found a marked decline in HIV prevalence rates in males and females age 18–29 with secondary to higher-level education but a much smaller decrease among those with lower educational levels (figure 2.1). Secondary education has a general preventive impact: by providing children and youths with skills to critically process information, it equips them to make decisions concerning their own lives and to bring about long-term behavioral change (de Walque 2004).

A similar association between educational level and health benefit is seen for smoking and education in the United States. These effects are thought to be a function of greater general ability to process information—a competence enhanced during the secondary school years—rather than a consequence of greater exposure to prevention messages alone.

Paradoxically, the secondary education system, which is the source of this "social vaccine," is itself being destroyed by HIV/AIDS in many African

Figure 2.1 HIV Prevalence by Educational Attainment, Age 18–29, Rural Uganda, 1990–2000

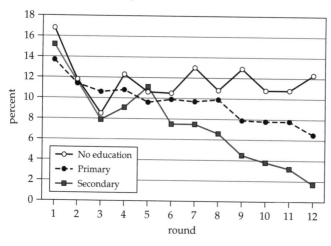

Source: de Walque 2004.

Note: The data are from a longitudinal study conducted over a 12-year period. Each round represents one year of data collection.

countries, through increased mortality and absenteeism of teachers. Ensuring the supply of education therefore implies a need for special efforts to protect both today's teachers and the young people now in secondary school who will be the teachers of the future.

Female education results in a number of beneficial health impacts for children. Better-educated women are more likely than their peers to delay marriage and childbearing and to have fewer and healthier babies. According to one estimate, a 10 percentage point increase in female primary enrollment lowers the infant mortality rate by 4.1 deaths per 1,000 live births, and a similar rise in female secondary enrollment is associated with another 5.6 fewer deaths per 1,000 live births (World Bank 2001a). Recent demographic and health surveys in 49 developing countries show that the mortality rate of children under five is highest in households where mothers have no schooling and lowest where mothers have some secondary schooling or higher (see figure 2.2).

Gender equality. In addition to the well-understood benefits to societies and to families of educating girls and women, there is evidence that women's education is a catalyst for reducing gender inequality and so benefits women themselves. The empirical literature on this topic begins with the assumption that education enhances women's well-being and gives

Figure 2.2 Under-Five Mortality Rates, by Mother's Educational Level, Selected Areas, circa 1998

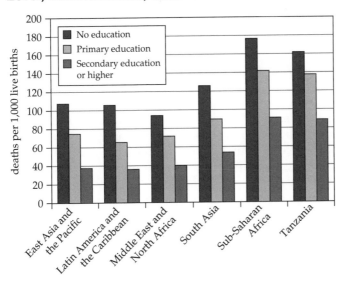

Source: Mahy 2003.

Note: Regional averages are population-weighted.

them a greater voice in household decisions, more autonomy in determining the conditions of their lives, and improved opportunities to participate in community affairs and the labor market. The literature spans a variety of social science and health disciplines, including economics, demography, sociology, and anthropology. The findings are that investments in female education do have a positive impact on gender equality, women's empowerment, and women's well-being (see Malhotra, Pande, and Grown 2003). In addition, the evidence indicates that relatively high levels of education (secondary or above) are consistently positively related to most aspects of gender equality, regardless of other conditions. The literature suggests a threshold effect of secondary schooling whereby women themselves are much more likely to be agents of normative and structural change when they have more education.

For example, higher levels of education (at least six years, or secondary schooling) always have a positive effect on a woman's use of a variety of prenatal and delivery services, as well as postnatal care, and the effect is larger than the effect of lower levels of schooling (Bhatia and Cleland 1995a, on India; Elo 1992, on Peru; Govindasamy 2000, on the Arab Republic of Egypt). Studies also find a protective effect of education on women's sexual and reproductive health, and the specific level of education matters. Some studies show that any education has a beneficial impact compared with no education but that the effects are stronger at higher than at lower levels of schooling (Bhatia and Cleland 1995b, on India; Yount 2002, on Egypt). Others find a threshold effect, suggesting that only at secondary or higher levels of schooling does education have a significant beneficial effect on women's own health outcomes for risks of disease (El-Gibaly et al. 2002, on Egypt; Fylkesnes et al. 2001, on Zambia).

Contribution to Realization of Democracy

Secondary education makes important contributions to the intergenerational maintenance and accumulation of human and social capital. As the society becomes increasingly complex and less traditional, secondary education tends to become a central builder of networks of civic engagement that form the core of the collective capabilities of communities to work for the common good (Welsh 2003).

Education contributes to the development of social capital by increasing individual propensity to trust and be tolerant. Research by Balatti and Falk (2002) and Schuller et al. (2002) shows that learning as a social activity not only has a strong influence on the development of shared norms and the value placed on tolerance and understanding within a community but is also an important determinant of the three key building blocks of social capital—building trust, extending and reconstructing social networks, and reinforcing behaviors and attitudes that influence community participation.

Research conducted by Dee (2003) on civic returns to education shows that in the United States additional secondary education "significantly increased the frequency of newspaper readership as well as the amount of support for allowing most forms of possibly controversial free speech" (page 3).

Secondary education also helps build social capital by raising the likelihood that citizens will participate in democratic institutions and will join community organizations and engage in politics. Findings of studies conducted in the United States and the United Kingdom (Dee 2003; Milligan, Moretti, and Oreopoulos 2003) show strong evidence that secondary education contributes to changes in attitudes and behaviors that enhance interest in politics, voter participation, and civic activity, thus helping promote active citizenship.

In addition to contributing to civic participation, secondary education can help reduce criminal activities and imprisonment, which in turn can yield important monetary benefits for society. In the United States Lockner and Moretti (2001) found that high rates of dropout from secondary school increase the probability of incarceration for both white and black males and that a 10 percent increase in the high school graduation rate reduces the arrest rate by 14 to 27 percent. According to the study, the social benefits of a 1 percent increase in the U.S. high school graduation rate could generate savings of about $0.9 billion to $1.9 billion per year. A similar study conducted by Feinstein (2002) in the United Kingdom found a comparable trend in crime reduction, which the author attributes to the positive impact of secondary school graduation on wages. According to Feinstein, in the United Kingdom the "benefit in terms of reduced crime through the effect on wages of a 1 point increase in the proportion of the working age area population with O Level or equivalent qualifications, is predicted to lie between £10 million and £320 million" (page 5).

Contribution to Primary and Tertiary Education

In addition to its effect on economic growth and the development of social capital, secondary education also makes a crucial contribution to both primary and tertiary education. The type of articulation between primary and secondary education, and between secondary and tertiary education, defines and depicts in an unequivocal way the overall features of a country's education system. Within an education system, secondary education is the bridge between primary schools and tertiary education institutions and serves as a bond between them. Secondary education can be a set of pathways for students' progress and advancement—or it can be the main bottleneck, preventing the equitable expansion of educational opportunities. In developing countries, despite all the efforts in recent decades, secondary education often acts as a bottleneck within the overall education system, inhibiting participation rates. The bottleneck is mostly manifested in the

---

Box 2.1 Mounting Pressures on Secondary Education in Cambodia

Secondary education in Cambodia can be described as a bottleneck. Education reforms enabled net primary enrollment to increase from 85 percent in 1996 to a reported 93 percent in 2002, but net enrollment at the secondary level declined from 23 to 20 percent during the same period and was reported to have plunged as low as 14 percent in the 1999/2000 academic year. As the primary education sector begins to exhibit greater efficiency in flow rates to grade 6, particularly with respect to declines in student repetition, the government anticipates that potential demand for places in lower secondary schools will double by 2006. This might cause transition rates to lower secondary school to drop from the current 83 percent to only 40 percent as base enrollment figures rise significantly.

Not surprisingly, such projections have led to calls for interventions in the country's secondary education sector to accommodate accelerating flow rates through the primary schools. For Cambodia there is a normative dimension to the dilemma of the static flow rates that characterize the transition to lower secondary school and the high incidence of dropout for the lucky few who actually get to lower secondary school. In 1996 the government introduced a major reform in the education sector that extended the basic education cycle from six to nine years, through the end of the lower secondary school cycle. Although Cambodia's constitution guarantees the right of every child to basic education, participation rates in lower secondary schools hover around 20 percent, in stark contrast to the desired social and political goals. This contrast has given the government a compelling reason to translate legal rights into real rights—an effort that underpins many of the ongoing efforts to introduce targeted pro-poor education reforms.

Source: ADE-KAPE 2003.

---

form of too few lower secondary education places, or too rigid tracking at the secondary education level, or both. (See box 2.1 for an example.)

Primary education and secondary education complement each other in many ways and so act as a two-way street. Increased primary education completion rates can boost demand for secondary education, and expansion of secondary education can be a powerful incentive for students to complete and graduate from primary school. Furthermore, in many developing countries primary school teachers are trained at the secondary level, so that the expansion and quality enhancement of secondary education has the benefit of providing more and better teachers for primary schools.

The two-way street analogy could be extended to secondary and tertiary education. Secondary education curricula; pedagogical practices; legal frameworks; the recruitment, selection, and status of teachers; student background; and so on mirror those in higher education. Given the right policies, well-trained secondary school graduates continue to university, and universities in turn prepare college graduates to be secondary school teachers. Appropriate policies to promote student retention through upper secondary education can help increase the number of qualified secondary graduates entering tertiary education.

The very structure of secondary education (the academic and vocational shares, for a start) and the corresponding curriculum choices and alternative student tracking have a strong impact on patterns of student demand and enrollment in tertiary education, notably on the distribution of higher education entrants by knowledge area. Put in a different way, the knowledge and skills acquired and accredited in upper secondary education may be the main determinant of student prospects and choices with regard to tertiary education. This is of critical importance when a country wants to increase the share of university enrollment in traditionally male-dominated studies such as engineering. In many cases reform of higher education should start by looking at the secondary school curriculum and the tracking structure of secondary schools. For instance, enabling vocational education students at the secondary level to enter tertiary education institutions at various points and levels would not only increase the flexibility and inclusiveness of the system but would also improve the balance between the professional and academic dimensions of higher education.

One outcome of the reforms of past decades has been a shift in partnership. Secondary education used to be linked only with higher education. Nowadays, secondary schools also create externalities for primary schools in their catchment areas by pressuring—or not pressuring—for quality of primary school graduates and simply by providing incentives for continuation, even if there is no quality pressure (Bregman and Bryner 2003).

The evidence presented thus far, based on economic, human, and social capital arguments, argues for appropriate secondary education policies. Demand-side evidence and arguments—the subject of the next section—confirm the need for appropriate policies for expansion of secondary education.

The Soaring Demand for Quality Secondary Education

The growing demand for secondary education can be directly attributed to (a) the success of efforts to achieve universal primary education and of equity-driven programs for females and minorities; (b) the increasing demand for new types of knowledge, skills, attitudes, values, and experiences originating from more pluralistic communities and the use of more sophisticated technologies in the workplace; (c) the decreasing role of the government and the rural sector as employers, together with the importance of the service sector, whose employment structure is dominated by "knowledge workers"; (d) the increase in elected representative governments and the concomitant need for better-educated citizens; and (e) the increasing private returns to secondary education as the labor market demands graduates with a more sophisticated set of skills, knowledge, and competence that can be acquired starting at the secondary education level.

Demand for More Educated Workers

To assess the demand for educated workers, trends over the past 20 years in the wages and supply of workers with secondary education relative to those with primary and tertiary education were analyzed, using household and labor force survey data. The countries selected were Argentina, Bolivia, Brazil, Chile, Colombia, and Mexico in Latin America (de Ferranti et al. 2003), Indonesia, Malaysia, and Thailand in East Asia (Abu-Ghaida and Connolly 2003), and Côte d'Ivoire, Ghana, South Africa, and Zambia in Sub-Saharan Africa (Abu-Ghaida and Connolly 2003). The research showed that several possible patterns can emerge when the interplay among relative wages, supply, and demand is taken into account. For example, while a rise in relative wages combined with an increase in relative supply is strongly indicative of increased relative demand, a drop in relative wages combined with an increase in relative supply may imply either increased or decreased relative demand.

The analyses reveal that the supply of workers with secondary education relative to those with primary education has undergone unmistakable increases in Latin America, East Asia, and Africa over the past 20 years and that relative wages dropped in the Latin American and East Asian countries but rose in the African countries. The resulting implications for trends in the demand for workers with secondary education relative to those with primary education were as follows: in Latin America, abstracting from crisis periods in Argentina and Brazil, relative demand for workers with secondary education increased; in East Asia relative demand increased in Indonesia and Malaysia but decreased in Thailand; and in Africa rising relative wages and supply led to a relative increase in demand for workers with secondary education.

The supply of workers with secondary education relative to those with tertiary education dropped in Latin America (except in Brazil), East Asia (excluding Thailand), and Sub-Saharan Africa. The findings on relative wages of workers with secondary education show a decrease in the Latin America countries and in Ghana, South Africa, and Thailand but an increase for

Indonesia, Malaysia, and Zambia, with Côte d'Ivoire showing much variability. The implications for trends in the demand for workers with secondary education relative to those with tertiary education were as follows: in Latin America the relative demand for workers with secondary education dropped (except perhaps in the case of Brazil); in East Asia relative demand fell in both Indonesia and Thailand but appeared to rise in Malaysia; and in Africa, despite the mixed evidence on relative wages, it decreased across the board.

The overall evolution of relative wages and labor supply shows that demand for workers with more education increased over time. In addition, there is some evidence from the sudden shifts in demand in favor of those with tertiary education. This trend was observed in Malaysia at the time of the 1997 economic crisis, when demand for more skilled workers increased. Finally, the evidence for Latin America is most consistent with the explanation that demand shifts confirm the complementarities between technology and skill—that is, the effect of skill-biased technological change on the relative demand for workers with different amounts of skill (de Ferranti et al. 2003).

Demand for Enhanced Relevance and Quality

A fundamental role of secondary education in the 21st century is to equip students and graduates to become active, contributing partners in their communities. According to Delors (1996), this active role encompasses the domains of political, economic, cultural, social, and religious life. The agenda is multidimensional and should not be confined to any one domain. Secondary education plays a crucial role in equipping adolescents and young adults to become active citizens, to exploit economic opportunities, to be capable of exercising their rights and duties, and to resist attempts to vitiate and abuse these rights and duties. The demand for enhanced relevance and quality of secondary education is discussed next from the perspectives of youths, civic life and socialization, and the workplace.

Youths. The transition from primary to lower secondary school comes at a difficult time for many adolescents. Just as the physical, emotional, and social changes of early adolescence begin to set in and young people begin to experience intense growth with new notions about identity and individualism, they find themselves in a school environment radically different from what they were used to (University of Pittsburgh 1996). The move from the protective setting of primary school to the more unstructured environment of secondary institutions can be smooth for some, but for many this is a period of intense conflict that could lead to academic failure, school dropout, and other serious problems. In many developed countries, for instance, between 15 and 30 percent of adolescents drop out before completing high school. In Sub-Saharan Africa the secondary completion rate has been estimated at 10 to 20 percent (Bregman and Bryner 2003). In general, in African countries the dropout rates are higher in the early grades of secondary education and decrease dramatically toward the end, indicating that students who stay long enough to begin the last year of secondary school are likely to finish their education. Unfortunately, the percentage that do so is, overall, very low (Liang 2002). A common phenomenon observed in Latin America is high levels of repetition in the initial grades of secondary education, making secondary education very inefficient (Cabrol 2002). The spin-off effects are that adolescents have the highest arrest rate of any age group and that an increasing number of them report regular use of alcohol or other drugs.

Hargreaves and Earl (1990) summarize well the main traits and needs of early adolescence. Young people in this stage of life have to (a) adjust to profound physical, intellectual, social, and emotional changes; (b) develop a positive self-concept; (c) experience and grow toward independence; (d) develop a sense of identity and of personal and social values; (e) experience social acceptance, affiliation, and affection among peers of the same sex and the opposite sex; (f) increase their awareness of, ability to cope with, and capacity to respond constructively to the social and political world around them; and (g) establish relationships with particular adults around whom the growth processes can take place.

To fully understand the secondary education needs of young people today, it is important to add to the above-mentioned considerations the current social context surrounding adolescents, which is characterized by constant changes in technology and lifestyle and by the presence of a strong worldwide adolescent subculture resulting from the global influence of communications, information technology, and multimedia. The information-rich environment surrounding adolescents' social and work lives makes additional demands on them, requiring them to think in progressively abstract, critical, and reflective ways, to gain experience in decision making and in accepting responsibility for decisions, and to develop self-confidence by achieving success in significant events and areas. Secondary schools, in turn, face an important challenge, as they are called on to provide relevant experiences to help youngsters develop their competencies.

Several typical characteristics of lower secondary education across the world appear to be at odds with the needs of contemporary adolescents and youngsters. They include the following:

1. *Increased control exerted by teachers in lower secondary school classrooms, as compared with elementary school.* In secondary school classrooms there is more teacher control and discipline and there are fewer opportunities for student decision making, choice, and self-management.[3] Yet this is the stage when students increasingly desire autonomy and avenues for self-determination.

2. *Less-personal student-teacher relationships.* Students in secondary school encounter teachers who are less friendly, less supportive, and less caring than their teachers in primary school. Their relationships are less personal and positive. For their part, teachers report that they trust students in this age group less.
3. *Less small-group and individual attention and mounting evaluation pressure.* Beginning in lower secondary school, there tends to be increased organization of activities for the entire class regardless of the varying abilities of students, rather than small-group work. In addition, secondary students have to deal with public evaluation of their academic achievement, sometimes in the form of high-stakes public examinations. This can alienate students, resulting in significant negative impacts on the motivation and self-perception of adolescents and youngsters.

Student disaffection and implications for civic life. Changes in the nature of the learning environment associated with transition to lower secondary school and eventually to upper secondary school seem to be a plausible explanation for the decline in students' engagement in school-related activities. But it can also be argued that such changes, seen from the students' perspective and in a context of quasi-universal secondary education, are tantamount to a de facto democratic deficit of contemporary secondary schooling. There is substantial research evidence (Cothran and Ennis 2000) that the current characteristics of secondary schools favor the creation of antischool student subcultures, school violence and antisocial behavior, increased dropout, and generalized student disengagement.

Schools also impart an image of ideal students, in terms of personal characteristics and behaviors. Those who do not fit that image and have very little chance or no real chance to ever meet the standard search for alternative ways, places, and institutions to construct and develop personal identity. Many educators view the growing problems of discipline in schools, and school violence in particular, as a sort of transnational epidemic that moves and extends from country to country, changing entirely the landscape of school systems and the self-perception of the teaching profession. Secondary school teachers' meetings are rife with significant and consistent worries about students' lack of motivation, widespread lack of discipline, and unwillingness to sacrifice part of their present in order to have a better future. In short, there appears to be a growing civic deficit among secondary school students.

International and national studies indicate that student absenteeism and disaffection (as manifested in lack of a sense of belonging or participation) are key challenges in secondary education. An OECD (2001b) report based on PISA results, which draw on data from 42 mostly developed countries, reveals a poor sense of belonging at school among, on average, one in four 15-year-old students, with one in five admitting to being regularly absent.[4]

Disaffection rates vary widely across countries. In Denmark and Spain a third of students, and in Canada, Greece, Iceland, New Zealand, and Poland, over a quarter, appear to miss school or skip classes regularly. In Japan and Korea, by contrast, the low-attendance category accounts for fewer than 1 in 10.

Even in countries with high secondary school attendance, students are not necessarily happy in school. A poor sense of belonging is greatest in Japan, Korea, and Poland, with over a third of students feeling they do not belong in at least one respect. Least affected are Hungary, Ireland, Sweden, and the United Kingdom, where the proportion is fewer than one in five. The prevalence of both types of disaffection is higher among non-OECD countries. Contrary to what might be expected, the findings reveal that disaffected students are not principally those with the lowest literacy levels; they are drawn from the full range of abilities. Students who feel the least sense of belonging at school have, on average, literacy skills somewhat above the norm. Students who are most frequently absent are often lower achievers, but they are not at the bottom; they perform, on average, at level 2 on a five-level literacy scale, showing at least a basic skill level. A youth survey conducted in Argentina (San Juan 2001) found that early adolescents (ages 13 to 15) have low levels of motivation and of engagement with school activities, resulting in a higher tendency to leave school early. In Canada a four-year national survey on student engagement in learning and school life (Smith et al. 2001) revealed that as students move through the grade levels from elementary to secondary, they become increasingly bored and alienated from school.

These findings raise important issues for policy makers. They indicate that disaffection from school (and as a possible outcome, antischool subcultures) is not limited to a small minority of students. These disaffected students do not achieve their full potential at school, may become disruptive in class, and may have a negative influence on other students, all of which could lead to early exit and permanent dropping out of school.

It has yet to be assessed whether disengagement from school during the adolescent years has longer-term effects. It can be expected, however, that students' attitudes toward school and their participation strongly affect their decision as to whether to pursue postsecondary studies. It is at the secondary level that a student's academic identity is defined and consolidated. Academic identity influences and shapes choices and opportunities as graduates face the labor market or seek to pursue further education.

Since secondary education coincides with a critical phase in students' lives, their engagement in the learning process and their overall well-being are vital components of academic achievement. These affective outcomes of schooling also need to be taken into account when dealing with curriculum, pedagogy, monitoring, and evaluation. There is an evident need to balance the current emphasis on academic and cognitive achievement with the affective dimension of achievement.

If secondary schools remain central agencies in the socialization of young citizens and workers, more emphasis needs to be placed on the role of the individual student and on his or her autonomy in steering the learning process. Teachers and principals must actively seek students' participation in areas such as curriculum choice, preferred methodological approaches, and quality-enhancing assessment practices. When drafting curriculum, pedagogy, monitoring, and evaluation, policy makers must take these aspects into consideration, since they affect schooling outcomes. Students are obviously the largest and most important asset in secondary schools, and they should become more actively involved in their fellow students' learning process. Participatory structures, mutual support, tutorial systems, and conflict mediation are good examples of measures that can foster direct involvement of students and so change the culture of a school, reduce dropout, and contribute to improving student achievement.

The workplace. Changes in the workplace resulting from technological improvements and the introduction of new technologies are creating pressures worldwide for upskilling the labor force, in terms of average educational attainment and of competencies obtained outside the formal education system (OECD 2001a; Stasz 1999). Core and foundational skills such as higher-order numeracy and literacy competencies are assuming importance equal to that of work-related skills and technical knowledge. In developed countries, having secondary education is making it easier for young adults to find employment or to shorten the period of unemployment. A comparative study of youth employment in eight OECD countries (Australia, Canada, Finland, Japan, Norway, Portugal, Sweden and the United States) found that youth-adult unemployment ratios fell from an average of 3.6 in 1977 to 2.6 in 1987 and to 2.4 in 1996 (OECD 1998).[5] The authors of the study observe that "this relative improvement in young people's position in the labor market can in large part be ascribed to rising educational levels among new labor market entrants, whose knowledge, skills and qualifications are better adapted to the needs of a knowledge society" (p. 54). What really makes the difference is not so much the number of years of schooling achieved but the quality of the schooling, since the same average number of schooling years may mask very different distribution patterns of qualifications across countries. Several studies have highlighted the importance of the quality of education for economic growth (Barro 1999; Dessus 1999; Hanushek and Kimko 2000).

An interesting caveat comes from a study in Latin America which confirms that education accumulation is good for growth but suggests that the degree of inequality in the distribution of education has a strong and robust negative effect on growth (Birdsall and Londoño 1997). This implies that the real challenge is to ensure equitable access to good secondary

⌣⌣ ₁tion. In order to prepare graduates for active participation in the labor market, secondary education must contribute to enhancing their skills and knowledge so they are better equipped to accomplish particular tasks and are able to absorb, use, and adapt new technical knowledge to respond to changing job requirements. In other words, secondary education should provide individuals with knowledge, skills, and attitudes so they can maintain a competitive edge. In a study on competitiveness and skills, Lall (2001) finds that as the industrial sector in a country becomes more complex and sophisticated, the demand for human capital formation accelerates. Good secondary education and technical schooling are prerequisites for staying competitive for countries at an intermediate level of industrial development and with export-oriented activities. In Uganda the findings of a firm demand study show that despite the advocacy for vocationalization, it is generic skills and knowledge, in addition to positive work attitudes, that employers most value (Liang 2002). Another study, on secondary education and employment in Thailand, found that managers rank work habits and attitudes above all other skills, followed by the ability to learn new occupational skills, and that they value people skills over specific occupational skills (World Bank 2000a).

Effects and Side Effects of the Expansion of Secondary Education

The expansion of secondary education has effects and side effects, and some of them can be problematic.

1. Secondary expansion has a direct impact on human capital development and on social equality. Unchecked expansion in countries with low secondary education participation rates has the potential to increase inequality, as measured by the gender and social background of students. Analysis of enrollment rates in secondary education in many developing countries such as Cambodia (ADE-KAPE 2003) shows that nontargeted investment in secondary education might be considered antipoor, since it has generated a situation where fewer than 10 percent of students from the lowest income quintile have access to secondary education (see box 2.2). In countries where access to secondary education is less restricted, further secondary expansion that pays insufficient attention to quality and relevance results in high dropout and low completion rates, turning the "open doors" of the system into "revolving doors" for a sizable proportion of students (UNESCO 2004b).

2. Secondary education has a strong effect on wages and the labor market. In theory, accessibility reduces the exchange value of an institution's educational credentials. This reduction strongly influences public perception of the value of secondary education, and the potential of the

Box 2.2 Inequities in Educational Attainment in Developing Countries

In a study of educational attainment using household survey data from 35 developing countries, Filmer and Pritchett (1999) show that the difference between the richest and the poorest households in median grade attained by students age 15–19 is as high as 10 years of schooling in India and between 3 and 5 years in many of the developing countries surveyed (see the figure).

In the Republic of Yemen enrollment in lower secondary education (grades 7 to 9) increased by 220 percent between 1998 and 2002, while enrollment in upper secondary education experienced a 46 percent increase in the same period. As a result, the gross enrollment rate (GER) in secondary education is now close to 45 percent. This rate, however, hides extreme disparities by gender, by urban and rural area, and among districts. The government estimates that in 2002/3 the GER was 57 percent for boys and 24 percent for girls. In large cities such as Aden and Sana'a secondary school enrollment rates for both girls and boys were over 70 percent, with girls' GER at 102 percent, exceeding that of boys. But outside these cities, the picture is entirely different: in half the country's governorates, the GER for girls was below 15 percent, and girls accounted for fewer than one in five secondary students.

Median Grade Completed, Youths Age 15–19 from the Poorest 40 Percent and Richest 20 Percent of Households, Selected Countries

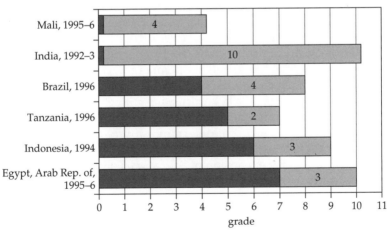

Median grade completed among the poorest
Gap between the richest and the poorest in the median grade completed

Source: Filmer and Pritchett 1999.

Note: The numbers on the bars show the size of the richest-poorest gap, in years of schooling.

credentials to provide graduates with a good chance of vertical mobility is severely reduced. By contrast, exclusivity enhances the value of credentials in the market. Goldin (2001) argues that the wage structure is the outcome of a race between technology and education. During most of the 20th century education outran technology, but during the past couple of decades, technology has outpaced education. This has introduced new variables, as well as new challenges to the employability of secondary graduates. Technological developments have demonstrated that expanding secondary education is simply not enough.

3. Expansion of secondary education has side effects within the education system itself. When a country decides to set and implement a goal of universalization of primary or basic education, an immediate and perhaps inevitable effect is that the next level tends to undergo significant internal differentiation and segmentation, reflecting sharply the divide between elite and mass educational opportunities. Ironically, this increased differentiation of, for instance, upper secondary education as a result of universalization of lower secondary schooling is often used in the political arena to question the benefits of expanding and democratizing education.

Conclusion

In today's world, acquisition of the enabling skills and competencies necessary for civic participation and economic success depends on access to good secondary education. Investment in secondary education in developing countries can be justified not only on the grounds of its contribution to productivity increases, which lay the basis for sustained economic growth and poverty reduction, but also for its contribution to human capital development and its associated effects on democracy, crime reduction, and improvement of living conditions.

Secondary education plays a key articulating role between primary schooling, tertiary education, and the labor market. The specific dynamics of this articulation is crucial because it determines future educational and job opportunities for young people. Secondary education can become a bottleneck constraining the expansion of educational attainment and opportunity, or, conversely, it can open a set of pathways and alternative channels for students' advancement.

Access to good secondary education entails having a system in which students have real opportunities to play meaningful roles in the enterprise of their own education. This ideal is at odds with the way secondary schools are currently organized—as large institutions that give youngsters few opportunities for self-management and participation. The result is disaffection among secondary students. This situation could become the main obstacle to increased participation in and graduation from secondary education. A policy challenge is to align secondary school curricula, pedagogy, and assessment with the demands and needs of young adolescents.

Unchecked expansion of secondary education, especially in countries with low participation rates at that level, could also give rise to increased inequalities in educational attainment by gender, social class, or region. Countries should consider targeted interventions to address this potential problem. Chapter 3 discusses in greater detail the challenges of expanding access to secondary education and improving its quality and relevance.

Notes

1. A balanced education system is one in which each level of education develops proportionally to prevailing access at lower levels.

2. In Angola, Botswana, Burkina Faso, Comoros, the Democratic Republic of Congo, Ghana, Sudan, and Zanzibar (Tanzania), basic education encompasses primary and junior (lower) secondary education and ranges from 7 to 10 years of schooling. In Benin, Burundi, Cameroon, the Central African Republic, the Democratic Republic of Congo, Eritrea, Guinea, Liberia, Madagascar, Mauritania, Mozambique, Rwanda, Senegal, mainland Tanzania, and Togo, only primary education is compulsory, and ages of children in compulsory education range between 5 and 11 years. In Chad, Kenya, Lesotho, Malawi, and Swaziland, primary education is not compulsory.

3. There is evidence that teachers in lower secondary schools spend more time maintaining order and less time actually teaching than do primary school teachers. In Greece 58 percent of students said that "more than five minutes go by at the start of each class without anything being done"; 46 percent, that there is noise and commotion; and 29 percent, that students do not listen to what the teacher says (OECD 2003d).

4. The report looks at two ways in which students can become disaffected. One is through a poor sense of belonging at school. For example, students may believe that their school experience has little bearing on their future, or they may feel rejected by their classmates or teachers. The other way is through low participation or absenteeism, calculated on the basis of the students' recent attendance at school.

5. The youth-adult unemployment ratio is defined as the ratio of the unemployment rate among those age 15–24 to the rate among those age 25–54.

3

The Twin Challenges in Secondary Education: Expanding Access and Improving Quality and Relevance

The central objective of secondary education is to provide young people with opportunities to acquire the skills, aptitudes, values, knowledge, and experience needed to continue their education and to be active citizens and productive workers. As a consequence of the accelerating pace of global integration and the accompanying changes in countries' socioeconomic conditions, objectives that focus on adaptation to the world of the future, with its changing and unpredictable labor markets and increasing labor migration, are receiving greater attention. One of the main challenges for policy makers is to ensure that secondary education is accessible to young people. Secondary schooling is intended to equip students with the education, knowledge, and skills that will prepare them for the constantly changing workplace. Such education would enable them to respond appropriately to emerging changes throughout their lives. Policy makers are, accordingly, striving to design policies and strategies suited to the particular country's sociocultural context and economic realities.

Depending on specific conditions in developing countries and transition economies, the challenges for secondary education can be broadly grouped into two priority areas: expanding access, and improving relevance and quality. A key policy objective is to ensure that both access and quality are enhanced for those generally excluded by poverty, ethnicity, gender, and other factors. This chapter lays out the magnitude of the challenges involved in this pursuit.

From Elitism to Inclusiveness: Expanding Access to Secondary Education

Despite significant growth in secondary school enrollments in recent years, developing countries face enormous challenges, especially in improving overall educational attainment. The primary reasons are limited access, low internal efficiency resulting from high repetition and dropout, and low overall quality. Developing countries have made concerted efforts to expand access to secondary education, and many are providing secondary education opportunities at a higher level than developed countries did when their income levels were similar. Yet developing countries continue to fall behind developed countries, for a number of reasons, and most developing countries need to make massive efforts to surmount the problem.

Of immediate importance is that developing countries need to establish a system of mass secondary education that (a) is responsive to countries' socioeconomic needs and capabilities, (b) can respond effectively to increased and diversified demand by expanding access to secondary education, (c) is able to retain enrolled students in secondary school, and (d) helps students graduate with the knowledge, skills, attitudes, and experiences needed to exercise their choices beyond secondary education.

Over the course of the second half of the 20th century, access to secondary education increased much faster in developing countries than it had in OECD countries between 1900 and 1950. Using 1990 data, Goldin (2002) compared real gross domestic product (GDP) per capita and the gross enrollment rate (GER) in a large number of countries with the evolution of these indicators in the United States beginning in 1900. She found that by 1990 developing countries had achieved higher participation rates than the United States had at the same level of per capita GDP in 1900 and 1920. Figure 3.1 shows that in 1990, even when their GDP per capita was significantly lower, only a few developing countries had GERs below the 1900 U.S. level; indeed, a large number had GERs above the 1920 U.S. GER. Goldin further showed that in 1990 many developing countries had higher secondary school GERs than most European countries had in the mid-1950s, when the latter had comparatively higher GDP per capita.

Nevertheless, the gap in access to secondary education has widened since 1990 because developing countries have not expanded opportunities in secondary education as rapidly as have developed countries. With the exception of Eastern Europe all developing regions are far behind developed countries.

In the 1990s some developing countries made concerted efforts to expand access to secondary education, with dramatic results (see figure 3.2). For example (taking one country in each region), between 1970 and 2000 Zimbabwe's GER increased from 7.5 to 44.5 percent; Brazil's rose from 26 to 108 percent; Thailand's, from 17 to 82 percent: India's, from 24 to 49 percent; and the Arab Republic of Egypt's, from 28 to 86 percent. Box 3.1 describes how India, with its large out-of-school population, has worked to extend the reach of secondary education.

Figure 3.1 Gross Enrollment Rates in Secondary Schools and GDP per Capita, 127 Countries, 1990

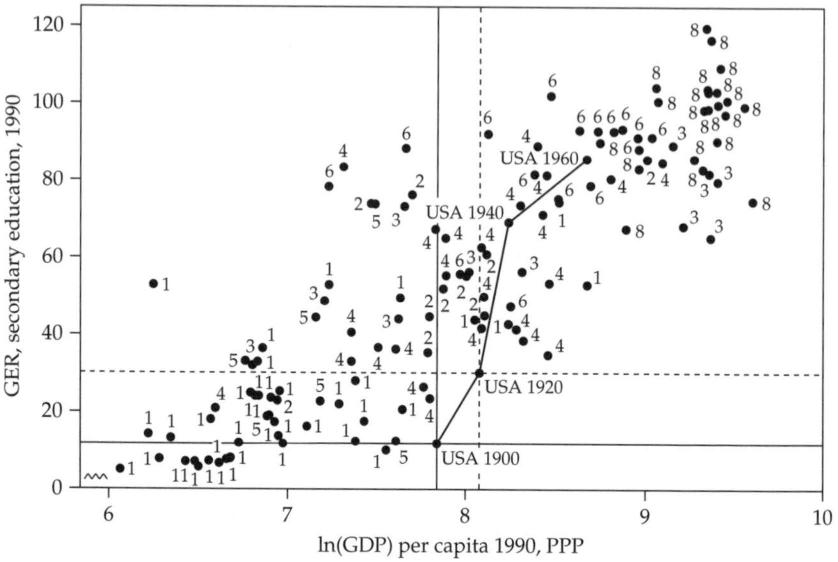

Source: Adapted from Goldin (2002).

Note: GDP, gross domestic product; GER, gross enrollment rate; PPP, purchasing power parity. Regional codes are as follows: Sub-Saharan Africa = 1; Middle East and North Africa = 2; East Asia and the Pacific = 3; Latin America and the Caribbean = 4; South Asia = 5; Eastern Europe and Central Asia = 6; developed countries = 8.

During the 1990s many Latin American countries designed and implemented important secondary education reforms in an attempt to improve access, equity, quality, and relevance. The results have been encouraging for access and equity but less so for quality and relevance. This is evident from poor student performance in countries participating in international tests such as the Trends in International Mathematics and Science Study (TIMSS), the Programme on International Student Assessment (PISA), and the International Assessment of Literacy Study (IALS). Regional policy makers have been preoccupied with analyzing the results to determine what "went wrong" and what can be done to achieve success (UNESCO 2002).

Equity Considerations

In many countries, inequities in access to secondary schooling may be a major barrier to human development and therefore to economic growth and poverty reduction. Historically, the initial expansion of access to

Figure 3.2 Gross Enrollment Rates in Secondary Education by Region, 1970–95

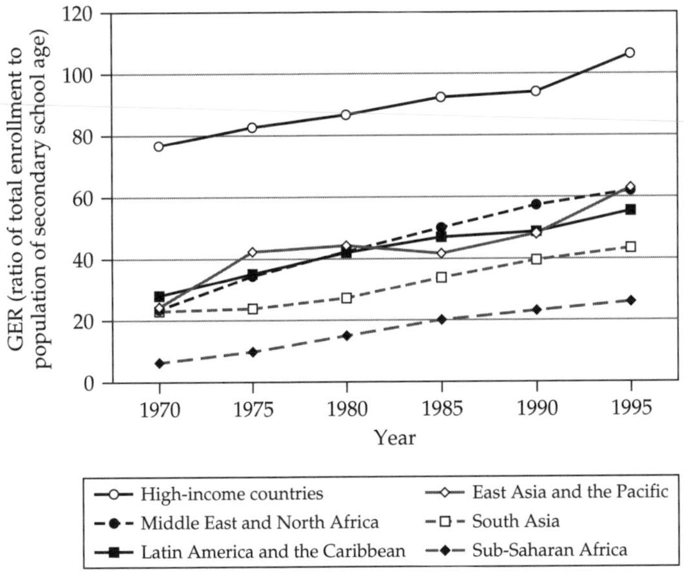

Source: World Bank, EdStats, 2004.

Note: GER, gross enrollment rate.

Box 3.1 Secondary Education in India: Building on Successes in Primary Schooling

India, a country of more than a billion people and a per capita GDP of over $520, has made remarkable progress in poverty alleviation and education. The 1990s saw a great push to expand and improve schooling. Significant advances were made in extending access to primary education to girls, scheduled castes, and scheduled tribes and in narrowing the gaps between urban and rural areas. Between 1993 and 2001 the GER for primary education (grades 1–5) increased from 82 to 96 percent, the GER for upper primary grades (6–8) increased from 54 to 60 percent, and the GER for secondary education rose from 31 percent to more than 49 percent. About 160 million students were enrolled in elementary education (primary and upper primary), 30 million in secondary education, and 1.5 to 2 million in vocational education and training institutions. By 2001 the efforts had been extended to upper primary education (equivalent to lower secondary education elsewhere).

(Continued)

Box 3.1 Continued

In 2002 the constitution was amended to make eight years of elementary education a fundamental right of every child. The government of India launched the National Program for Universal Elementary Education, which aims at ensuring that all children between ages 6 and 14 complete eight years of education of satisfactory quality by 2010. Since the states have primary responsibility for providing and financing education, the Elementary Education Program provides for fiscal transfers from the union government to state governments to support their efforts, in a cost-sharing arrangement in which 75 percent from the center is to be matched by 25 percent from the states. This would provide additional resources of about 9 percent over the existing operating expenditure on elementary education.

Although the National Program for Universal Elementary Education began only a few years ago, preliminary results show a dramatic reduction in the number of out-of-school children—from 25 million in 2003 to fewer than 10 million in 2005. This outcome is the fruit of intense social mobilization and concerted efforts at all levels of government. Dropout has also been reduced modestly, as a consequence of some improvement in school quality. It can be expected that the demand for secondary education (grades 9 and 10), senior secondary education (grades 11 and 12), and vocational education and training (VET) will increase manyfold within a few years. By 2010 it is envisaged that an additional 10 million primary school graduates will be seeking admission to secondary school. A few years later, this demand will spread to tertiary education.

For the vast majority of youths, secondary education or VET is the last stage of formal schooling. Fewer than 10 percent of secondary graduates go on to the tertiary system, while most of the remainder seek to enter the labor market. An effective school-to-work transition for these youths, made possible by enhancing the quality of secondary education and VET, will improve their employment prospects and lifetime earnings. At the same time, India needs to maintain very high quality secondary and higher education to keep its cutting edge in the information technology and business services sectors. But India's secondary education and VET systems face numerous challenges, including those of access, quality, and relevance. Recognizing this, the government has devised strategies that include increasing private sector participation; providing financial assistance for girls to encourage them to enroll in secondary school; revising and updating the curriculum, with a focus on mathematics and science; and improving teacher quality. The government plans to proceed with greater vocationalization of secondary education and upgrading of vocational training institutions and facilities to make them more responsive to labor market demand.

Source: World Bank staff, South Asia Region, 2005.

secondary education has not equally benefited boys and girls. As expansion reaches an initial threshold, gender differences begin to emerge. Cultural factors that favor sending boys to school while keeping girls at home to look after younger siblings, combined with low expectations that girls will enter the job market, are often cited as the primary reasons for gender differentials in secondary school enrollments.

Close analysis of the gender parity index (GPI) in figure 3.3 reveals that in all regions disparity in access between boys and girls has been decreasing over time, to an extent that in most regions it is almost indiscernible. Still, in South Asia 52 percent of boys but only 33 percent of girls are enrolled in secondary school. In the Middle East and North Africa the figures are 64 percent for boys and 55 percent for girls, and in African countries, 28 percent for boys and 22 percent for girls (UNESCO 2004b). And although the gender gap in enrollments has narrowed, intraregional and intercountry differences persist. In regions where access is still low, policies to improve coverage might result in gender differentials unless accompanied by appropriate policies to address equity issues.

Figure 3.3 Gender Parity Index in Secondary Education by Region, Selected Years, 1970–2000

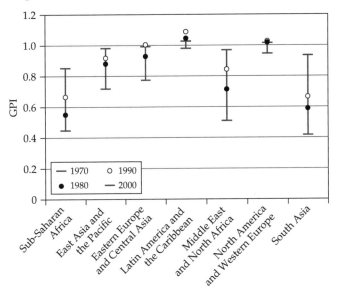

Source: World Bank, EdStats.

Note: The gender parity index (GPI) is the ratio of female to male gross enrollment rates in secondary education. A GPI of 1 indicates parity; a value between 0 and 1 indicates disparity in favor of boys; and a value greater than 1 indicates disparity in favor of girls.

Regional and Country Disparities

Use of the Cohen-Soto dataset developed by Bloom (2003) shows that the encouraging history observed in the evolution of access to primary education has not been duplicated for secondary education. Worldwide improvements in secondary education enrollment hide wide interregional and intraregional disparities. GERs in East Asia and the Pacific, Latin America and the Caribbean, and the Middle East and North Africa were around 42 percent in 1980. By 1996 they had risen to 69, 52, and 64 percent for the respective regions. In South Asia between 1980 and 1996, GERs rose from 27 to 48 percent, and in Sub-Saharan Africa, from 15 to 27 percent (*World Development Indicators*, 1998, 1999). Figure 3.4 reveals widening gaps across regions between those who have at least some secondary education and those who do not.

Intraregional comparisons show similar disparities. In Africa, for example, GERs in secondary education in Burkina Faso, Chad, Guinea, Mozambique, and Niger are still below 13 percent, whereas South Africa has a GER of 87 percent.

Figure 3.4 Share of Population with at Least Some Secondary Education by Region, 1960–2000 and Projected to 2010

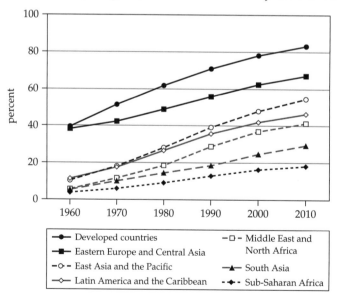

Source: Cohen and Soto 2001.

Demand-Side Interventions

Affordability is a principal reason children either do not go to school or drop out early. The primary constraint is household income forgone because of the loss of the school-going child's earnings. Under these circumstances, supply-side initiatives such as improving schools, augmenting teachers' salaries, and reforming the ministry of education are not likely to have significant effects. Demand-side interventions such as conditional transfers for education may be more effective because they go directly toward achieving program objectives—higher school enrollment and retention levels.

Until recently, little was known about the role of targeted education subsidies in improving educational outcomes in developing countries, although these programs have taken root rapidly, especially in Latin America (Morley and Coady 2003). Examples of targeted subsidies include cash-for-education programs such as Brazil's Bolsa Escola (Scholarship Fund), Chile's SUF (Unitary Family Subsidy), Honduras's PRAF (Family Allowance Program), Mexico's Progresa (Education, Health, and Nutrition Program), and Nicaragua's RPS (Social Safety Net), as well as the food-for-education program in Bangladesh, which has now been monetized. These programs represent, on average, a commitment of between 0.1 and 0.2 percent of gross national income. Of particular interest is the size of the programs in relation to what governments spend on education. In Latin America governments are committing about 2.5 to 5 percent of total education spending to these programs, which have contributed significantly to increasing school enrollments (Morley and Coady 2003). Providing demand-side financing to secondary school students can thus have significant direct and indirect benefits. Mexico's cash-for-education program (box 3.2) is a good illustration.

Low Retention and Completion in Secondary Education

Not only are developing countries having problems with providing opportunities to attend secondary education; they are also doing a poor job at keeping and graduating those who enter secondary school. The situation is worse for the poor and for girls.

Using 1995–96 household data from 41 countries, Filmer (2000) studied the interactions of gender, wealth, and educational attainment and showed considerable within-country inequalities in educational attainment. Filmer's findings reveal a significant gap in completion rates among young adults from poor, middle-income, and rich households. For example, in Egypt among males age 15–19, 99 percent of those from rich households had completed grade 1 or higher, 94 percent had completed grade 5 or higher, and

---

Box 3.2 Progresa, Mexico's Cash-for-Education Program

Progresa, which serves students enrolled in secondary education as well as primary school, began in 1992 as a pilot project of the Ministry of Social Development and was scaled up in rural areas countrywide in 1997. In 1999 monthly benefits started at 80 pesos ($8.37) in grade 3 of primary school and increased with each grade. This approach was adopted because enrollment levels decline with age, especially after primary school, partly as a consequence of the rising opportunity costs associated with forgone income and travel costs. In junior secondary school (grades 7–9), benefits are higher for females, with the aim of reducing the gender gap in educational outcomes, especially in secondary education.

The Progresa program interacts with supply-side government expenditures on schools. Progresa works closely with the Ministry of Education to ensure that extra schools, teachers, and materials are made available in areas that experience increased enrollments. As a result, higher enrollments have not led to higher student-teacher ratios. Furthermore, because new schools have been built in program areas, the distance to secondary school has been reduced by about 10 percent.

The effect of Progresa on educational outcomes is greatest during the transition year between primary and junior secondary school, where there has been a 20 percent increase in enrollment for girls and 10 percent for boys. A child in the program receives, on average, 0.66 extra years of education—from an average level of 6.8 years of education before the program to 7.46 years. Providing demand-side financing to secondary school students thus has had significant direct and indirect benefits.

Source: Morley and Coady 2003.

---

81 percent had completed grade 9 or higher. Among young males from middle-income families, the respective proportions were 96, 83, and 64 percent. Young males from poor families had considerably lower attainment: 87 percent for grade 1 or higher, 74 percent for grade 5 or higher, and 47 percent for grade 9 or higher. This type of scenario is observed in other parts of the world as well, as demonstrated by the figures in appendix B and by the data results in appendix C. The countries included in the study experienced a significant decrease in enrollments during transition from primary to secondary education, and the decline was more dramatic in rural than in urban areas. One positive outcome was that most rural students who reached secondary education remained in the system until graduation.

The income and gender differentials manifest themselves in significant variations between urban and rural areas. A study of four countries that

Figure 3.5 Share of Rural and Urban Cohorts Reaching Next Grade in School, Dominican Republic, Ecuador, Mexico, and Peru, Early 1990s

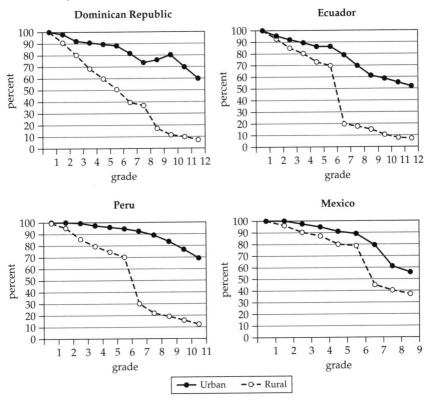

Source: Cabrol 2002.

are representative of the reality in most of Latin America shows large differences in graduation rates between students from rural and urban communities. Figure 3.5 illustrates how in the early 1990s in Peru, of the original cohort of rural students enrolled in grade 1, 70 percent reached grade 6, less than 40 percent entered grade 7, and only 20 percent entered grade 11. A large proportion of students from rural families do not continue to secondary education, although the few who do are quite successful. Students in urban schools did better: close to 98 percent entered grade 6, 95 percent entered grade 7, and 75 percent reached grade 11.

In a large country such as Mexico the difference in primary school completion between rural and urban areas is not nearly as dramatic; there, almost 75 percent of rural students and 85 percent of urban students enter grade 6. In secondary education there is a stark difference, with fewer than 50 percent of rural students going on to secondary education and only 40 percent graduating from lower secondary education (grade 9), whereas 68 percent of students from urban families continue to secondary education and 64 percent graduate from grade 9.

The two main factors responsible for the low levels of participation in secondary education in Latin American countries are loss of interest on the part of parents and students because of high repetition levels, and the perception that the quality and relevance of education are low. Mexico has been addressing this problem through a special distance education program, Telesecundaria, that targets rural areas. Telesecundaria began over 30 years ago as a television-based educational program. In its initial phase it used microwave and later moved to broadcast satellite programming. Telesecundaria provides rural teachers and students with a complete package to support teaching and learning, together with a comprehensive instructional model, enabling schools to deliver a full junior secondary curriculum at costs comparable to those in more populated urban areas (Calderoni 1998).

In East Asia, China has made great strides in expanding access to secondary education in a very short period of time, as described in box 3.3.

Incorporating Adults into the Secondary Education System

Although the focus of this paper is on school-age youths, it is important to note that in many developing countries adult education, training, and retraining are inadequate for the challenges of a knowledge society. Using average years of schooling of the population older than age 25 as an indicator of adult educational attainment helps highlight the magnitude of this problem. In South Asia in 1990 the figure was 3.3 years, and in Sub-Saharan Africa it was only 2.5, but in OECD countries it was, on average, 9.4 (Barro and Lee 1996). In recognition that secondary education is an important vehicle for national skills formation, countries in recent years have expanded second-chance education for the adult population in both formal and non-formal educational settings.

Most countries tend to rely on distance education to give adults opportunities to complete general secondary education. For example, the National Open School of India serves as an alternative to formal secondary education and reaches out to learners of all ages in the country with its flexible educational programs. Vocational upper secondary education, which may offer supplementary courses for secondary school students, has also been used to provide continuing education for adults. Finland has a noteworthy adult education program: except for basic university education, adults can participate in all levels of certificate-oriented and non-certificate-oriented education in courses designed specifically for adults (World Bank 2003c).

Box 3.3 Policies for Expansion of Secondary Education in China

In China a drive to expand secondary education led to a dramatic increase in lower secondary enrollment between 1990 and 2002. During those years the GER increased from 66.7 to 90.0 percent as a result of the implementation of three intertwined policies in support of expansion:

- *Education legislation to promote enrollment.* In 1986 the Chinese government promulgated the Compulsory Education Law (CEL), which established rights and obligations of individuals and governments with respect to compulsory education. The CEL contained two main provisions for promoting enrollment in lower secondary education: (a) all children reaching age six had to enroll in school and receive nine years of compulsory education—that is, lower secondary education became mandatory; and (b) local authorities were given the responsibility for compulsory education, including operating funds, capital investment, and teachers' salaries. The central government was responsible for increasing per-pupil expenditures at a faster rate than the increase in regular state expenditure on education.
- *Mobilization of resources in rural areas.* In the early 1990s, as the income of farmers in wealthy areas increased rapidly, the central government introduced a 2 percent education tax in rural areas. This tax, together with other types of parental contribution, yielded RMB 100 billion ($12.5 billion), which was added to the budgetary resources of local governments for the development of nine-year compulsory education.
- *Increased government expenditure for rural education.* Since the mid-1990s government spending on basic education has increased, in terms both of regular budgetary expenditures and of special funds for rural areas. As a result, between 1996 and 2001 recurrent expenditures for lower secondary education grew at a rate of 151 percent. The national government began allocating about RMB 5 billion–10 billion annually to rural areas for construction, renovation, and Internet education. This central special fund is provided as a cofinancing contribution to participating local governments.

Sources: China, *National Education Finance Statistics Yearbook* 1997, 2002; National Center for Education Development and Research 2003, 26–27.

Incorporating the adult population into the education system requires strategic thinking on many policy and education issues. The significant differences in learning styles and needs between young and adult learners have to be taken into account. A country that has a large number of adults with limited education and wants to increase investment in more technologically advanced industries would need to analyze how to respond to the training needs of individuals who have only primary education and who are mainly employed in the informal sector. Important questions for policy makers arise in this context: What role should secondary education play? Should adults be streamed into formal secondary schools? Should adult programs embrace education and training that lead to secondary school certificates or some other form of recognition?

Secondary Education Attainment

Educational attainment has improved steadily over the past 40 years in all regions of the world (see the data on selected countries in appendix C). But despite the progress, many developing countries still lag behind. Although the average number of years of schooling has increased steadily in all regions, the rate of growth shows significant variation (figure 3.6). Sub-Saharan

Figure 3.6 Average Years of Schooling, Population Age Five and Older, by Region, 1960, 1980, and 2000

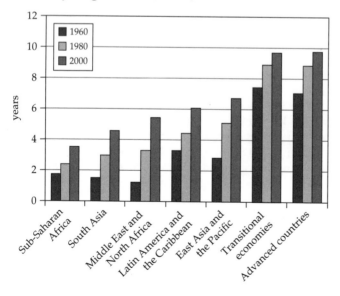

Source: Barro and Lee 2000.

Africa has fallen alarmingly behind in spite of tremendous efforts and some achievements in the past decade.

Average years of schooling is commonly used as an indicator of educational attainment. It is incorrect, however, to assume that the more years of schooling, the better will be the quality and depth of the knowledge acquired.

Compared with advances in primary education, increases in the share of the population achieving secondary education have been rather slow. Low provision of secondary education has been the bottleneck to increased educational attainment in most developing countries. As figure 3.7 shows, Sub-Saharan African countries have lagged in providing secondary education, in part because of neglect in the 1970s, and the trend continues. In 1960 the proportion attaining the secondary education level in Sub-Saharan Africa was larger than in South Asia and in the Middle East and North Africa, but by 2000 the proportion of its population with some secondary education was significantly lower than in other regions. A similar trend can be observed when comparing East Asia and Latin America: in East Asia the population

Figure 3.7 Educational Level of Population Age 15 and Older by Region, 1960 and 2000

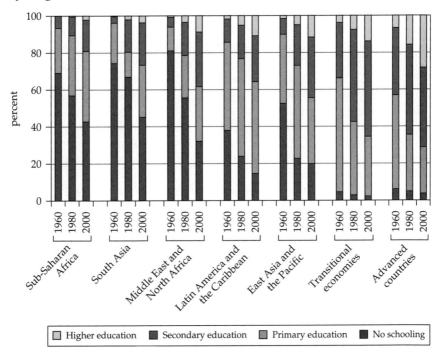

Source: Barro and Lee 2000.

ıth secondary education expanded significantly, but Latin America made only modest gains. Most countries in these regions will need to continue making significant and concerted efforts in the next 10 to 20 years to reduce the current schooling gap. Both transition and advanced economies showed dramatic improvements, with nearly full enrollment of primary-school-age children and, at the same time, an increase in the student population attaining at least secondary education.

Can the secondary education gap among regions be reduced? The experiences of, for example, Finland, Hong Kong (China), the Republic of Korea, Malaysia, Singapore, and Taiwan (China) demonstrate not only that it is possible but also that the gap can be reduced in a relatively short time. Between 1960 and 2000 these economies increased their average years of schooling by more than 4.5 years (World Bank 2003a). Finland and Korea achieved this by taking strong measures to reduce the fraction of the adult population that had only primary education while increasing the opportunities for all to attend secondary education.

Over the past 40 years, both Finland and Korea have implemented active education policies that have led to a large increase in the number of adults with at least a secondary school education (figure 3.8, panel A). The education transition in Korea is illustrated by the change from an education pyramid with a large base, implying a large number of adults with less than primary education, to one that is larger in the middle (representing adults with some secondary schooling) than at the base. Korea's policies took only 20 years to achieve this result, whereas the same process took 40 years in Finland. (See box 3.4 for a fuller discussion of Korea's success.) Educational upgrading in the East Asian "tigers" and in Finland and other Nordic countries began with improvements at the bottom of the pyramid, through strong and sustained efforts to provide secondary education. The education policies of these countries resulted in a widening of the middle section of the pyramid and a considerable reduction of the base, initially leaving the top (adults with some tertiary education) almost unchanged.

By contrast, the education transitions of most countries in Africa, South Asia, and East Asia show very slow or almost no progress over the past 40 years (see the examples in figure 3.8, panels B–C). South Africa has advanced significantly during the past 20 years after a period of stagnation. The Philippines experienced a considerable expansion of the populations with secondary and with tertiary education (panel D). Its relatively equal efforts toward expanding tertiary and secondary education have been impressive.

Overall, the expansion of secondary education in Latin America has been weak. In most countries a large fraction of the population still has primary education or less. Latin America is distinctive in that it has invested heavily in increasing access to tertiary education. Costa Rica presents an extreme

Figure 3.8 Distribution of the Population over Age 15 by Educational Attainment, Selected Countries

A. Finland and Republic of Korea

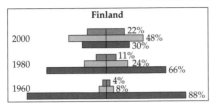

B. South Africa and Kenya

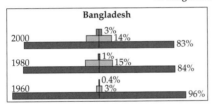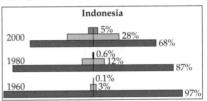

C. Bangladesh and Indonesia

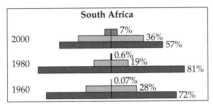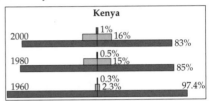

D. Philippines and Poland

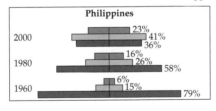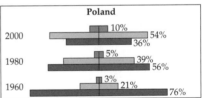

E. Colombia and Costa Rica

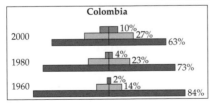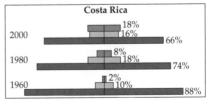

■ Percentage of population over age 15 with tertiary education or higher
■ Percentage of population over age 15 with secondary education
■ Percentage of population over age 15 with primary education or no schooling

Source: Authors' compilation.

Box 3.4 The Drive for Universal Primary and Secondary Education in Korea

Emerging from a bitter war in the early 1950s, the Republic of Korea, at that time one of the world's poorest countries, achieved nearly 100 percent coverage in primary and secondary education in just four decades. Korea now has a tertiary education sector comparable to that in developed countries. Average years of schooling almost doubled between 1970 and 1995, from 5.74 years to 10.25 years. The illiteracy rate fell dramatically, from 13 percent in 1970 to 2 percent in 1999. Results from the most recent PISA and TIMSS studies (1995 and 1999) show that Korean students are among the top performers in both mathematics and science in OECD member countries. It is no coincidence that Korea has become the world's 12th largest economy.

The rapid expansion of education is attributable to a number of factors:

1. In the late 1950s the government embarked on a comprehensive development plan that included a strengthened and broadened education system. In the 1960s the plan emphasized universal primary education as a top priority; in the 1970s policy emphasis shifted to secondary education, and in the 1980s, to the tertiary level.

2. Equity considerations were important for a balanced expansion of the education system. In 1968 the government abolished the entrance examination for middle schools and introduced a lottery system for student placement. The lottery was perceived as fair because placement was based mainly on residence rather than on test scores, which may be influenced by economic means or other socioeconomic factors. The new system, which virtually eliminated all elite middle schools, was well accepted by students, parents, and other stakeholders without much controversy. In 1974 the government introduced the similar but more controversial High School Equalization Policy (HSEP), which was intended to equalize or level school inputs such as operating expenditures, student intake, class size, and education facilities across schools. The HSEP contributed to the expansion of upper secondary education. Thanks to the subsidy and to other measures under the equalization policy, there is no discernible quality difference across public schools or between private and public schools.

3. Government spending increased substantially to finance the expansion. Between 1954 and 1959 government spending on education rose threefold. By 1960 four-fifths of the education budget was focused on primary education. The education budget has increased steadily, from 14.3 percent of the total government budget in 1963 to 17.5 percent in 2003. Education expenditure as a percentage of GDP increased from 2.9 percent in 1970 to 4.97 percent in 2003.

(continued)

Box 3.4 Continued

4. Private participation has been significant in sustaining the expansion. As of 2000, the enrollment shares of the private sector were 20 percent for middle schools, 55 percent for high schools, and 78 percent for four-year colleges and universities. Private providers of secondary and tertiary education were supported largely by government tax incentives (for example, property tax exemptions), fees, family contributions, and foreign aid until growing government revenues could be reinvested in education. The government started to provide direct financial assistance to private providers following the introduction of school-leveling policies.

The significant social and economic demand for education was pivotal in helping Korea achieve its education goals. The Korean case demonstrates that political commitment at the inception of a national education development plan and throughout its implementation is critical in pushing the education frontier from the lower to the upper levels of the system and that access and equity can be achieved simultaneously if the government resolutely addresses potential trade-offs between the two goals in the planning and implementation stages.

Source: Authors' compilation.

example of this situation, with a larger proportion of adults having tertiary education than secondary education (figure 3.8, panel E). Additional examples of education pyramids are presented in appendix D.

Low Quality and Relevance

We have seen that developing countries today have higher levels of access to secondary education than did developed countries when the latter were at similar levels of per capita income. What can be said about the quality of secondary education in developing countries? How do country averages and within-country distribution compare with those in developed countries? Is there evidence that countries that have expanded access to secondary education very quickly have education of lower quality than others?

Cognitive performance can be considered a reasonable proxy for quality. In recent years there has been an attempt to assess cognitive performance through international assessments such as TIMSS and PISA. It is widely acknowledged that more developed than developing countries

Figure 3.9 Student Performance and GDP per Capita, Selected Economies, PISA 2000, Reading

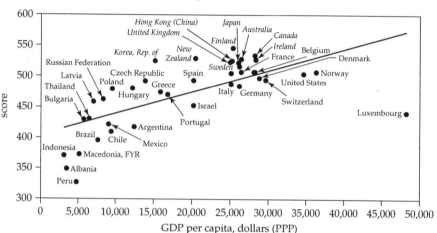

Source: OECD 2003b.

Note: GDP, gross domestic product; PISA, Programme on International Student Assessment; PPP, purchasing power parity. Italics indicate countries that are statistically significantly above the OECD average.

participate in comparative international assessments. Among those countries that do participate, the test results indicate that developing countries do relatively poorly compared with developed countries and that middle-income countries do relatively less well than high-income countries. Since the poorest countries do not typically participate in comparative international assessments, it is difficult to come to objective conclusions as to how they fare in the comparison. Notwithstanding low overall performance, the variance in scores between high and low performers within developing countries is much higher than that observed for developed countries.

The results of the PISA study on access to quality education show that in general, students from high-income countries tend to perform better than those from low- and middle-income countries (see figure 3.9).[1] The wealth of a nation, however, is not always a good predictor of test achievement. For example, high-income Italy has a mean performance in reading that is almost 40 points lower than Korea's. Thailand, with half Argentina's GDP per capita, scores slightly higher than that country. What appears to matter most is how a county's education system deploys and uses resources in order to provide good learning opportunities.

Figure 3.10 shows the percentage of students at each proficiency level on the PISA reading literacy scale. In OECD countries 60 percent of 15-year-olds can perform reading tasks of at least moderate complexity, such as locating multiple pieces of information, making links between different

Figure 3.10 Percentage of Students Age 15 at Each Level of Proficiency on the PISA Reading Literacy Scale, Selected Economies, 2000

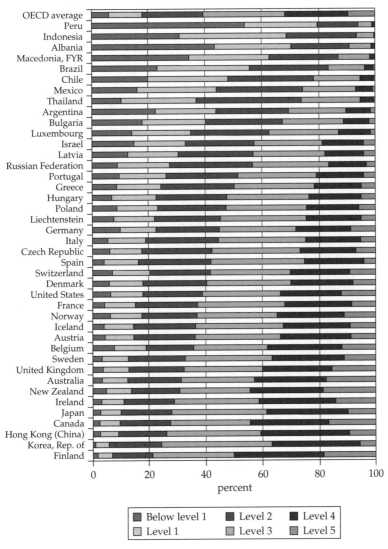

Source: OECD 2003b, table 2.

Note: PISA, Programme on International Student Assessment. Students who score below level 1 are considered to lack the most basic skills that PISA assesses. Students proficient at level 3 on the combined reading literacy scale are able to perform reading tasks of moderate complexity, such as locating multiple pieces of information, making links between different parts of a text, and relating text to familiar, everyday knowledge; 60 percent of the students in the OECD average are at or above level 3.

parts of a text, and relating text to familiar everyday knowledge (that is, they are either at or above level 3 in the PISA study). In most participating developing countries 15-year-olds do not show this capacity. Ten low-income and middle-income countries—five in Latin America, plus Albania, Bulgaria, Indonesia, the former Yugoslav Republic of Macedonia, and Thailand—have the largest percentages of students below level 3.

Comparison of average scores provides a good overview of a country's performance relative to others, but it masks variance in student performance within a country. Here again, developing countries perform poorly. The variance between low and high performers in developing countries is significantly higher than in high-income countries. Developing countries face the challenge of raising the average level of performance while at the same time reducing the disparity between high and low achievers. Policy makers need to design and implement targeted interventions with the overall objective of improving the quality of secondary education and reducing the quality and relevance gap.

The three top scorers in the PISA study—Finland, Hong Kong (China), and Korea—exhibit relatively low variance between high and low performers. This signals that their education systems have had considerable success in eliminating socioeconomic segregation and have provided high-quality learning opportunities to all. As discussed earlier, over the span of the 40 years 1960 to 2000, these countries significantly increased average years of schooling by improving secondary education attainment while at the same time providing high-quality education for all.

Panel A of figure 3.11 presents the cumulative frequency of student achievement by proficiency level on the PISA test. The figure shows that in poorer countries few students perform at the OECD average. In Peru and Indonesia, for example, even students at their country's 95th percentile are below the OECD average.

Panel A also shows that not all middle-income countries are the same. In particular, of the examples chosen, Mexico and Thailand are clearly "better" at improving quality at the left-hand end of the distribution. Children who are poor performers compared with their own top performers and with the OECD average are fewer in number in these countries, whereas in Peru (in particular), Brazil, and Indonesia very large numbers of students are at the lowest level of proficiency. Panel B of figure 3.11, which shows the simple frequency distributions by level of proficiency, illustrates these dynamics even more dramatically.

Taking Peru, Indonesia, Brazil, Mexico, Thailand, and the OECD total as being in a sort of spectrum, it can clearly be seen that as countries improve in quality, the most dramatic changes are seen at the left-hand end of the distribution. In Peru more than 50 percent of children are below level 1 on the PISA scale, but in Mexico the figure is only about 15 percent and in Thailand, about 10 percent. Not by coincidence, in a recent compendium of good

Figure 3.11. PISA Achievement, OECD Average and Selected Developing Countries, 2000

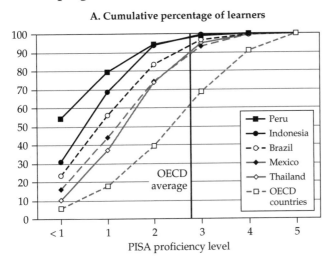

A. Cumulative percentage of learners

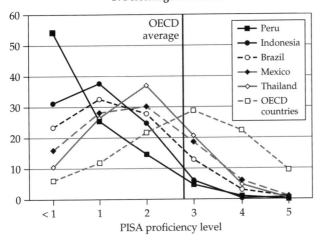

B. Percentage of learners

Source: Based on data in Mullis et al. (2001), table 2.3.a.

Note: PISA, Programme on International Student Assessment. For PISA proficiency levels, see the note to figure 3.10.

practices in education (de Andraca 2003), Mexico is listed as having several programs oriented toward improving the educational performance of the poor—programs such as Progresa, which provides conditional cash transfers for attendance, and Telesecundaria, which is aimed at improving quality among the poor through distance education.

Figure 3.12 Relative Performance of High-Income Countries and Selected Middle-Income Countries (South Africa, Morocco, and Chile) on the TIMSS-R

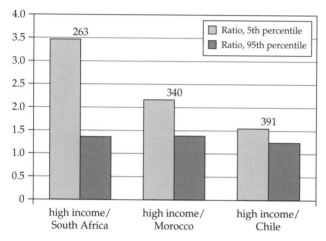

Sources: Based on data in OECD and UIS (2003), exhibit D.1; and on World Bank classification of countries by income group.

Note: TIMSS-R, Trends in International Mathematics and Science Study, repeat data set. The numerals above the bars represent the average score for each country.

Figure 3.12 makes the same point, using data from TIMSS and a somewhat different approach. Three countries—Chile, Morocco, and South Africa—are selected as representative of a spectrum among middle-income countries. The figure shows relative performance of high-income countries and the selected country at the 5th and 95th percentiles, as well as the average performance of each country. As countries' average performance improves, the ratio of high-income country performance to each country's performance drops, as one would expect. But the important thing to note is that the ratio of high-income performance to selected country performance falls much faster for performance at the 5th percentile. As countries improve their averages, it is the gap between their worst performers and the worst performers in the OECD countries that narrows the most. Indeed, using TIMSS data, for middle-income countries, the ratio between high-income and selected country performance decreases seven times faster at the 5th than at the 95th percentile, as average performance improves.

Figure 3.13 shows that income, access, and quality go together; that is, higher income, greater access, and higher achievement tend to be correlated. Furthermore, the lower the income level, the higher is the correlation between access and achievement, and the steeper the relationship. (The central

Figure 3.13 Access, Learning, and Income by Country Income Group

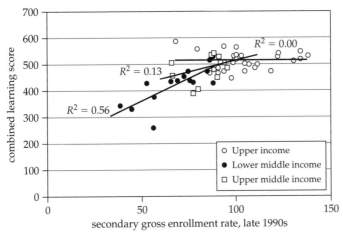

Sources: EdStats; elaborations by the authors using World Bank classification of countries by income group.

Note: PISA, Programme on International Student Assessment; TIMSS, Trends in International Mathematics and Science Study. The combined PISA, TIMSS99, and TIMSS95 index was crafted as follows. The correlation between the average of all three PISA areas and TIMSS99 performance in mathematics and science was 0.85, and that between TIMSS99 and TIMSS95 (grade 8) was 0.92. A simple regression was used to create TIMSS99-equivalent scores for countries reporting PISA but not TIMSS99 data, and similarly with TIMSS95.

tendency lines flatten and show lower correlation coefficients as income increases.) This result is to some degree an artifact of the data: high-income countries have very high quality and access, both of which tend to have natural upper limits (either because of the measurement approach or by definition), and so the relationship between the two becomes less significant.

The correlation between access and achievement should not be taken to mean that access automatically leads to higher achievement. Excessive expansion would generally be expected to lead to decreased quality, if nothing active is done to maintain quality. The data do, however, suggest that as access has expanded, countries and international organizations have in fact generally taken steps to focus on quality and achievement issues more or less in tandem. These steps, as noted above, generally include conscious schema and management systems that improve quality and performance at the lower end of the performance distribution. Such efforts clearly need to continue, and in countries such as Peru or Brazil they need to improve. Figure 3.13 also makes it clear that both access and quality are improved by a third factor—income per capita. Again, this improvement is not automatic: better-off countries have put in place the right processes and systems to improve quality, particularly of the poorer performers in their own societies.

Conclusion

Depending on specific country conditions, the principal challenges in secondary education in developing countries and transition economies can be grouped into four, not mutually exclusive, priority areas: (a) expanding access for all, paying special attention to issues relating to gender- and ethnicity-related exclusion; (b) increasing retention and graduation; (c) improving efficiency; and (d) improving relevance and quality. Countries have to address these issues in resource-constrained environments, within hard budget constraints. The reality is that either developing countries and transition economies lack the capacity to raise the additional resources necessary to address most of these priorities, or the fresh new resources they can raise are simply not sufficient. Another crucial aspect is that available resources could be utilized more efficiently. The challenge is to find ways of increasing efficiency and effectiveness in resource allocation and utilization. Tailored solutions are required to address the particular needs, capacities, and conditions of each country. Greater capacity for policy formulation, planning, and performance assessment is required in order to develop and implement feasible options through programs that are sectorwide in scope but at the same time are focused on clear, achievable outcomes. Chapter 4 describes how developing countries and transition economies worldwide face similar challenges but differing realities.

Note

1. The OECD, through PISA, conducted an assessment on reading, mathematics, and science in 2000 and 2002 (PISA+). PISA assesses 15-year-old students' ability to apply acquired knowledge to real-life situations; it does not assess levels of knowledge and skills as specified in the national curriculum of the participating countries. It has six levels of reading proficiency, from below level 1 to level 5. Students who score below level 1 are considered to lack the most basic skills that PISA assesses. Students proficient at level 3 on the combined reading literacy scale are able to perform reading tasks of moderate complexity, such as locating multiple pieces of information, making links between different parts of a text, and relating the text to familiar, everyday knowledge.

4

Similar Challenges, Differing Realities

What possesses a high probability in one country, or period, or civilization, may possess no probability in another; and the ground of the difference may lie only slightly in outward and palpable material factors and almost entirely in the set of insights that are accessible, persuasive, and potentially operative in the community.

—Bernard J. F. Lonergan (1983), 211

The challenges around middle years schooling are not unique to this country. Indeed this has become a major preoccupation of those concerned with school improvement in many other countries. While the analysis of the challenge has been similar, the nature of the response has been subtly different. In the United States, there has been a particular focus on supporting 11–14 year olds in coping with the emotional and social challenges they face. In Australia, much effort has been focused on looking at the institutional environment in which middle years learning is set.

—Estelle Morris, former U.K. Minister of Education (2001)

Developing countries, by and large, have similar long-term goals for secondary education. But countries differ in their historical experiences, cultures, and economic situations, even though they may appear similar when measured by traditional indicators. Consequently, they will also have diverse responses to the challenges facing secondary education.

Investment policies and plans for secondary education must be related to a country's current state of development, the flow of direct investment, and the evolving economic, governance, and social environment. Failure to manage the interplay of these variables can arouse unrealistic expectations, leading to sociopolitical problems. There is no magic formula for handling this multifaceted challenge, but it is possible to set out useful guidelines, to be applied as appropriate to country conditions. This chapter presents a framework to help identify the main socioeconomic realities that could shape a country's and assistance agencies' specific responses to the twin challenges described in chapter 3.

A Framework for Grouping Countries

Traditional classification by income level implies that all similarly classified economies have the same absorptive and innovative capacity and would respond to demands for change in similar ways. The perspective presented here represents an attempt to combine the two dimensions of the secondary education challenge—access, and quality and relevance—and design a classification system that takes into account a country's capacity to manage and absorb innovations.

As a starting point, combining *stock indicators* such as educational attainment with *flow indicators* such as the gross enrollment rate can help summarize a country's present situation with respect to access. The stock indicator shows the state of a country's educated population; it reflects past efforts. The flow indicator provides information about the current efforts being made by the government and citizens to provide and take advantage of opportunities to acquire a secondary school education.

Figure 4.1 illustrates how countries can be ranked on these stock and flow indicators. As the figure shows, a large number of low-income countries have a low stock of population with secondary education or more, and their current efforts to provide secondary education are relatively modest (quadrant I). Most of the countries in this situation are in Africa and South Asia, but some are in Latin America and East Asia. Quadrant II identifies the countries that are currently investing in improving educational opportunities but still need to take corrective measures to elevate educational attainment. Most of the countries in this situation are middle-income countries. Countries in quadrant IV have historically provided good access to secondary education and continue to do so. With a few exceptions, countries in this group are typically upper or middle income. Because of their significant previous investment in education, all transition economies are in this category.

This categorization does provide a dynamic view of countries, but it tells very little about what kind of education developing countries should provide to equip their young people for the world they will face. In other words, it is not informative about aspects relating to relevance.

Porter's work (1998b) suggests a system of categorization that classifies countries by economic status and addresses their absorptive capacities for innovation.[1] The following discussion describes this system and examines how it can be used to design policies and target the efforts needed to move toward a system of mass secondary education in developing countries that is responsive to those countries' development needs and capabilities.

Figure 4.1 Education Stock and Current Efforts to Increase Educational Attainment by Country Income Group, 2000 or Latest Year Available

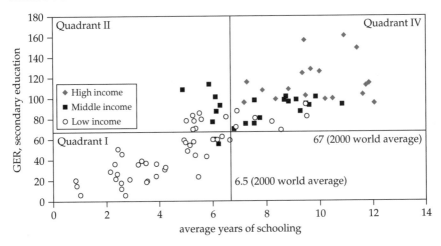

Sources: For world mean for average years of schooling and school attainment, Barro and Lee (2000); for world mean GDP, *World Development Indicators* (2003); for income category, World Economic Forum definition.

Note: GER, gross enrollment rate. See appendix E for gross enrollment rates and educational attainment by income level for countries in each quadrant.

The fundamental challenge of mass secondary education is to generate effective demand for schooling, ensure access to meet the demand, and devise systems that enable student retention and transition while ensuring quality. At the same time the graduates produced by the system must have skills and competencies that are relevant and appropriate both to the current level of development and to the changes that will result from competition and integration into global markets.

Porter offers a threefold model. The framework proposed employs the triple-axis taxonomy shown in box 4.1. At the heart of this taxonomy is the degree to which the national economy is embedded along the economic, political-legal, and domestic-regional-global axes. As the dotted circles expand to the limits, the nation or community becomes more deeply embedded in the global, innovation-driven, open value system.

The more deeply an economy is embedded within the domestic-regional-global axis of activities, the greater is its capacity and capability to absorb new learning and initiate innovation, leading to national development. This capacity and capability increase the effective demand for educated manpower and improved education systems. The broader and deeper

Box 4.1 Triple-Axis Framework for Grouping Countries

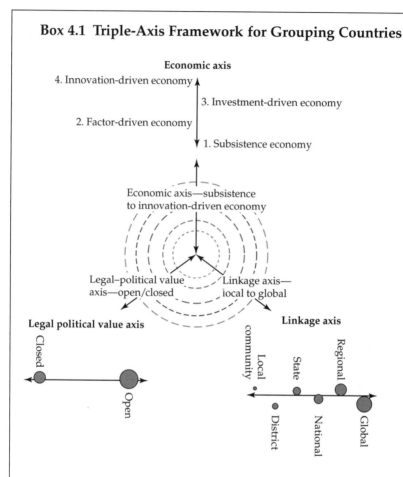

A country can be located at any place within the space formed by
the axes. However, as the economy of the country becomes more
innovation- and knowledge-driven, as local communities become
more integrated into an increasingly globalized world, and as legal
and political institutions become more transparent and open to
change, the demands for an educated citizenry become increasingly
complex. The challenge for education policy makers is to handle that
demand by putting in place education strategies that are responsive
to the movements that occur along the axes.

What this framework illustrates is that there is no single best
strategy for developing high-quality mass secondary education
systems.

Source: Welsh 2003.

the linkages across the axis are, the greater the dependence on an educated citizenry. It is important to note that within a nation there can be both pockets and populations who are differently positioned with respect to this taxonomy.

From the perspective of capacity to absorb and be innovative, a country's economy can be classified as factor driven, investment driven, or innovation driven.

1. In the *factor-driven economy* basic factor conditions such as low-cost labor and access to natural resources are the dominant sources of competitive advantage and exports. Firms produce commodities or relatively simple products designed in other, more advanced countries. Technology is assimilated through imports, foreign direct investment, and imitation. A factor-driven economy is highly sensitive to world economic cycles, commodity price trends, and exchange rate fluctuations. This sensitivity in turn dictates the sensitivity of effective demand for education, especially secondary education.

The concept of cluster, as used here, is singular; there is one education cluster containing several educational institutions. The educational cluster (network) and content at the secondary education level are very limited and are usually locked into basic education.[2] Demand for technologists, especially high-level technologists, is so low that a "dense" system along the triple axes is not required. Until the economy is more deeply integrated along the triple axes and achieves significant and sustainable economic growth, investment in secondary education will be limited, reflecting low effective demand. There can exist subregions within a country that are not factor-driven but subsistence economies.

2. In the *investment-driven economy* efficiency in producing standard products and services becomes the dominant source of competitive advantage. Heavy investment in efficient infrastructure, a business-friendly government administration, and strong investment incentives and access to capital allow major improvements in productivity. The products and services produced become more sophisticated, but technology and designs still largely come from abroad. Technology is accessed through licensing, joint ventures, foreign direct investment, and imitation. Countries at this stage, however, not only assimilate foreign technology but also develop the capacity to improve on it. Companies serve a mix of original equipment manufacturer (OEM) customers and their own customers. An investment-driven economy is concentrated in manufacturing and outsourced service exports. It is susceptible to financial crises and to external, sector-specific demand shocks.

Here the three axes are becoming more extensive and denser, and the country is contributing to the density of the network rather than being merely a recipient. The country is a visible partner in the global export-led economy. In addition, some of these countries may have pockets of innovation that are competitive along the global axis. These enriched political-economic linkages across the triple axes bring with them an effective demand for a more sophisticated political-bureaucratic system, which in turn is supported by increased educational investment in the public and private sectors. At this stage there is a growing need for a better-educated and better-trained citizenry.

The increasing demand for education leads to the recognition of the importance of the secondary educational cluster by the public and private sectors. Growing industries and firms need higher-quality labor, and the country's political processes require better-informed, participating citizens. The volume of training taking place in the private sector is significant at this stage. The domestic secondary cluster becomes more effective and integrated across the public and private sectors. The challenge is to accelerate the enrichment of the secondary cluster and its links to the political economy. The priority accorded by the national government to this effort, effective demand by business, and effective demand by parents are the three forces that, acting together, will essentially determine the flow of resources to meet the challenge.

Investment-driven economies may be subdivided into full investment-driven economies (FIDEs), which satisfy all the characteristics identified by Porter, and partial investment-driven economies (PIDEs), which do not fully satisfy the FIDE criteria but are carrying on manufacturing and have moved beyond factor-driven economy status. The differences lie in the PIDEs' absent or very restricted capacity and capability to adapt and improve imported capital and in some cases in the persistent pull of the factor-driven economy model.

Table 4.1 illustrates the fine separation that can be achieved by applying and elaborating on Porter's framework. For example, there is little to be gained by grouping Kenya and Burkina Faso together (as in the conventional classification by income) when assessing the potential for secondary education reform programs. The taxonomy could be helpful in ensuring that lessons learned from similar countries are taken into account in similar efforts to reform secondary education. Finally, this more sophisticated method helps qualify the tendency to homogenize countries on the basis of regional proximity.

3. In the *innovation-driven economy* the ability to produce innovative products and services at the global technology frontier using the most advanced methods becomes the dominant source of competitive advantage. The national business environment is characterized by strength in all areas and by the presence of deep clusters. Institutions and incentives supporting innovation are well developed. Companies compete by pursuing unique strategies that are often global in scope. An economy of this type has a high share of services and is resilient in the face of external shocks.

Table 4.1 Illustration of Classification by Economic Status and Absorptive and Innovative Capacity

Traditional economic classification	Subsistence economy[a]	Factor-driven economy	Partial investment- driven economy	Full investment- driven economy
Transition economy	Albania	Moldova	Estonia	Poland
Poor economy	Benin, Burkina Faso, Chad, Guinea, Somalia	Ghana, Mali, Mozambique, Nigeria, Tanzania, Uganda, Zambia	Côte d'Ivoire, Kenya, Senegal	Botswana, Mauritius, South Africa

Sources: Welsh 2003; authors' compilation.

a. Subsistence economies lie outside the factor-driven economy category and are almost exclusively oriented toward family consumption and a small local market. These economies focus exclusively on basic education that might not even include a significant secondary component. They will need extensive assistance to achieve any level of successful educational investment. The focus of such economies will be basic education, possibly extending as far as the ninth grade.

Application of Porter's Model to Secondary Education

The tables in this section show how Porter's framework can be helpful in understanding the policy issues countries may face when transforming their secondary education systems in order to provide relevant, high-quality secondary education. Factor-driven and investment-driven economies are discussed in some detail. Innovation-driven economies are not analyzed here because all are high-income economies that no longer face the same secondary education choices as countries in the other categories.

Factor-driven economies (table 4.2) have generally failed to meet Education for All targets. In many cases claims of success are not bolstered by convincing evidence on the ground. For example, in many Sub-Saharan African countries children attend schools without equipment, furnishings, or materials. Too often, the problem is one of teacher absenteeism rather than student dropout. Secondary education is problematic in this setting because of inadequate coverage and access, irrelevance of the curriculum due to colonial and elite historical momentum, and bad management. In many cases the situation is exacerbated by overt competition among aid agencies. In times of high commodity demand these economies can appear to be successful, but they are basically not sustainable.

The partial investment-driven economy (table 4.3) is a transformational stage from which a country can either advance to full investment-driven economy status (table 4.4) or regress to factor-driven economy status. If the

Table 4.2 Secondary Education Supply and Demand in Factor-Driven Economies

Characteristics of economy	Supply of secondary education	Demand for secondary education
(*Examples*: Afghanistan, Bolivia, Ghana, Nepal, Nigeria, Paraguay, Zambia)	Low overall supply.	Low overall demand.
Dependence on *primary products*, extraction exports, capital imports, and luxury imports for urban elites.	Low levels of all forms of capital.	Low effective demand because of
Social capital structure and content: subnational, tribe and family, authoritarian-paternalist. Social capital in this setting is probably an inhibitor of change, as it sustains traditional relationships and reduces mobility.	Failure to achieve Education for All. Inadequate stock of basic schools and poor basic educational infrastructure. Low stock of secondary schools and infrastructure. Elite secondary participation; male biased.	• Poor economic performance and declining returns to educational investment for the poor • Low cash income levels and lack of employment opportunities, compounded by the existence of inefficient or corrupt product cooperatives • Limited access and low basic education completion rates • Inadequate education and health services for the poor, especially for poor females
Human capital: informally transmitted—oral-experiential, conservative-conformist transmission system.	Weak educational governance structure with little regard for the law governing education.	• Limited female attainment of secondary education, negatively affecting mothers' capacity to motivate and direct children
Physical capital: traditional agricultural plus export cash crops or imported extraction and limited processing capital. Luxury-good capital.	Ministries focused on administration and control rather than on management and performance.	• Competitive basic education programs advocated and supported by aid agencies rather than integrated set of programs supporting government strategy.
Education: Low quality of educational cluster hinders provision of quality education.	Low commitment and capacity of local government; failure to invest in human resource development and social capital. Weak taxation system and revenue base.	

Source: Authors' compilation, 2004.

Table 4.3 Secondary Education Supply and Demand in Partial Investment-Driven Economies

Characteristics of economy	Supply of secondary education	Demand for secondary education
(Examples: Bangladesh, Bulgaria, Croatia, Ecuador, Guatemala, Honduras, Kenya, Pakistan, Romania, Tajikistan)	Increasing stock of secondary public schools. Teacher training institutions still traditional.	Effective demand for secondary education stable or declining.
Transition phase that can be regressing or progressing. Areas of investment-driven economic activity are few. Some transition economies may be regressing to factor-driven economy status.	Slowly increasing nonschool learning and experience opportunities, mainly via nongovernmental organizations. Slow deepening of learning infrastructure.	Stable demand attributable to • Slow growth of foreign direct investment • Rapid urbanization.
Social capital structure and content: mostly national, with relatively weak representative governments still in their infancy.	Increased but limited access to information and communication technologies. Weak educational governance structure with little regard for the law governing education.	Declining effective demand attributable to • Demographic collapse • Youth emigration • Economic decline, regressing to factor-driven economy status.
Human capital: transmitted via formal systems; value increasingly placed on literacy.	Ministries predominantly focused on control and administration, but with some departments innovating by introducing small accountability initiatives.	
Physical capital: becoming more oriented toward manufacturing for the local market. Its foundation is the introduction of basic technologies from abroad.	Low investment in human resource development and social capital in the education bureaucracy.	
Education: low quality, with educational cluster supporting access.	Taxation system improving but still predominantly centralized.	

Source: Authors' compilation, 2004.

Table 4.4 Secondary Education Supply and Demand in Full Investment-Driven Economies

Characteristics of economy	Supply of secondary education	Demand for secondary education
(*Examples*: Southeast Asia, Chile, Estonia, Hungary, India, Mexico, Poland, Slovenia, South Africa)	Increasing stock of secondary schools, private and public.	Growing effective demand for secondary education attributable to • Higher returns to secondary education investments as compared with investments in primary education • Diminishing returns to investments in basic education • Increasing levels of foreign direct investment, expanding the wage economy • Increasing diversity of opportunities in the growing economy • Rapid urbanization • Mass, almost universal, basic education • Relatively high access to higher education • Enhanced female secondary education, positively shaping mothers' capacity to motivate and direct children • Better educational and health services for the poor, especially poor females.
Social capital structure and content: increasingly national and often regional. Although in some cases authoritarian-paternalist styles still persist, there is increasing acceptance of effective management. Social capital in this setting is an enabler of change, as it focuses on modernity and greater mobility.	Increasing nonschool learning and experience opportunities (economic and social corporate human resource development) and deepening of learning infrastructure. Increased access to information and communication technologies. Increase in stable representative governments. Areas of investment-driven activity emerging, such as India's software industry. Stronger educational governance structure with more regard for the law governing education.	
Human capital: transmitted via formal systems; value increasingly placed on basic education.	Ministries increasingly performance focused; greater role for local government.	
Physical capital: imported manufacturing and extraction, producing for both the domestic and foreign markets; physical capital being adapted to new products.	Increasing investment in human resource development and social capital in the education bureaucracy.	
Education: improving quality, with cluster evolving to support quality provision.	Stronger taxation system and revenue base, in some cases decentralized.	

Source: Authors' compilation, 2004.

country regresses, it reverts to the conditions outlined in table 4.2.[3] If it makes progress, it is likely to assume the distinguishing characteristics of a partial investment-driven economy.

First in this process comes recognition of the need for import substitution for standard services and products. This forces recognition of the need for significant infrastructure development and improvement, initially limited to basic power and transport—better roads and a reliable supply of electricity. Next, a reform movement gathers momentum. The necessary reforms in national governance (institutional and bureaucratic) are initiated, and the legal framework is overhauled to remove barriers and provide incentives for new investments and new educational initiatives. Because of lack of relevant domestic know-how, the governance and legal reform frameworks need to be supported by international bodies. A critical element that can be at work here is the existence of an economically dominant minority, domestic or expatriate, that already has considerable linkages from local to international levels. The presence of such a minority can accelerate the country's evolution, but at the risk of creating political instability later, when the economy is at the FIDE level. Examples of such economically important minorities are Indians in East Africa, Lebanese in West Africa, Chinese in Southeast Asia, Russians in Moldova, and Europeans in Latin America (Bacevich 2002; Chua 2002). At this stage the PIDE nation is embarking on the initial step of assimilating foreign technology for import substitution.

It is important to recognize that the evolution to the PIDE stage is likely to be unevenly distributed within the country. Initially, it will be urban centered and mainly focused on the capital city. As a general rule, the underlying movement that typifies the shift to PIDE status is one from centralized bureaucratic control through regulation and licensing to a more open system of legal relationships supported by a more transparent institutional framework. Overall, the PIDE stage is characterized by reform and investment programs primarily driven by economic objectives.

Finally, PIDE nations have limited connectedness above the national level. The reforms manifest themselves in growing national coherence derived from infrastructure improvements and increasing economic opportunities in urban locations. The emerging coherence has a downside in that it demands the recasting of social relationships into new forms that transcend family, tribe, and other traditional affiliations. It is here that education plays a major role, in that the school, especially secondary education, forces exposure to new elements outside the traditional context.

For politicians, policy makers, and managers involved in transforming the provision of secondary education, this framework offers a structure for thinking about the associated challenges. First, it emphasizes the need to accept and prioritize national economic conditions as the basis for reform policy and planning. Second, it calls attention to the need for effective assessment of the capacities and capabilities of the domestic and external economic and education clusters and the efficiency of their interactions. Third, it highlights the necessity for realism about the absorptive and innovative capacity of national systems. Education policies and plans must address what will be required to increase absorptive and innovative capacities and capabilities efficiently and effectively. Finally, it must be recognized that the supportive environment of the constitution, the rule of law, the institutional framework, the effectiveness of the bureaucracy, and the participatory capacity of civic society influence policy and program choices and formulation.

Conclusion

Developing countries are under enormous internal and external pressure to develop mass secondary education systems that are responsive to the needs and capabilities of the society and economy. In addition to the growing aspirations of their populations for more and better education, countries face the challenge of responding without delay to the imperative of becoming active and productive participants in a global economy, and sustaining that response. This challenge calls for an ongoing effort as the nation's links to the global economy evolve at an ever-increasing pace. Although most countries face like challenges, there is no single best strategy or policy that fits them all. To sum up: similar challenges, different realities.

Education policy makers need to weigh two questions in designing secondary education strategies and policies for appropriate expansion and quality improvement: What is the country's absorptive and innovative capacity for incorporating new technologies and creating new knowledge and products? To what degree is the national economy integrated along the economic, political-legal, and domestic-regional-global axes? The broader and deeper the linkages across the axes are the greater the dependence on a highly educated citizenry. Stronger linkages yield greater complexity, demanding a better educated and participating citizenry.

From the perspective of their capacity to absorb and be innovative, economies can be categorized as factor driven, investment driven, or innovation driven. From the perspective of integration along the domestic-regional-global axis, they can be placed on a continuum extending from being mere recipients to becoming active contributors to the density of the network. As the linkages along the axis become richer, the need for investment in education in order to be able to contribute to the network through a more educated and trained citizenry will grow. The increasing demand for education will lead to the recognition of the importance of having a strong, well-developed secondary education cluster with robust backward and forward linkages with the other levels of education, as well as with the labor market and the political system.

The framework presented in this chapter shows how important it is for countries to develop home-grown secondary education strategies and policies. Education policy makers should not assume that imported solutions will generally work in their countries. The emphasis should be on defining and better targeting the type of secondary education reform needed in the specific country context. The design of appropriate solutions must be based on solid knowledge obtained through policy research and assessment—tasks that demand the collaborative efforts of professionals and experts from many disciplines.

Notes

1. "There are three main contributors to a nation's overall innovative performance: the common innovation infrastructure that supports innovation in the economy as a whole (e.g., investment in basic science); the cluster-specific conditions that support innovation in particular groups of interconnected industries (e.g., automotive, information technology); and the strength of the linkages among them (e.g., the ability to connect basic research to companies and the contribution of corporate efforts to the overall pool of technology and skilled personnel)" (Porter and Stern 1999, 5).

2. In the business literature, *clusters* are geographically proximate groups of interconnected companies, suppliers, service providers, and associated institutions in a particular field, linked by commonalities and complementarities. Cluster industries are geographically interconnected by a flow of goods and services that is stronger than the flow linking these industries to the rest of the economy (Porter 1998a). As applied to secondary education, this concept refers to a network of educational institutions that supports the effective provision of responsive, high-quality mass education. It comprises the entire value chain involved in the provision of educational services in a given region, including primary and secondary schools, universities and teacher training institutions, local (and national) bureaucracies, private sector business and training systems, and professional associations, trade unions, and civic organizations.

3. Albania, Armenia, Georgia, the Kyrgyz Republic, Moldova, Mongolia, and Tajikistan could be viewed as nations in danger of reverting to factor-driven economy status.

5

Responding to the Twin Challenges: Curriculum and Assessment

That education should be regulated by law and should be an affair of state is not to be denied, but what should be the character of this public education, and how young persons should be educated, are questions which remain to be considered. As things are, there is disagreement about the subjects. For mankind are by no means agreed about the things to be taught, whether we look to virtue or the best life. Neither is it clear whether education is more concerned with intellectual or with moral virtue. The existing practice is perplexing; no one knows on what principle we should proceed—should the useful in life, or should virtue, or should the higher knowledge, be the aim of our training; all three opinions have been entertained.

—Aristotle, *Politics*, B.VIII

The soaring demand for access to high-quality, relevant secondary education is forcing secondary school systems everywhere to react and adapt. Secondary education is becoming massive and nearly universal in many countries, and this is translating into increasingly complex challenges. This chapter and the next address the response to the twin challenges—expanding access to secondary education while enhancing its quality and relevance—from the perspective of four separate but interrelated sets of issues: (a) changes in curriculum; (b) the changing role of monitoring and evaluation policies in secondary education, beginning with the role of external or public examinations; (c) the professional development of secondary education teachers; and (d) the introduction and use of information and communication technologies (ICTs) in secondary schools. These four sets of issues have been selected because of their critical implications for the response to the twin challenges and because contemporary secondary education reform efforts worldwide tend to focus on them. Other factors and policy issues also need to be considered, and these are dealt with elsewhere in this book.

Curricula—Intended and Implemented

Within the context of the knowledge economy, changing work patterns are leading to radical new approaches in the way curriculum knowledge is selected, organized, and sequenced. In addition, greater emphasis on the democratization of access to worthwhile knowledge and on the formation of social capital, better understanding of youth issues and of how adolescents learn, and the very evolution of academia toward increasingly hybrid research areas, to name but a few trends, are affecting the way curricular knowledge is arranged in secondary education. As a result, new forms of school knowledge are emerging. This development requires a new balance in curriculum focus and emphasis, impelling curriculum-based reform in secondary education.

It is commonly asserted that there is a knowledge gap between the subject matter currently being taught and the knowledge and skills that are required if individuals and countries are to be competitive in the globalized world. It is also said that there is strong demand for a much closer intertwining of theoretical and practical elements and styles of learning throughout the educational experience. The convergence of the theoretical and the practical, and of the general and the vocational, would provide students in the compulsory and postcompulsory school years with greater possibilities for taking advantage of the full range of educational and job opportunities.

Tensions have arisen from, among other causes, the curriculum expansion, particularly in secondary education, that has come about through the internal logic of formal education systems. This trend implies that more types of knowledge are becoming socially, politically, and economically relevant and have a claim to a place in the curriculum. In principle, the only response to the increasingly important role of knowledge in 21st century societies seems to be to increase the number of years of compulsory education. The challenge now is to expand access to secondary education while providing high-quality, relevant educational opportunities for all. Needless to say, the financial implications of such expansion are enormous, given the soaring demand for secondary education.

The Unbearable Irrelevance of the Secondary School Curriculum

Today in many countries, both adults and young people share a feeling that the secondary education curriculum is profoundly inadequate (Abelmann 2001; Levy and Murnane 2001). The worsening of employment opportunities for the young, the increased competition resulting from credentialism, and the perception that curricula are inadequate converge in the day-to-day routine of educational establishments and give rise to apathy, school disaffection, and antisocial behavior on the part of students (see chapter 2). It can even lead to complicity between students and teachers, who are also at a loss when faced with the novelty and scope of challenges that they were never trained to handle.

In many developing and transition countries the secondary education curriculum remains profoundly abstract and alien to social and economic needs. It is almost completely driven by high-stakes public examinations that in many of these countries were introduced by the colonial powers and that still hold the key to university access and to elite professional jobs. Abstract, fact-centered, and decontextualized narrative knowledge prevails in the secondary curriculum and continues to be used for selective purposes in a setting of scarce educational and job opportunities, causing high dropout and high failure rates among secondary school students.

The endemic irrelevance of the secondary curriculum is one of the greatest obstacles to successful expansion of secondary education via curriculum reform. Curriculum relevance is a condition not only for improving the quality of secondary graduates but also for retaining youngsters in school. Yet the secondary school curriculum is a resilient cultural artifact in most societies; it takes much more than *White Papers* and expert groups to change it in a meaningful and sustainable way.

Comparative analysis of national secondary education curricula carried out by Benavot (2004), in work cosponsored by the World Bank and the International Bureau of Education (IBE), provides persuasive evidence for extreme curriculum stability. If there is a period in contemporary history when one could have expected major changes in school curriculum, particularly at the secondary level, it would have been 1985–2000. These years marked the advent of mass secondary education in many countries and

Figure 5.1 Mean Proportion of Total Instructional Time Allocated to Curricular Areas, Grades 7 and 8, by Region, 1985 and 2000

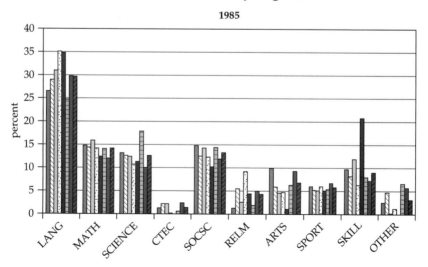

Figure 5.1 Continued

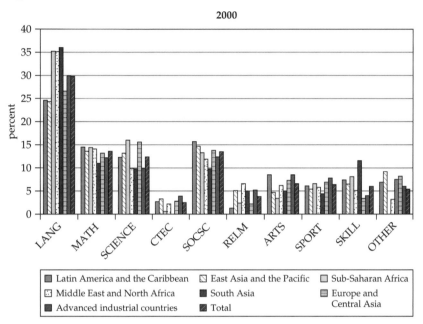

Source: Adapted from Benavot (2004).

Note: The 10 general curricular areas used in the figure incorporate the following school subjects:
- LANG: language education; includes instruction in national, official, local, and foreign languages and literature
- MATH: mathematics; includes all math-related subjects
- SCIENCE: science; includes all general science subjects (for example, natural, physical), as well as chemistry, biology, and physics
- CTEC: applied science; includes computers and technological subjects
- SOCSC: social science; includes social studies, history, geography, social sciences, environmental studies, civics, and citizenship education
- RELM: religious or moral education; ethics
- ARTS: aesthetic education; includes art, music, dance, singing, and handicrafts
- SPORT: sports and physical education
- SKILL: subjects such as health education, hygiene, agriculture, manual training, vocational education, domestic science, and life skills
- OTHER: all remaining subjects, especially electives and required-optional subjects

regions; moreover, it was exactly during this period that awareness of the knowledge society and, in particular, the impact of globalization on education systems set in. Yet when the proportions of total instructional time allocated to various curricular areas in lower secondary education in 1985 and 2000 are compared (see figure 5.1), overall curriculum change appears to have been much more modest and limited in every region of the world than might have been expected.

In fact, the mean time allocated for each major curricular area has remained virtually unchanged in all regions. In order to spot interesting trends over time, one has to look at the least central curriculum areas. First, probably the most visible change is the decrease in the curriculum area Skill, which for the most part reflects the trend toward deferring vocational content until the upper secondary level. Second, in all regions except Africa the time allocated to elective or required-optional classes (listed as Other in figure 5.1) has increased, reflecting more curriculum diversity and flexibility and greater opportunities for individualized and student-centered instruction. Third, an important, albeit modest, change is the upward move of technology and ICT instruction, a trend that is likely to be making further progress during the first decade of the 21st century.

Building Metacognitive Capital and Creative Capital

While the deeply conservative secondary school curriculum, reminiscent of medieval times, lingers and persists into the 21st century, the context for future opportunities for individuals, communities, and entire countries is radically different. The 21st century workforce is less and less involved in industrial production and increasingly concentrated in services, ideas, and communication. At the same time, adolescents and youths, even in the most isolated corners of the world, are subject to strong media influence and are part of a global youth culture. The challenge is to build up metacognitive capital that can position individuals and countries to adapt to and succeed in knowledge-intensive economies and a globalized world.

An emphasis on metacognitive abilities and skills means that learning to think and learning to learn become priorities. Metacognitive skills include the abilities to

- integrate formal and informal learning, declarative knowledge ("knowing that"), and procedural knowledge (know-how)
- access, select, and evaluate knowledge in an information-soaked world
- develop and apply forms of intelligence beyond strictly cognitive processes
- work and learn effectively and in teams
- face, transform, and peacefully resolve conflict, which involves participatory and active citizenship skills
- create, transpose, and transfer knowledge
- deal with ambiguous situations, unpredictable problems, and unforeseeable circumstances
- cope with multiple careers by learning how to locate oneself in a job market and to choose and fashion the relevant education and training.

Increased competition in the labor market and rapid change in economic situations have created the need for individuals who can produce creative and innovative ideas, who are flexible, and who expect to change career paths several times in the course of their working lives. Such development has led OECD governments to place high value on building "creative capital" and to pursue appropriate reforms in curricula and teaching methods (World Bank 2003d). For instance, the arts are now seen as making a significant contribution to creativity and cultural development and so are progressively gaining ground in the contemporary secondary school curriculum.

It is precisely these types of skills and competencies that are increasingly in demand in the knowledge society, and their continuous development and acquisition pose a permanent challenge to education and training systems in general and to secondary education in particular. Research carried out by Levy and Murnane (2004) on the skills requirements for the tasks performed in the U.S. labor market is revealing. The authors divide the tasks performed by a labor force today into five broad categories:

- *Expert thinking:* solving problems for which there are no rule-based solutions, such as diagnosing the illness of a patient whose symptoms seem strange
- *Complex communication:* interacting with others to acquire information, to explain it, or to persuade others of its implications for action; for example, a manager motivating the people whose work she supervises
- *Routine cognitive tasks:* mental tasks that are well described by logical rules, such as maintaining expense reports
- *Routine manual tasks:* physical tasks that can be well described using rules, such as installing windshields on new vehicles in automobile assembly plants
- *Nonroutine manual tasks:* physical tasks that cannot be well described as following a set of "if-then-do" rules and that are difficult to computerize because they require optical recognition and fine muscle control; for example, driving a truck

Figure 5.2 shows trends for each type of task in the U.S. labor market. Tasks requiring expert thinking and complex communication grew steadily in frequency during the 1970s, 1980s, and 1990s. The share of the labor force employed in occupations that emphasize routine cognitive or routine manual tasks remained steady in the 1970s and then declined over the next two decades. Finally, the share of the labor force working in occupations that emphasize nonroutine manual tasks declined throughout the period.

Current approaches in the way curriculum knowledge is selected, organized, and sequenced have important implications for methodology and pedagogy. The need to build metacognitive and creative capital is reflected in the growing predominance of interactive teaching methods and active learning, case-based training, simulations, and team projects—in short, of

Figure 5.2 Economywide Measures of Routine and Nonroutine Task Input, United States, 1969–98

$(1969 = 0)$

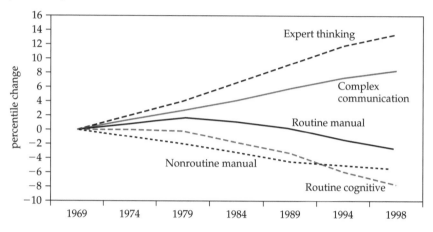

Source: Reproduced from Levy and Murnane (2004), 50, figure 3.5.

Note: Each trend reflects changes in the numbers of people employed in occupations emphasizing that task. To facilitate comparison, the importance of each task in the U.S. economy is set to zero in 1969, the baseline year. The value in each subsequent year represents the percentile change in the importance of each type of task in the economy.

a problem-oriented curriculum. The influence of academic research and of higher education is also at work here, since many pedagogical innovations and approaches are imported from universities.

Building Social Capital, Preventing Social Conflict, and Learning to Live Together

The irrelevance of the secondary education curriculum contributes to the widening gap between school and the youth culture, to the extent that school is not sufficiently attractive to youths and does not effectively address their needs. In both developed and developing countries (although to a greater extent in those countries with mass secondary school systems), this gap tends to give rise to antischool cultures and antisocial behavior among young people and to an overall lack of commitment by students to secondary school life (OECD 2003d).

In light of the need for people to individually and collectively contribute to life and work in modern societies, the growing importance of civic knowledge and life skills has led to citizenship education being embedded in secondary education curricula. Given the worldwide goal of universal access to (at least lower) secondary education, the role of secondary schools as institutions for preventing, processing, and dealing with social and political conflict takes on paramount importance. The curriculum of every core area is being enriched to incorporate historical and cultural background and social applications, beginning with the international dimension of knowledge, its environmental implications, and the ethical aspects of scientific thinking and the use of technology in the contemporary world.

Physical education was traditionally tied to military training for boys and was virtually nonexistent for girls. That approach is being replaced by more comprehensive physical education and training closely interacting with emotional skills and with the joy of movement and open-air activities. The practice of sports has become a part of school life instead of an optional extracurricular activity, and new themes (such as information on drugs, alcohol, and tobacco; sex education; HIV/AIDS prevention; and nutrition) have been introduced as cross-curricular issues to provide students with the knowledge and skills they need to adopt a healthy lifestyle.

The Shifting and Fading Frontier between the General and Vocational Curricula

No matter how much countries differ in their approach to secondary education reform, the balance between general and vocational programs and curricular content has consistently been at the core of every policy choice. Decision makers have long struggled with issues such as determining the optimal size of the vocational sector, ensuring that secondary vocational tracks or schools do not become dead-end streets, and making the right curriculum choices in vocational programs to ensure smooth and successful transition of graduates to the labor market.

The broad historical and global overview presented in table 5.1 provides evidence for a long-term trend leading to new directions and solutions for the academic-vocational balance in secondary education. Structurally speaking, historical models of secondary education were and are segmented into tracks, curriculum specializations, and even completely different institutional modalities. Thus, general (mostly academic) secondary education usually coexisted with vocational secondary education tracks or specialized schools, teacher training tracks, specialized institutions for sports or the fine arts, and, in some specific regions and countries, religious or theological schools and special schools for the gifted.

Whereas high segmentation was clearly the norm in the 1960s and even in the 1980s, the data in table 5.1 point to a worldwide trend toward a reduction in the segmentation or fragmentation of secondary education curricula by 2000. This trend takes on significance as secondary education becomes both compulsory and increasingly universal in countries around the world. The structural merging of secondary education over the past four decades has led to a renewed and ever-changing balance between general and

Table 5.1 Percentage of Countries Offering Secondary-Level Programs of Study in Selected Educational Fields by Region, 1960s, 1980s, and 2000

	Academic/general			Vocational/technical or technological			Teacher training			Religious/theological training			Other[a]
	1960s	1980s	2000	1960s	1980s	2000	1960s	1980s	2000	1960s	1980s	2000	2000
Latin America and the Caribbean	100	100	100	96	85	93	86	38	17	20	3	0	10
East Asia and the Pacific	100	100	100	92	86	87	67	36	7	25	29	13	7
Sub-Saharan Africa	100	100	100	100	98	84	93	54	13	29	9	0	8
Middle East and North Africa	100	100	100	100	100	94	93	53	12	43	56	41	29
South Asia	100	100	100	100	75	75	75	38	0	25	50	0	13
Europe and Central Asia	100	100	100	100	100	96	88	44	4	0	13	0	15
Advanced industrial countries	100	100	100	92	96	85	46	15	19	39	23	4	19
Average	100	100	100	97	92	89	77	40	12	29	21	6	14

Source: Benavot 2004.

Note: Country coverage is as follows: for the 1960s, 105 to 116 countries; for the 1980s, 141 to 159 countries; for 2000, 160 to 162 countries.

a. Refers, generally, to specialized schools in the fine arts, music, and sports.

vocational education. In addition, it has brought about the upgrading of some other segments of education, such as teacher training, specialized schools, and religious and theological schools, which tend to be housed in postsecondary or even higher educational institutions.

In interpreting the data in table 5.1, characterizing the vocational and technological education subsector is tricky. Overall, there appears to be some movement away from institutionally distinct secondary vocational schools and programs, although most countries still have such arrangements. But many of the schools have lost their terminal (labor force–directed) character and have added elements traditionally associated with the academic-general sector. Other schools have been upgraded by being redefined as technical or technological programs. As a consequence, in both cases previous limitations placed on students who wished to sit for national matriculation examinations or to enter postsecondary educational frameworks have been rescinded. This measure is critical for breaking away from social perceptions of vocational options as being low-prestige and dead-end.

With progress being made toward mass secondary education, and with knowledge becoming the basic economic resource of society, curriculum issues today involve not so much how to impart vocational skills to secondary graduates as how to add basic vocational content to the general curriculum. At the heart of the new debate is the reconceptualization of which school subjects are vocationally relevant. Science, mathematics, English, and philosophy—all traditionally viewed as fully academic, college preparatory subjects—are in increasing demand because of their career and work relevance. This shift has blurred, perhaps irreversibly, the hitherto well-delineated frontier between the general and the vocational in secondary education. The critical dilemma and the traditionally hard-to-strike balance between vocational and general education at the secondary level are coming to a point of compromise and, in a way, are being superseded. Even countries that are decidedly seeking to enhance the labor market relevance of graduates through a secondary education curriculum that strongly emphasizes occupationally oriented skills and competencies tend to ensure at the same time that a strong and updated general content remains the central component of the curriculum. This new balance could be the best possible answer to the key question every education decision maker has to tackle: which curriculum best prepares students for an uncertain future?

In the past two decades a goal of secondary-level curriculum reforms the world over has been to emphasize the applied dimension of all sorts of knowledge, beginning with the most traditional curriculum areas. This objective is critical for ensuring that secondary curricula and the skills and competencies acquired by students are not subject to a short-term expiry date. But this vocationalization of the general secondary curriculum has not proved easy, particularly at the upper secondary level. The deep historical roots of the secondary curriculum make it essentially abstract and discipline based, and abstract knowledge is by definition difficult to apply. Nevertheless, the secondary school curriculum is becoming more diversified and, in a way, also more eclectic, adding new sources of valid curriculum knowledge that are not discipline based. This is also the outcome of demand-side pressures. Since students are highly aware of the choices that could enhance their employability, more academically oriented students in secondary education, in the general track leading to higher education, are demanding vocational options (that is, electives) to widen their training and increase the range of their skills.

In addition, previously terminal and dead-end vocational tracks have been upgraded. This has permitted graduates to take school-leaving examinations in which general knowledge is tested and has given them access to tertiary education institutions, as well as to the acquisition of professional qualifications. Conversely, vocational elements in the secondary curriculum have tended to materialize and to assume the status of general elements. Examples include Work-Related Education in England and Wales and the more generalized, and indeed increasing, emphasis on counseling and guidance services to support secondary education students (Watts and Fretwell 2004).

Dialectics of General and Vocational Secondary Education

Some research evidence indicates that rates of return for academic and general curricula at the secondary level are higher than those for vocational education. Accordingly, some developing countries are shifting away from classical vocational options and toward a general curriculum for all secondary school students. (Brazil may be the best example; see Larach 2001.) A study of secondary education in Thailand, however, finds that rates of return are higher for vocational than for general secondary education and concludes that investment in improving access to vocational schooling may be beneficial (Moenjak and Worswick 2002). Mundle (1998) discusses the policies that the advanced Asian economies of Japan, Korea, Singapore, and Taiwan (China) adopted in their efforts to increase access to and improve the quality of secondary education. One of these policies was to concentrate investment effort on vocational education at the upper secondary school level until per capita incomes reached about $8,000 (1992 rates) and then to shift to a more general curriculum.

In short, evidence from rates of return is contradictory. One can truly speak of the dialectics of general and vocational education at the secondary level, as the balance between general and vocational at that level is a moving target within and across countries. The key appears to be that demand for vocational education and the market value of the credentials gained through it also depend on public and labor market perceptions of its quality. Most of all, they depend on the extent to which students, families, and employers no longer feel that vocational education is a second-class, dead-end, low-status option for working-class children and for those who fail at school.

The cases of the United Kingdom and France are telling with respect to the complex and paradoxical nature of secondary education policy issues. The U.K. Department for Education and Skills (DES) has adopted the approach of using vocational options at the lower secondary level, which is traditionally comprehensive in nature (U.K. DES 2004). In France, although overall enrollment at the secondary level is declining for demographic reasons, enrollments in vocational and technical lycées are climbing rapidly. France is also moving in the direction of introducing vocational elements and optional subjects at the lower secondary level (CNDP 2004). After more than a generation with quasi-universal coverage of secondary education, these countries can afford to fine-tune the duration of the common curriculum in secondary education and to introduce vocational elements and vocational choices in earlier grades. Such elements and choices have a different status than they did earlier because of the altered nature of the institutional settings in which they are being taught. These countries are able to adopt this approach in response to demand from students and employers and in a context of increased social recognition of and market reward for transformed, high-prestige vocational education.

The Rise and Fall of Curriculum Knowledge Areas: The Politics of Knowledge and Its Market Value

Contemporary secondary curriculum reforms reflect the emergence of new subject areas and, as a consequence, a continuous realignment of the weight of traditional types of knowledge in school curricula. As noted above, more and more subjects, disciplinary and interdisciplinary, have become socially and economically relevant and seek to occupy a significant place in the curriculum. This is the case, for example, for technology, economics, citizenship education, second foreign language, environmental education, and health. Other areas that had been at the periphery of the school curriculum have been promoted from elective to compulsory status in several countries; examples are foreign language, music, arts, and physical education. In some other cases the reverse has taken place, as with religion or classical languages. In many countries, subjects such as geology, earth and space, and astronomy, in the natural sciences, and sociology, political science, anthropology, and economics among the social sciences have steadily gained ground (World Bank 2003d). Today there is probably no education system that refrains completely from teaching economics at the secondary level.

The growing demand for a scientifically and technologically literate workforce presents additional challenges. Efforts are being made to discontinue the practice of using science and technology education to develop future scientists and technologists and instead to retrain science teachers to impart knowledge about science as a process of inquiry rather than a collection of discoveries.

The importance of rapid and easy communication in labor markets and the increased need for understanding among peoples of different cultures and nationalities create demand for competence in more than one foreign language. Competence in foreign languages is directly related to a country's overall marketing capabilities. To respond to this need, recent curriculum reforms in many developed countries have made the teaching of at least two foreign languages compulsory.

Curriculum expansion, differentiation, and overload. Massive access to schooling and greater differentiation among students are forcing secondary schools to take into account the diversity in students' interests and capabilities. This has become especially important in maximizing students' potential. As student populations grow and become increasingly diverse, responding to differentiated demand may be the only way to prevent student dropout and achieve high completion rates. In a broad sense, policy choices for curriculum differentiation include tracking students according to academic ability or achievement or permitting students to choose from a variety of electives, options, or curriculum modules that can be sequenced and accredited in different ways. In many subject areas common tasks can be set with the expectation of differing levels of achievement. Many outcomes can be achieved via different routes and different content. Particular attention is now being given to students who need special support and a longer period to discover and learn important concepts, methods, and relationships in core subjects. Similarly, attention to the special needs of more able and gifted students is required.

Needless to say, diversification and profiling are terms with strong political connotations in many countries. They are at the core of the heated political debate that usually surrounds equal access to secondary education and recurring waves of reform. Tracking, streaming, banding, and other student grouping arrangements are the practical outcomes of political and ideological stances pertaining to secondary education.

Table 5.2 presents a relatively complete picture of the organization of curricular programs in upper secondary education in contemporary education systems. It highlights the overwhelming fact that upper secondary education curricula increasingly take the form of comprehensive and general tracks and programs. The prevalence of such tracks, together with experiments that combine two or more traditional tracks, strongly supports this conclusion. Paradoxically, the data presented in the table make it clear that the number of tracks in upper secondary education is increasing, with new specializations emerging, some of them of a hybrid nature and with no precedent in traditional secondary curricula. Comprehensiveness

Table 5.2 Prevalence of Upper Secondary Track Types by Region, circa 2000

(percentage of countries in the region whose upper secondary academic sectors include at least one curricular track of the type specified)

Region	General/ comprehensive	Classical	Modern languages	Humanities, arts, letters	Math and sciences	Social sciences	Economics, business, commerce	Religion, theology	Technological, technical, computer
					Basic classification of track types				
Latin America and the Caribbean (n = 29)	52	0	0	24	31	3	14	0	17
East Asia and the Pacific (n = 14)	79	0	8	14	29	21	0	8	8
Sub-Saharan Africa (n = 14)	57	0	22	24	46	8	11	0	5
Middle East and North Africa (n = 14)	16	0	5	84	89	5	11	21	26
South Asia (n = 14)	88	0	0	13	25	13	13	0	0
Eastern Europe and Central Asia (n = 14)	92	4	15	16	27	12	0	0	4
Advanced industrial countries (n = 14)	57	4	11	25	36	7	7	0	14
Average	60	1	11	29	41	9	8	3	11

(Continues on the following page.)

Table 5.2 Continued

Region	Tracks that combine track types					Other	
	Humanities and sciences	Combination of two humanities	Humanities and social sciences	Combination of two social sciences	Combination of science and technology	Teacher training	Other[a]
Latin America and the Caribbean (n = 29)	21	3	3	0	3	10	10
East Asia and the Pacific (n = 14)	7	0	0	7	8	0	0
Sub-Saharan Africa (n = 14)	0	0	0	3	3	0	3
Middle East and North Africa (n = 14)	0	5	0	0	3	0	5
South Asia (n = 14)	0	0	0	0	0	13	0
Eastern Europe and Central Asia (n = 14)	4	4	4	0	0	0	12
Advanced industrial countries (n = 14)	0	7	7	11	4	0	7
Average	5	2	2	3	4	3	6

Source: Benavot 2004.

Note: Countries were coded by number of tracks (none, one, or more than one) for each track type.

a. Includes a mix of uncategorized tracks, including hotel and tourism, home economics, agriculture, sports, music, and aesthetics.

is balanced with, and in a way reinforced by, growing curriculum flexibility and adaptability to student needs and to social, academic, and labor market requirements.

Alternatives for dealing with or responding to increasing student diversity in secondary education always involve the widening of the curriculum in every dimension: expansion of the knowledge areas taught in school, variation and flexibility in teaching and learning situations, more choices of common and elective subjects, the use of a variety of teaching materials and curriculum resources in different and more flexible ways, more and alternative formulas for grouping students, efforts to multiply and make flexible school time and space, more skills and competencies to be acquired beyond cognitive ones, greater variety of material to be learned beyond conceptual content, and more flexibility in assessment and grade promotion criteria (UNESCO 2004a). In short, coping with student diversity entails deepening the process of curriculum expansion, and this appears to be the key to the democratization of secondary education.

Curriculum expansion has changed the balance of time allocated to different areas and subjects. Expanding and differentiating the secondary curriculum without causing curriculum overload can be difficult (see box 5.1). Some countries have increased the daily hours of instruction at the secondary level to introduce new subject areas. Others have attempted to relieve curriculum overload by reducing the number of school days and teaching hours per week. Between these two extremes are countries that try to rebalance the school day, reinforcing subjects considered to be most important by increasing the time allocated to them without exceeding the predetermined total number of school hours.

Summary: Trends in Secondary Education Curriculum Reform

Over the past decades, trends in secondary education curriculum reform in developed countries and in many developing countries have evolved in the following directions:

- Deferring selection and specialization as the duration of compulsory education has increased. Taking higher education as the reference, if there is a generalized trend in higher education toward delaying specialization and promoting wide-ranging and interdisciplinary studies, it would be sensible to eliminate early specialization at the secondary level.
- Avoiding grouping by ability through tracking and streaming (which tend to raise the attainment of higher achievers at the expense of low achievers; see Ireson and Hallam 2001) to promote equity and develop human social capital.
- Increasing the status recognition of traditional vocational education, in part by pushing it to the upper secondary and postsecondary levels.

Box 5.1 Secondary Curriculum Overload in Eastern Europe and Central Asia

Over the past 15 years, in most Eastern European and Central Asian countries, and particularly in the countries of the former Soviet Union, curriculum reform has been a hectic and intense issue. During the early 1990s the focus was on cleaning up the ideological slant embedded in official curricula and on reviewing textbooks in some key curricular areas. A few years later, traditional subjects were revisited to introduce national elements, and new subjects were added in line with curriculum reforms then being carried out in "mirror countries," especially those of the European Union. Currently, reformers are incorporating the discourse of standards-based, skill-centered, and outcome-oriented curricula. Despite this appearance of progress and curriculum modernization, the practical outcome has been widespread curriculum overload and a de facto increase in academic demands and requirements for secondary school students.

Curriculum overload in secondary education is a chronic disease in Eastern Europe and Central Asia, and it stands in the way of successful reform of secondary education. Curriculum design and development is a zero-sum game. If school days and school hours are reduced and at the same time the number of compulsory subjects keeps growing, the number of weekly hours per subject will have to be cut. In Ukraine secondary students deal with up to 17 different subjects, and in some tracks or streams almost half of the students receive only one hour or class session per week in many subjects. In Uzbekistan the average secondary school student may be taking 28 different subjects. Teachers in Romania and Bulgaria believe that secondary curricula are "highly overloaded in terms of volume and highly demanding in terms of knowledge" (World Bank 2003d). In these countries the school week was reduced at the beginning of the decade from six to five days, but new subjects and an extra year were added to upper secondary school. Instead of reducing the number of existing subjects and developing a core curriculum of relevant knowledge, the trend has been to add more time and more subjects to an already congested curriculum.

Sources: World Bank 2003d; authors' compilation.

- Departing from the disciplinary tradition of curriculum design and development and moving toward broader curriculum areas, skill-centered approaches, and nonacademic sources of relevant knowledge, with the aim of constructing more relevant and inclusive secondary curricula.

Secondary education curriculum policy can be disaggregated into three variables: selection and specialization, the academic-vocational balance, and the disciplinary or nondisciplinary nature of curriculum design and development. A matrix of policy choices and trade-offs is implicit, resulting in a broad framework for policy analysis of secondary education systems. Combining and balancing the three variables yields a complete set of alternative policy choices for secondary education, with clear implications for the financing of secondary education.

- *Scenario 1.* Highly specialized (tracking) and highly selective (tracking and examination at age 11–12, resulting in attendance at different types of school). Vocational education a main option in lower secondary school. Emphasis on traditional disciplines in academic tracks and on job preparation and practice in the vocational track.
- *Scenario 2.* Specialization and selection deferred to the end of the lower secondary level. System of elective subjects as a device to introduce limited internal differentiation. Vocational education pushed to the upper secondary level. Some emphasis on introducing vocational elements in the common curriculum. Cross-curricular issues and interdisciplinary approaches are considered, but traditional areas continue to frame the secondary curriculum.
- *Scenario 3.* Specialization and selection deferred to the end of upper secondary school. System of electives and homogeneous student grouping form the internal system of selection within a given secondary school. Vocational education is a fully postsecondary enterprise, and vocational elements are increasingly built into the academic curriculum. Apart from languages and mathematics, the rest of the curriculum departs from traditional disciplines by including widespread use of skills-based, project-based, and cross-curricular alternatives.

These are all classical options within the framework of an industrial-based model of secondary education provision. The issues of balancing uniformity and diversity in secondary education are perennial and will remain a challenge for development of secondary education policy. Meanwhile, knowledge-based secondary education and secondary curriculum are urgently calling for new alternatives. These entail the development of systems that allow students to take more control of their learning, through modularizing the curriculum, creating individualized study programs, featuring multiple and ever-changing options for student grouping, combining project work, and introducing e-learning course components, to mention a few possibilities. The issue remains as to how these alternatives can be evaluated and, more important, accredited and certified. Credit systems of the kind used at universities will be introduced into secondary schools, providing a more flexible, rational, and equitable approach to secondary education certification.

Measuring What Students Learn and Master

He is good at examinations; if there were no examinations for him to be good at there would be little special about him. Examinations create in him a heady, trembling state of excitement during which he writes quickly and confidently.

—J. M. Coetzee, *Boyhood* (1997)

National Examinations: The Way Into and the Way Out of Secondary Education

The role of national examinations is arguably the most characteristic and peculiar feature of secondary education. For many students and their families all over the world, secondary education is for the most part a matter of dealing with national, external, public, high-stakes examinations. In fact, the exact duration of secondary education in a country could be assessed by identifying the points at which students sit for the entry examination and for the graduation or school-leaving examination. The latter conditions the transition to further education and job opportunities. In many developing countries secondary education is "guarded" by examinations at both entry and exit.

Examinations can be used to distribute opportunities for further education and as a condition for accessing labor markets. They are a powerful tool for influencing and shaping the secondary school curriculum. Decision makers and education planners can steer examinations in the directions considered to be most appropriate. In many developing countries the political and economic importance of examinations is often so great that it is impossible to understand the operation of the education system without looking through the lens of examinations.

The centrality of examinations has manifold implications. For a start, policymakers need to acknowledge that any reform proposal, especially curriculum reform, needs to deal with the role of examinations as the major shapers of secondary education. Expansion of equitable access to secondary education may not be viable unless entry examinations are thoroughly reformed, postponed to the entry point of upper secondary education, or altogether eliminated. It is the exit examination, however, that is usually the biggest stumbling block, requiring much-needed curriculum reform, and in many countries it is the main source of social discontent and unrest. In fact, absence of transparent and fair evaluation practices governing access to higher education, among which the secondary school–leaving examination is always a key element, is probably the number one corruption trigger in education all over the world (Noah and Eckstein 2001).

High Stakes and the Signaling and Screening Functions of Examinations

Secondary education is more high-stakes and last-chance than is primary education, for at least two reasons. First, in most countries the difference in opportunity costs of attendance is much higher between secondary school and university than between primary and secondary school. This means that there is likely to be a steeper enrollment decline between secondary and tertiary than between primary and secondary, particularly in countries where secondary education has expanded beyond elite status. Second, in most countries secondary education school-leaving examinations are higher-stakes than primary education school-leaving examinations. The former are important labor market signals and serve as entrance filters for tertiary education. As a result, secondary education is more likely to be highly politicized, or at the least to attract considerable policy attention. Parental anxiety is heightened, and the risks of fraudulent and corrupt practices related to external public examinations are becoming widespread.

A phenomenon that deserves particular attention in analyzing the implications of high-stakes secondary examinations is the rise of private tutoring, especially in Asian countries (Bray 1999, 2003; Kwok 2004; see also table 5.3). Private tutoring and cram schools, mostly dealing with what Kwok labels "examination-oriented knowledge," make up an entire shadow education system. In Korea parents are reported to be spending more on tutoring than the government spends on public schooling, and 60 percent of Japan's secondary school students attend *juku* (after-school private tutoring services). The numbers are even higher in economies as different as Hong Kong (China), the Arab Republic of Egypt, and Mauritius (Bray 1999). The Japan-coined expression "examination hell" could also be used in countries such as China and India, where families are willing to invest heavily in private tutoring to enhance their children's chances of success.

The New Wave of International Comparative Studies of Student Achievement

Policy makers and the public have become interested in international comparative studies of student achievement because of concern about the competitiveness of countries' current and future labor force in the global market and the extent to which citizens can adapt to rapidly changing societies. The results of these studies easily make front-page headlines and have a definitive influence in shaping public opinion about education around the world. The 1990s marked the advent of a new generation of international and regional initiatives on student achievement. Most popular among them are two large-scale studies, the Programme on International

Table 5.3 Private Supplementary Tutoring in Selected Economies

Economy	Indications of scale
Brazil	A study in Rio de Janeiro public schools found that over 50 percent of students received tutoring and saw it as a way to reduce the likelihood of having to repeat grades.
Cambodia	Respondents in 31 percent of 77 primary schools indicated that pupils received tutoring. Among urban schools the proportion was 60 percent, and at postprimary levels the proportions were higher still.
Egypt, Arab Rep. of	One study showed that 54 percent of 9,000 grade 5 students (300 schools) and 74 percent of 9,000 grade 8 students (another 300 schools) were receiving private tutoring. Another survey, covering 4,729 households, found that 65 percent of urban primary school children and 53 percent of rural primary school children had received tutoring.
Hong Kong (China)	A survey of 507 students found that 45 percent of primary, 26 percent of lower secondary, 34 percent of middle secondary, and 41 percent of upper secondary students were receiving tutoring. A later study of four schools serving different population groups found an average of 41 percent of grade 3 and 39 percent of grade 6 pupils receiving tutoring.
Japan	A survey found that 24 percent of primary pupils and 60 percent of secondary students were attending *juku* (after-school tutoring). Another 4 percent received tutoring at home. Nearly 70 percent of all students had received tutoring by the time they had completed middle school.
Korea, Rep. of	A survey indicated that in Seoul 82 percent of primary students, 66 percent of middle school students, and 59 percent of academic high school students received tutoring. In rural areas the respective proportions were 54, 46, and 12 percent.
Malaysia	Among 8,420 secondary school students surveyed, the proportions receiving tutoring were 59 percent in form 3, 53 percent in form 5, and 31 percent in form 6. About 83 percent of students had received some form of tutoring by the time they reached the upper secondary level.
Malta	A survey of 2,129 students found that 52 percent of primary and 83 percent of secondary students had received tutoring at some time during their careers; 42 percent of grade 6 and 77 percent of grade 11 students were currently receiving tutoring.
Mauritius	A survey showed that 56 percent of students in secondary form 2 were receiving tutoring. The proportions rose to 98 percent in forms 3 and 4 and to 100 percent in forms 5 and 6. Another survey, of 2,919 grade 6 students, reported that 78 percent received extra lessons.

Table 5.3 Continued

Economy	Indications of scale
Myanmar	A survey of 118 grade 9 and 10 students in Yangon Division found that 91 percent were receiving tutoring, as were 66 percent of 131 students in grades 5–8.
Singapore	A survey of 1,052 households, plus interviews with 1,261 students, found that 49 percent of primary and 30 percent of secondary students were receiving tutoring. The findings matched an earlier study of tutoring in languages among 572 primary and 581 secondary students.
Sri Lanka	Among 1,873 students in years 6, 11, and 13 surveyed, 80 percent in year 6 and 75 percent in year 11 were receiving tutoring; in year 13 the proportions, by program, were 62 percent for arts students, 67 percent for commerce students, and 92 percent for science students.
Taiwan (China)	Government statistics indicate that in 1996 Taiwan had 4,266 tutoring centers with 1,505,491 students, not counting unregistered, illegal centers. A 1998 survey found that 81 percent of 397 upper secondary students were receiving private tutoring.
Tanzania	A survey of grade 6 pupils in three urban and four rural schools in mainland Tanzania found 26 percent receiving tutoring. In a Dar es Salaam school 70 percent of grade 6 students received tutoring. A separate survey of 2,286 grade 6 students in Zanzibar found 44 percent receiving extra lessons, although not all students paid for the classes.
Zimbabwe	A survey of 2,697 grade 6 pupils in all nine regions of the country reported that 61 percent received extra lessons. The regional range was from 36 to 74 percent.

Source: Bray 1999, 2003.

Student Assessment (PISA) and the Trends in International Mathematics and Science Study (TIMSS).

The two studies focus on different aspects of learning. TIMSS is a curriculum-based assessment of mathematics and science designed to measure student ability with respect to what is intended to be learned, what is actually taught, and what is actually learned. TIMSS also seeks to analyze the underlying factors that affect student performance (Dager and Blank 1999; Mullis et al. 2001). PISA, which is based on the notion that acquisition of literacy is a lifelong process, aims to measure "real-life" skills pertaining to reading, mathematics, and science, as well as cross-disciplinary competencies (OECD 2003b). For instance, instead of classrooms or laboratories, scientific literacy in PISA focuses on everyday life and on fields in which science is applied, such as health, earth and the environment, and technology.

Table 5.4 Key Competencies Identified by the Definition and Selection of Competencies Project

Interacting in socially heterogeneous groups	Acting autonomously	Using tools interactively
Relating well to others	Acting within the big picture or the larger context	Using language, symbols, and text interactively (written and spoken communication, and mathematical skills in multiple situations)
Cooperating	Forming and carrying out life plans and personal projects	Using knowledge and information interactively
Managing and resolving conflict	Defending and asserting one's rights, interests, limits, and needs	Using technology interactively (understanding the potential of technology and identifying technological solutions to problems)

Source: Rychen and Salganik 2003.

The OECD's Definition and Selection of Competencies (DeSeCo) Project has identified three key competencies that are essential for the personal and social development of people in modern, complex societies: interacting in socially heterogeneous groups, acting autonomously, and using tools interactively (table 5.4). Assuming that these competencies do reflect a global trend, and that a general consensus about them even exists, the question then is, how many of the key competencies are actually measured by the current generation of international comparative studies of student achievement? Existing studies mostly focus on the third competency, using tools interactively. Under ideal conditions the studies should enable countries to determine the fraction of their secondary school graduates who reach labor force age with competencies and skills that minimally equip them for a global economy. Considering that demand for new skills and competencies has surfaced only in recent years, it is understandable that these studies do not deal with many of the key competencies. As the plan is to repeat the assessments every few years, measurements of some key competencies may become available in the future, but others may remain unavailable (Rychen and Salganik 2003).

Despite the current limitations of international assessments, the studies, in addition to yielding information on whether students are actually acquiring the skills specified in standards and curriculum, provide tools for education reform. By identifying the strengths and weaknesses of education systems in comparison with those in other participating countries, they give policy makers a means of further examining their education systems. (See box 5.2 for an illustration from Jordan.)

Box 5.2 Jordan's Secondary Education Reform Based on IAEP Data

In the 1970s and 1980s Jordan, with significant human resources but few natural resources, faced economic crises. The country nevertheless rapidly achieved its goal of instituting compulsory basic education, although at the price of deteriorating educational quality. In times of global technological advances and economic change, the education system was no longer producing a labor force with relevant skills to meet the demand. To reverse the trend, Jordan conducted a diagnosis of its education system with a view toward improving quality and realigning education to match the changing socioeconomic reality.

In 1990 Jordan participated in the second International Assessment of Educational Progress (IAEP II). The study results showed that only 40 percent of questions in mathematics and 57 percent of questions in science were answered correctly. This triggered an investigation; each item in the test was scrutinized carefully, as were the school curricula and the administration of practice tests. On the basis of the findings, Jordan readministered the tests. The results were almost identical to those from the previous round. This led to the 1995 education reform.

Data from IAEP II were used to (a) establish benchmarks for 13-year-olds' achievements in mathematics and science vis-à-vis performance in 19 other countries; (b) show the areas of weakness and strength in each subject; (c) compare performance of students in schools managed by different education authorities within Jordan, in different administrative regions and in urban and rural areas; (d) identify certain cognitive processes involved in learning; (e) inform preservice and in-service teacher training programs; (f) analyze family and home characteristics associated with student achievement in mathematics and science; and (g) target the negative and positive influences of various classroom practices, out-of-school student activities, and student attitudes on achievement in mathematics and science. Participation in IAEP II was, furthermore, instrumental in developing national capacity to independently conduct national surveys of educational progress. This has enabled the National Center for Human Resources Development to administer sample-based national assessments of educational achievement on a regular basis.

Preliminary findings of a World Bank economic and sector work study on education costs show some evidence of quality improvement. Jordan's case indicates the importance of government commitment to use the results of international assessments for education reform and to build national capacity for future assessment studies independent of international assessments.

Source: Koda 2002.

Data from international assessments are helpful in analyzing the relationship between education system variables and student achievement. Using TIMSS 1995 data, Wössmann (2000) studied the relationship between educational institutions and student achievement. His model examines the effect on student achievement of three sets of factors: student's background, use of resources, and the characteristics of the institution in which learning takes place. The results indicate that 75 percent of cross-country variation in mathematics and 60 percent of the variation in science are explained by institutional differences in education systems.

PISA data have provided key empirical evidence on the relationship between performance standards and socioeconomic distribution of student performance, and the studies have shown that countries can achieve good results without creating inequalities (OECD 2004c). Countries such as Finland, Japan, and Korea demonstrate that excellence is attainable at a rational cost and that it is possible to combine good results with socially equitable distribution of learning opportunities.

National Assessments of Student Achievement

In the context of increasing demand for secondary education, policy makers need to make informed decisions about how to invest limited public resources to improve the quality of education and yield cost-effective outcomes. Many countries are now conducting their own national studies of student achievement.[1]

In the 1990s many countries either created new standards or overhauled their national curriculum and assessment systems within the framework of a renewed agenda for educational quality. At the same time, the use of national assessments as tools for school and teacher accountability became prominent, especially in countries such as Australia, Canada, the United Kingdom, and the United States. The approach was to use the hard evidence from national comparable data on student achievement to hold local actors (school councils, principals, and teachers) accountable for both successes and failures in students' skills and competencies as defined in the national curriculum standards.

Since 2001, the practice has become prominent in the United States under the No Child Left Behind Act. While the National Assessment of Educational Progress (NAEP) conducts sample-based studies at the national level, most U.S. states have been developing state-mandated assessment systems to monitor student achievement. All students in certain grades are tested on the skills and competencies specified in state standards. Although the particular forms and functions of state assessment systems vary widely, the norm is that teachers, schools, and districts should be held accountable for student performance. A number of states also hold other actors, including students, accountable (Kellaghan and Greaney 2001). Teachers' unions, school leaders, principals, and teachers tend to oppose policies linking assessments and accountability, on various grounds. Among them are the perverse effects, including the narrowing of the curriculum, the practice of "teaching to the test," and incentives for teachers to cheat (Evers and Walberg 2003). Technical difficulties include the issue of identifying who is accountable for whom, since many teachers change schools within a short time span.

There is also evidence showing that the existence of external examinations, especially high-stakes examinations, is one of the variables associated with higher student achievement (Bishop 1998; Phelps 2001; Wössmann 2000). Bishop reports that students in countries with curriculum-based external exit examination systems had considerably higher scores in TIMSS than those in countries without exit examination systems. An explanatory variable for the results could be the impact of widespread private tutoring.

Large-scale summative assessments are considered unsuitable for assessing some of the key competencies needed by labor markets, such as ability to interact in socially heterogeneous groups and to act autonomously. These can only be measured using more serious and sophisticated classroom-based assessment systems. Classroom-based student achievement monitoring is considered important but still does not receive enough attention. Some researchers lament the current emphasis on large-scale summative assessments and urge policy makers to pay more attention to what takes place in classrooms if they really wish to raise standards (Black and William 1998). According to the National Research Council (NRC), the organization that developed the National Science Education Standards in the United States, frequent classroom assessments have been found to have positive effects on student achievement (Committee on Classroom Assessment and the National Science Education Standard 2001). The NRC recommends that this type of assessment be aligned with more formal assessments and that teachers be trained to conduct them properly. Such capacity building could help teachers regain control of their professional practice.

Summary: Assess Locally, Examine Nationally, and Compare Globally

In the effort to expand secondary education and improve its quality, the role and implications of national examinations cannot be taken for granted. Secondary education reform may be unviable if examinations do not receive targeted attention from the outset of the reform effort. Broadly speaking, entrance examinations to secondary education are disappearing or are being used for purposes other than competitive selection. They are being moved to the end of the compulsory phase of secondary education (usually, lower secondary school), and the results are increasingly being used as a counseling tool and for sorting students into different tracks or paths at the upper secondary level, when they are about 16 years of age.

The shift from uniformity toward diversity in secondary education is well illustrated by changes in assessment policy over time. Examinations that once involved only a tiny fraction of the population now interest a much wider public. In some cases examination systems have demonstrated great adaptability to changing circumstances, on the assumption that the quality of curriculum reforms cannot be ensured without equally good evaluation methods. As work content increasingly demands specific technical knowledge and skills, school curricula and examinations have moved to incorporate more applied and vocational elements into subject matter that was once almost exclusively academic and abstract. To avoid accusations of subjectivity and unfairness in grading (or of outright fraud), national examination agencies have tended to develop what they claim are objective, standardized tests. Further reinforcing the trend from norm-referenced to criterion-referenced assessment, there are now strong and visible signs of movement away from reliance on one-shot, time-limited tests toward the incorporation of such nonexamination practices as portfolios, profiles, and school records in the final evaluation of secondary school leavers. These trends in secondary education reform deserve praise, as they symbolize the way forward in building a new culture of educational evaluation and assessment that is both technically sophisticated and socially inclusive.

The utilization of various kinds of assessment and monitoring tools appears to be the optimal and balanced approach toward enhancing the role of these systems in improving educational quality and relevance. International studies such as PISA and TIMSS measure different things in quite different ways. Policy makers need to be clear about what needs to be measured and to decide which international studies best fit the needs of the education system. National systems can have a direct impact on student achievement, especially when their results are used as the only available proxy for educational quality. Decision makers should be aware of the potential risks and implications of using national assessments as tools for teacher and school accountability. The potential effect of classroom-based student assessment on achievement seems to be great, but this method is inherently more costly and takes time to implement because teachers need to be trained and national curriculum standards need to be reformulated accordingly.

Note

1. National assessments and public examinations both assess students' ability, but whereas the former mainly focus on the system level, the latter measure individual students' ability and are normally used for selective purposes.

6

Responding to the Twin Challenges: Teachers, Teaching, and Technology

Teacher repertoires have been shaped by the crucible of experience and the culture of teaching. Policymakers need to understand that altering pedagogy requires a change in what teachers believe. Getting professionals to unlearn in order to learn, while certainly not impossible, is closer in magnitude of difficulty to performing a double bypass heart operation than to hammering a nail.

—Larry Cuban (1986)

The teaching profession is charged with the immense task of creating conditions and developing processes for building the human skills and capacities that are considered to be indispensable for economic growth, prosperity, social well-being, and individual development. It is no surprise that in any national education system teachers are considered the most important element where educational quality is concerned. Reform efforts in both developed and developing countries assume that the most direct and effective way of raising instructional quality is to introduce changes in teacher education and recruitment, to improve the knowledge and pedagogical skills of in-service teachers, and to ensure that the organizational conditions under which teachers work promote effective instruction and focus on student learning outcomes.

The shift from industrial- to knowledge-based school organization has a direct impact on teacher training and teacher deployment. More flexible arrangements are needed that, among other things, allow teachers to break away from the isolation in their classrooms. For example, team teaching to larger and flexible student groups is a worthwhile contemporary trend. The demand is for a teacher who is a knowledge worker, a designer of learning environments, with the ability to take advantage of the various areas in which knowledge is produced.

Within the context of knowledge-based, knowledge-intensive teaching, the latest revolution in the education sector has to do with the potential role of information and communication technologies (ICTs) in introducing radical change to teaching and learning processes. ICTs include radio, television, computers, and the Internet. For some decades now, technologies have been seen, in both developing and developed countries, as tools for expanding the provision and coverage of education at a reduced cost. Although this has been true in several cases, ICTs nowadays are considered preferably as a means of offering high-quality education that is centered on student learning and geared toward relevant skills in demand in the knowledge economy. ICTs offer a means of reducing costs while expanding coverage (as in traditional distance education), but they can also increase costs without necessarily expanding coverage—an example is sophisticated online course tutoring at the tertiary level. So ICTs hold the promise of expanding access to education, but they can also be an avenue for new forms of inequity. For secondary education in particular, ICTs appear to be at the core of the twin challenges of expanding access and, at the same time, improving quality and relevance.

Secondary School Teachers: Shortages, Professional Identity, and Training Issues

Qualified secondary school teachers are becoming a precious commodity in many developed and developing countries. They tend to be the hardest segment for the teaching profession to attract, the most expensive to educate, and the most difficult to retain. The numbers of unqualified teachers tend to be much higher in secondary than in primary education in almost every developing country. And the attrition rates of secondary education teachers are the highest in the teaching profession, especially for male teachers and for those in high-demand fields such as mathematics, science, and technology (OECD 2004a).

Since, almost everywhere, preservice teacher education for secondary school tends to be consecutive (that is, teachers are educated first in a curriculum area or specialized discipline and then go on to receive some pedagogical training), the professional identity of secondary teachers is not constructed around teaching but, rather, around their discipline of specialization. But as mass secondary education spreads, more and more teachers who at the start of their careers had thought of themselves as *pretertiary* teachers are confronted with the hard fact that they are, rather, *postprimary* teachers. In contrast to the days when secondary education had elite status, student motivation can no longer be taken for granted. This fact entirely changes the conditions of day-to-day teaching for secondary school teachers. Instead of being trained to develop the new competencies required to deal with today's students, secondary teachers see their professional identity questioned and experience a loss of control over their own professional practice. And insofar as training is concerned, secondary teachers seem to be increasingly tempted to trade off opportunities to learn to innovate in favor of survival toolkits.

Education decision makers today face the problem of attracting able graduates to the teaching profession and retaining them there. In developing countries, and especially in Africa, shortages of teachers, particularly in areas such as mathematics, science, and technology, pose a major threat to the goals of expanding education and enhancing its quality. For example, whereas in some African countries, such as Uganda, qualified teachers are unemployed (Lewin 2002), in Zambia the 1996 national education policy estimated that the numbers of teachers retiring, dying, or chronically ill would equal the entire output of teacher training colleges in the years to follow. In Lesotho it was estimated that almost half the school completion cohort would have to choose teaching in order to meet predicted demand (Lewin 2002, 229). The shortage of teachers will continue to be the main challenge for teacher policies in the near future. This will be the case worldwide, although the reasons vary—demography, labor market trends, the impact of HIV/AIDS, and so on. Comprehensive incentive policies to attract and retain high-quality teachers need to be designed taking into account the effective and dynamic integration of teacher professional development and career issues, teacher deployment policies, class size, and monitoring and evaluation practices. Such policies could commence with measures to make the teaching profession more attractive by increasing the salaries and compensation of secondary school teachers. (The case of Chile is probably the best illustration of success in this regard.) Alternatively, or in addition, measures to alleviate teacher shortages could include investments in teacher education and changes in teacher certification and recruitment policies.

Broadly speaking, solutions to teacher shortages in developing countries have taken two directions. One is to accelerate preservice teacher training, thus reducing the duration and the cost of training. In some countries, such as Guinea, training has been cut down to three months. The other solution is to institute policies that permit recruitment of unemployed graduates with no formal teacher training, graduates from teacher colleges, or secondary school graduates fresh from the classroom on a contract basis at a lower monthly salary than regular teachers receive.

Accelerated preservice training has greatly reduced the cost of preservice teacher education and has helped place more teachers in classrooms in a relatively short time. In some cases, however, it has negatively affected teaching quality, particularly when students' academic background is weak. Contract teacher policies can also lead to increased regional disparities, since contract teachers tend to be deployed to rural and remote areas. More empirical evidence is needed about the effects of these policies, and governments need to weigh the options carefully before putting them in practice. There are no easy shortcuts to achieving the goal of an appropriately trained teaching force, particularly at the secondary education level.

Developed countries are also attempting to respond to shortages of secondary education teachers, in some cases with imaginative and innovative solutions. For example, in the Netherlands the Unqualified Teaching Interim Act makes it possible for professionals with a higher-education degree to choose a career in education. Interested professionals are required to go through an assessment process before they can begin teaching in a school, and they take a tailor-made two-year training program. On successful completion of the training, they earn the formal qualification to teach.

To What Extent Is Investment in Preservice Teacher Training for Secondary Education Worthwhile?

Teacher shortages are becoming severe in some countries and in some curriculum areas, particularly mathematics and science. Many educators, researchers, and policy makers are convinced that investment in preservice education is not yielding the expected results and that resources would be better utilized if redirected to other, more productive areas. The fact that in many countries preservice training has remained virtually unchanged is raising even more doubts about its effectiveness. This is particularly so where secondary school teachers are concerned, since their preservice training relies almost exclusively on specialized knowledge training at universities, with very little, if any, practical training in teaching and learning processes. To a great extent, this has meant that secondary teachers have to be responsible for their own training and professional development once they start teaching in schools. In addition, and especially in developing countries, teachers generally have to teach alone, with students the only witnesses of their professional activity. Few jobs are characterized by greater solitude and isolation. Teachers labor on their own to decide what instruction works, what standard of student work is acceptable, and what additional knowledge, skills, or insights would best serve them and their students. "It is probable that this version of private, is the modal one across most school settings and at most points of the career. Both the architectural and the social organization of schooling make it difficult to work otherwise" (Huberman 1995, 207).

There is, moreover, a profound mismatch between the radically new key competencies demanded of students in the knowledge society and the teaching skills acquired from teacher training colleges and in-service training programs (World Bank 2004a). For developing countries, designing appropriate policies for selecting and training teachers who can help students acquire the new competencies required by society and labor markets is an extraordinary challenge. The new competencies clearly require that teachers behave in classrooms in a way contrary to the training they receive.

Conservative and strongly academically oriented teacher training systems are unable to facilitate such a shift. But the inefficiency and high cost of traditional preservice teaching training do not justify abandoning such training altogether.

At least two dilemmas emerge for developing country decision makers. The first arises from the growing tension and potential conflict between the drive to raise the status of the teaching profession and the perceived need to bring teacher education back from academia and closer to schools and classrooms. Efforts are being made to upgrade the academic status of teacher education programs (which could result in greater access restrictions, thus paradoxically worsening teacher shortages). At the same time, there is a need to base and concentrate both preservice and in-service teacher training in schools and classrooms if it is to be relevant and efficient.

The second issue, which is closely related to the first, arises from the research evidence suggesting that school-based in-service training and mentoring of novice teachers is more effective and less costly than traditional preservice training (Lewin 2003). A policy move in that direction could lead to the shortening of preservice periods in teacher colleges, which would at least partially reduce university control over teacher education and access to the teaching profession and might jeopardize the academic status of teacher education programs. Such a risk might be dealt with through renewed teacher accreditation systems that sanction qualifications regardless of the duration of formal studies. Notwithstanding the caveats implicit in the trade-offs involved, a prudent and gradual shift in resource allocation from preservice to school-based training could be a change worth considering in teacher education policy in some countries.

Matching Teaching Skills with Required Key Competencies for Secondary School Graduates

A teaching skill or competency is the capacity to mobilize a variety of cognitive resources to deal with a specific type of teaching situation. Rather than relating to the teaching of a particular content or type of knowledge, teaching competencies and skills integrate and articulate cognitive resources that are relevant to a given situation. They are constructed through training and through daily practice in the classroom. Teaching competencies are common to every curriculum area and school level; they cut across subjects and disciplines, in primary, secondary, and tertiary education.

The debate about the professional, nonprofessional, or semiprofessional nature of school teaching has been going on for decades, but today the issue is more controversial and crucial than ever. In the contemporary knowledge economy, knowledge management is seen as the key to the flexibility of operations, the training and professional development of employees, and even the overall productivity of an institution. The implicit challenge is that knowledge of teaching is for the most part tacit, difficult to articulate and systematize, and strictly practical and context based. These characteristics reinforce the traditional isolation of teachers and schools, making the transfer and full utilization of knowledge very difficult. In short, teacher education institutions, schools as organizations, and education systems in general are still very far from meeting the needs of a knowledge-management society. This is why the curriculum of teacher education, especially preservice training, remains an open, controversial, and puzzling issue, with contradictory evaluation results and research evidence.

Linkage between curriculum reforms and in-service teacher training. The implementation of curriculum reform is basically a problem of in-service teacher training. And such training is difficult because of the "stickiness" (resilience) of teachers' preexisting know-how. Other professions have constructed highly specialized knowledge capital that permits the establishment of a considerable distance between the professional and the customer. (This is the key to the classic sociological category of professional prestige.) Professional knowledge of teaching cannot be constructed in the same manner. Being close to students, caring about them, and building learning communities that are responsive to students' needs are part of the essence of the teaching profession. An entirely new approach to professional knowledge has to be developed (Hiebert, Gallimore, and Stigler 2002)—one that allows for the conceptualization of teacher education and teacher professional development in terms of lifelong learning.

The debate about the curriculum of teacher education programs has taken place around two fundamental and conflicting stands: (a) that the emphasis should be on subject-related knowledge (*content knowledge*) and (b) that the most pertinent knowledge for teachers is obviously *teaching-and learning-related knowledge*. Teaching- and learning-related knowledge includes professional knowledge about students themselves (in secondary education, understanding adolescence is vital) and about classroom management, pedagogy, and evaluation and the school as a learning and knowledge-producing institution. Contrary to common wisdom in education, there is strong research evidence that knowledge about teaching and learning processes is even more closely associated with student achievement than is content knowledge of the discipline (Darling-Hammond 2000).

Educational research in several related fields has pointed out the existence of a third category of knowledge that is at least as relevant for teacher education as the other two: *pedagogical content knowledge*—that is, specific and specialized knowledge about teaching and learning processes in a particular discipline (see figure 6.1). Pedagogical content knowledge is a teacher's understanding of how to help students understand specific subject matter. It includes specialized knowledge of how particular subject-matter topics can be organized, represented, adapted to the diverse interests of learners, and presented for instruction. According to some recent

Figure 6.1 Categories Contributing to Pedagogical Content Knowledge

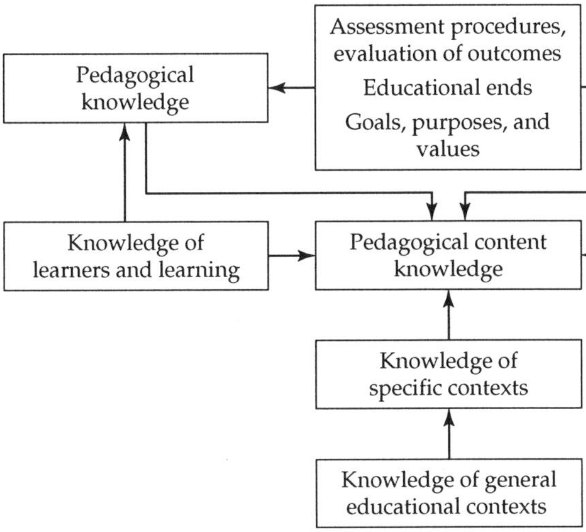

Source: Morine-Dershimer and Todd 2003.

reviews, this is the type of knowledge most clearly linked to student achievement and the one with the greatest potential vis-à-vis the professional development of teachers. Pedagogical content knowledge is not only a renewed and advanced source of a new identity for the teaching profession; it can also promote better student results and a more equitable school system. Emphasis on pedagogical content knowledge results in more productive and inclusive secondary schools.

Competencies relating to the work of teachers in the classroom are those that should be considered core elements in preservice teacher education. Research evidence shows the importance for beginner teachers of developing a repertoire of abilities and basic knowledge that allows them to make a good start in their professional lives (see figure 6.2).

Lifelong learning is more than just a good axiom. Fundamentally, a change is required in the way the teaching profession is viewed: a teacher must be seen as a professional, a knowledge worker who does not spend his or her entire professional life in just one education system or even in a single country. Like students, teachers must be prepared to work in changing and unpredictable environments in which knowledge is constructed from different sources and viewpoints. The ability to teach challenging content to learners with different experiences and conceptions depends on the capacity of practitioners to create powerful and diverse learning experiences that connect with what students know and how they can most effectively learn. In addition to addressing pedagogical and subject-matter knowledge and skills, secondary school teachers are expected to develop skills for communicating

Figure 6.2 Secondary School Teacher Competencies

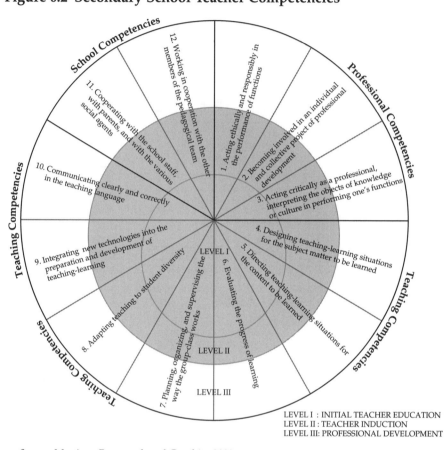

LEVEL I : INITIAL TEACHER EDUCATION
LEVEL II : TEACHER INDUCTION
LEVEL III: PROFESSIONAL DEVELOPMENT

Source: Martinet, Raymond, and Gauthier 2001.

Note: Appendix F provides a road map of teacher competencies for a knowledge-based secondary school.

with parents, dealing with dropouts, grade repetition, and poor attendance, and working in disadvantaged communities. Teacher education programs should enable teachers to teach in multiple contexts to diverse groups of children and should help them understand how to build effective school-community partnerships.

Teaching and Learning with Technology

In low-income countries the strategic use of ICT potentially provides a means of leapfrogging in educational development. The mere availability of computers and other technology, however, does not replace the core business of teaching and learning, nor is it in itself a guarantee of gains in educational quality. Education, not connectivity, is the challenge here, but the two need not be sequential or in conflict.

There is still a long way to go before the potential of ICT in actual classroom learning processes is realized. In both developed and developing countries there is mounting skepticism about the learning outcomes of massive investments in ICT.

The challenge concerning full utilization of ICT in education closely concerns the teaching profession. ICT teachers seem to be especially hard to attract, recruit, and retain in secondary schools (OECD 2004a), and the ICT training needs of secondary school teachers with no or little knowledge of ICT in teaching and learning are enormous. Institutional innovation within educational institutions has not kept up with the pace of technological innovation in education, and this gap creates problems with the implementation and full utilization of ICT. Policies for ICT in education should be set within the framework of a precisely defined strategy for the entire education sector, entailing a new cultural framework for educational institutions. These policies should emphasize new forms of access to education and new channels for social participation. Careful review of the organizational, managerial, and financial features of educational institutions is a precondition for the successful implementation of any ICT education policy.

If anything, ICT means networking and collaboration. Institutional partnerships at all levels are the key to sustainable success. Quality control and quality assurance mechanisms become crucial. The supply of ICT education can potentially be of the highest quality but also of the poorest.

Use of ICT for Distance Education to Expand the Venues for Learning

ICTs have brought about a new approach to institutionalizing education by providing alternative venues for knowledge dissemination and learning, beyond the constraints of space, time, or physical structure. Technologies such as interactive radio broadcast, satellite and cable television, computers, and the Internet have become available for educational use (see table 6.1). These technologies have the potential to provide learners with a highly interactive, synchronous and asynchronous multimedia learning experience from geographically dispersed organizations and schools via vast national and international networks (Haddad and Draxler 2002).

Radio broadcast and interactive radio instruction (IRI). Although radio lacks the visual effects of television and computers, distance education programs via radio have many advantages: broad outreach can be attained without complex infrastructure, radio is easy to use, and the programs are less expensive to produce than television and computer-assisted programs. The first IRI program in a developing country was initiated in Nicaragua in the 1970s

Table 6.1 Distance Education for Secondary Equivalence in Africa

Country	Subjects offered	Enrollment, 1999–2000	Technology used
Botswana	All subjects	600 junior secondary	Print, radio
Burkina Faso	French, math, physics	—	Radio, television
Ethiopia	Eight subjects	8,400	Print, radio, television
Ghana	English, math, science	—	Print, radio, television
Guinea	French, math, science	300 secondary teachers	Print, radio, audio-tapes
Malawi	—	80,000	Print, audiotapes
Namibia	All subjects	18,325	Print, radio, audio-tapes
Nigeria	All subjects	—	Print
Zambia	—	11,138 (1990)	Print, radio
Zimbabwe	Academic subjects	25,000	Print

Source: World Bank 2002a.

Note: —, Not available.

to teach mathematics to students in grades 1 to 4. Since then, IRI has been used to teach a variety of subjects, including language arts, second languages, science, and environmental studies, in 20 countries, mostly in Africa and in Latin America and the Caribbean.

Experience has shown the potential of IRI for expanding secondary education. Program evaluations in Bolivia, South Africa, and Thailand have indicated that IRI programs make a substantial impact on urban-rural equity gaps and educational quality, as reflected in achievement gains by targeted students (Bosch, Rhodes, and Kariuki 2002). Studies on IRI programs in Honduras, Papua New Guinea, and South Africa have identified the potential of IRI to reduce gender equity gaps (Hartenberger and Bosch 1996). Other studies have consistently demonstrated IRI's cost-effectiveness across programs (Haddad and Draxler 2002). Although IRI requires relatively high initial fixed costs, recurrent costs are markedly lower. Initial costs include production of audio and print materials and development of management and training systems; recurrent costs include staff salaries, program dissemination, maintenance, and training of teachers and program staff. Because of the wide reach of radio broadcasts and the insignificance of the variable costs (new school and broadcast facilities, textbooks, teachers, and maintenance staff) required for additional learners, the cost per learner of IRI programs decreases proportionally with an increase in users. Thirteen of the twenty countries that launched IRI between 1974 and 1999 continue to implement the original programs. Three countries are using different applications from those launched initially, and four have abandoned the program (World Bank 2002a).

Educational television. Television has been used in secondary education since the late 1960s, with mixed results. The most important advantage of educational television is that complex or abstract concepts can be illustrated through visual effects. Notable disadvantages include high production costs associated with relatively sophisticated production facilities, equipment, and technical skills, and inflexibility in updating programs once they have been developed.

Programs implemented in Côte d'Ivoire and El Salvador with the support of international agencies did not succeed. The program in Côte d'Ivoire came to an end soon after external financing was discontinued, the victim of high per-student costs, teachers' resistance to centralized institutions, and weak local capacity resulting from overreliance on foreign or expatriate technical assistance. By contrast, two educational television programs in Latin America and one in Asia—Mexico's Telesecundaria, Brazil's Telecurso, and the National Open School of India—have succeeded in providing secondary education to students who would not otherwise have had the opportunity. The success of television-based educational programs in these three countries, despite the high initial fixed-cost investments, is attributed to their large populations of potential secondary school students, which permit economies of scale.

Telesecundaria was developed in 1968 by Mexico without external financing. Its main objective was to solve the problem of access in rural areas. (The urban delivery version became financially unviable because of low demand.) Telesecundaria targeted students in the 200,000 rural communities with populations of less than 2,500. In 1998, 15 percent of Mexico's junior secondary students were educated through the program (World Bank 2002a).

Brazil's Telecurso was developed in the late 1970s by the Roberto Marinho Foundation and was supported by the country's largest commercial network, Rede Globo. Its purpose was to provide young working adults with the opportunity to acquire primary or secondary equivalency certificates. To respond to the new demands of the labor market, a new program, Telecurso 2000, was developed in the early 1990s by the Roberto Marinho Foundation, the Globo media company, and industrialists. Telecurso 2000 is a condensed version of a basic secondary education curriculum, with an optional curriculum on basic mechanical skills. The guiding principles of its design are job-oriented education, development of basic skills, citizenship education, and contextualization (Haddad and Draxler 2002).

The National Open School of India was established in 1989 as an autonomous institution under the Ministry of Human Resources Development to support India's National Policy on Education. The school mainly caters to the educational needs of out-of-school children and of socially and economically disadvantaged students in general. Although it started with academic courses at the secondary level (including the senior secondary level), it currently offers courses in vocational and other life-skill areas. It has also extended its range from elementary to preuniversity programs. Over 400,000 children from physically, socially, economically, and geographically disadvantaged groups have enrolled in the school.

Computers and the Internet. The major investments made over the past two decades have brought modern ICTs into nearly all secondary schools in the most advanced OECD countries (OECD 2004b).[1] In some middle-income countries too, computers and the Internet have been introduced in a large number of secondary schools; for example, in Chile the student-computer ratio is 33 to 1 (Hepp et al. 2004). Computers and the Internet are used for educational purposes in three basic ways: (a) as teaching tools (simulations, courseware, online learning communities, professional development of teachers); (b) as content delivery tools (online libraries, journals, and books); and (c) as management tools (Education Management Information System, or EMIS, assessment, record keeping). Examples of how computers and the Internet have been used to expand access to secondary education include community telecenters, for the most part in developing countries, and virtual high schools, mainly in developed countries.

Community telecenters in poor rural areas provide computers and Internet access to the public. They are diverse in structure, clientele, services provided, financing, and availability of hardware and software. Some serve as nonformal education centers providing basic literacy courses and training to school dropouts and adults. For instance, LearnLink telecenters in Ghana offer supplementary educational programs beyond those available in public and private institutions. In the three years 1998–2001 the program provided more than 14,000 individuals—students, teachers, businesspeople, and even national telecommunications staff—with useful ICT skills (USAID and AED 2003).

Virtual schools offer courses to students over the Internet. Since 1997 many new virtual schools have been established in Australia, Canada (British Columbia and Alberta), Europe, and the United States. Virtual schools vary significantly in their curricula and in how they are structured and funded. Some have individual courses that students may take to receive credit from their school districts toward a regular diploma. Others offer a complete program and diploma. In the United States about 300,000 students, mainly high school students, were enrolled in virtual schools during the 2002/3 academic year. It is estimated that more than 520,000 students were enrolled in 2004/5 (Revenaugh 2004). More than half of the U.S. states offer some form of virtual education. In addition, 67 virtual charter schools in 17 states served 21,000 students in 2003/4 (see box 6.1).

Box 6.1 Types of Virtual School
in the United States, with Examples

- *State-sanctioned, state-level.* Sanctioned by the state government to act as the state's own virtual school. *Example:* the Florida Virtual School, which is state funded as an independent entity and offers a full online curriculum but not a diploma.
- *College and university based.* Virtual introductory college-level courses have been made available to upper-division high school students through dual or concurrent enrollment. *Example:* the University of Nebraska–Lincoln Independent Study High School, which has developed, under a federal grant, CLASS online diploma program courses that are marketed through the for-profit CLASS.com.
- *Consortium and regionally based.* Virtual school consortia can be national, multistate, state-level, or regional. Many regional education agencies have added virtual K–12 courses to their service menus for schools. Most consortia act as brokers for external provider opportunities or share courses among members. *Example:* the nonprofit VHS Inc. (formerly Concord VHS) in Massachusetts, which is seeking sustainability through its broad network of participating schools.
- *Local education agency based.* A large number of local public schools and school districts have created virtual schools, mainly to serve their own supplemental or alternative educational needs and to reach out to homeschool populations. They usually employ their own regular, certified K–12 teachers, either within the regular course of instruction or on the side. *Example:* the HISD Virtual School in Houston, which offers middle school curricula for enrolled and homeschool students, as well as advanced placement courses to supplement its high school offerings.
- *Virtual charter schools.* State-chartered entities—including public school districts, nonprofit organizations, and for-profit organizations—operate public charter schools that are exempt from some rules and regulations. Charter school legislation has a major impact on how these schools operate. *Example:* the Basehor-Linwood Virtual Charter School in Kansas, which focuses on providing state-funded public education opportunities for K–12 homeschoolers across the state. It delivers self-developed courses in a full diploma program, using a certified district teacher for each elementary grade level and secondary content area.
- *Private virtual schools.* Like local public schools, many private schools have developed virtual school programs, mainly designed to provide supplemental courses and instructional materials for homeschoolers. A limited number offer state-approved or regionally accredited high

(Continued)

Box 6.1 Continued

school diplomas. *Example:* the Christa McAuliffe Academy in Washington State, where student cohorts meet weekly with their mentor in an online virtual classroom meeting and students follow online mastery-based learning curricula facilitated by academy mentors and developed by external providers.

- *For-profit providers of curricula, content, tools, and infrastructure.* Many for-profit companies have played an important role in the development of virtual schools. *Example:* companies such as Apex Learning and Class.com have supplied starter courses for many new virtual school efforts. Blackboard and eCollege have provided delivery platforms that are used by many virtual schools. Many companies are broadening their original focus and are making available expanded curricula or comprehensive services to meet the needs of this growing market. Web development software companies such as Macromedia have provided the tools used by virtual schools to self-develop courses.

Source: T. Clark 2001.

The greatest benefit of virtual schools lies in the increased opportunities for students in small rural districts. Often, these districts cannot offer a full range of courses such as advanced placement (specialized preuniversity) courses and enrichment courses. This explains the prevalence of virtual schools in some of the less-populated areas of Australia, Canada, and the United States. Another noteworthy benefit of virtual schools is that they provide learning opportunities for individuals who cannot attend school because, for example, they have severe medical problems or are incarcerated. It also helps parents who decide to homeschool their children.

Three main factors need to be taken into account when considering the virtual school as an alternative venue for secondary education:

1. *Technology requirements.* The more closely a course resembles a real classroom with frequent simultaneous interactions, the more bandwidth is required. Equity concerns arise immediately: the higher the technology infrastructure requirements, the lower the number of students who will be able to participate, especially those who are economically disadvantaged. This issue needs to be carefully thought out during the design stage so that alternative technologies can be used to avoid heavy reliance on the Internet and on Web sites. For instance, CD-ROMs can be used to disseminate high-volume course materials and resources, and dedicated

listservs, newsgroups, and discussion boards can be used for asynchronous discussion and conferencing.
2. *Teachers and instructors.* Because the online teaching environment is quite different from the traditional classroom, different skills and pedagogy are required. It is important that teachers and instructors receive appropriate training on pedagogy, course design, and the use of technology.
3. *Students.* Not all students are prepared for online learning. Some may lack motivation, some may have a learning style unsuitable for online learning, and some may not be proficient in using the technologies. Lessons learned from existing virtual schools can be drawn on: readiness assessments of students, provision of support mechanisms, and good online technical support are all useful.

Integrated approach with multimedia. All the programs mentioned so far utilize mainly one type of technology, whether radio, television, or computers. But programs may also use a blend of technologies, each serving a specific purpose. National General Upper Secondary Distance Education in Finland is an example of this integrated approach.

The program was developed in 1997 by the National Board of Education (NBE) and the Finnish Broadcasting Company together with 12 educational institutions as pilot institutions. Encouraging results from the pilot schools led to the extension of the project to all of Finland's provinces. By February 2003 nearly 90 upper secondary institutions with approximately 3,200 students were participating. The objectives of the project are to improve educational equity by expanding access to general upper secondary education, to increase citizens' ability to use ICTs, and to meet the challenges of lifelong learning by offering students an open and flexible educational track.

All students in the Finnish program are enrolled at a participating educational institution and draw up their personal study plans in consultation with the institution's principal and the subject counselors. Students use textbooks and other written materials, distance learning programs on radio and television, audiocassettes, e-mail, and Web-based and other online learning materials. The success factors for this integrated approach are the nationwide scale and the NBE's partnerships with the business sector, which includes publishers, hardware suppliers, network operators, and the national public service broadcasting company.

Use of Computers and the Internet to Improve the Quality and Relevance of Education

Computer literacy is becoming a baseline requirement for many jobs, and demand for highly skilled ICT workers has increased where new technologies have been introduced (World Bank 2003a). To measure the quality of ICT skills of students and employers, educational institutions and government agencies in over 100 countries have adopted international competency standards such as the International Computer Driving License (ICDL) and the European Computer Driving License (ECDL). Some countries are setting up their own ICT literacy standards for secondary students; Chile, for instance, is establishing national accreditation for ICT skills in secondary schools based on the ICDL (Hepp et al. 2004).

More specific skills are also being taught at secondary schools around the world. A network company, Cisco, distributes to schools through the Internet the Cisco Networking Academy curricula, allowing students to be certified as Network Associates and Network Professionals. The program, launched in 1997, has evolved from a high school network support curriculum to a worldwide educational program. Over 450,000 students have enrolled in more than 10,000 Cisco Networking Academies located in high schools, technical schools, colleges, universities, and community-based organizations in over 160 countries (see http://www.cisco.com/en/US/learning/netacad/index.html).

Potential and Promise

Studies and evaluations of the effect that the use of computers and the Internet in the classroom has on student learning have yielded mixed results. Some studies show no clear or substantial evidence of improved academic achievement or cite negative evidence (Angrist and Lavy 2002; Cuban 2001; Wood, Underwood, and Avis 1999). Other studies have shown that the use of computers and the Internet can help build effective learning environments and improve student learning (Earle 2002; Honey 2001; Mehlinger 1996; Van Dusen and Worthen 1995). More recent surveys (OECD 2004b) indicate that actual levels of computer and Internet use in secondary schools are much lower than expected, even in developed countries that have made huge investments in ICT in secondary schools. These results obviously raise questions about the significance of impact evaluation studies in the field. There is a need for more rigorous studies and evaluations in different school contexts and different teaching and learning environments. Some of the recognized contributions of technologies to building effective learning environments are summarized here using the categories identified by Bransford, Brown, and Cocking (2000): learner-centered, knowledge-centered, assessment-centered, and community-centered environments.

Learner-centered environment. Some computer and Internet programs provide individualized instruction and present content beyond what has traditionally been available to a classroom teacher through textbooks. The programs motivate students through collaborative learning activities and by building a network of learners. They put students in the driver's seat, providing them with structure and giving them responsibility for their own learning.

Computer simulation programs can be used to teach core topics and to provide science students with theoretical or simplified models of real-world phenomena. (An example is the GenScope Project for genetics in precollege biology.) Such programs allow learners to investigate scientific and mathematical concepts through direct manipulation and experimentation. These scientific video- and computer-based simulations and visualization tools have been shown to lead to increased understanding of core scientific concepts (Honey 2001).

Knowledge-centered environment. Computers and the Internet make curricula more exciting by bringing real-world problems into the classroom. For example, through the Global Learning and Observations to Benefit the Environment (GLOBE) project, over a million students from more than 12,000 schools around the world have taken part in gathering data about their local environments using protocols specified by principal investigators. Students submit their data to a GLOBE data archive through the Internet, which both scientists and the students use to conduct their analyses. Visualization tools such as maps, graphs, and digital photos on the GLOBE Web site enable students to see their own data and to make comparisons with data collected in other locations. These knowledge-centered environments, which provide access to a vast array of information, including digital libraries and real-world data for analysis, as well as connections and interactions with meteorologists, geologists, astronomers, computer scientists, and other practitioners, make students enthusiastic about their work while producing impressive intellectual achievements (Means et al. 2000).

Assessment-centered environment. Computers and the Internet can help create a self-assessment-centered environment that gives students and teachers more opportunities to receive feedback, reflect, refine their understanding, and build new knowledge. For instance, networked technologies for communication such as the Computer-Supported International Learning Environments (CSILE) developed at the Ontario Institute for Studies in Education provide opportunities for students to collaborate on learning activities by working through a communal database that has text and graphic capabilities. Within the networked multimedia environment, students create "nodes" that contain an idea or piece of information about the topic they are studying. The nodes are available for other students to comment on, leading to dialogue and knowledge accumulation (Bransford, Brown, and Cocking 2000).

Community-centered environment. The Internet is especially effective in enabling teachers and students to build local and global communities that include teachers, administrators, students, parents, practicing scientists, and other interested people. For example, Internet-based international collaborative learning programs such as the International Education and Resource Network (iEARN) and the World Links program (see box 6.2) offer an online platform through which students work with peers in their

---

Box 6.2 World Links: A Global Learning Community

The World Links program was launched in 1997 by the World Bank Institute (WBI) as an effort to pilot-test the impact of information and communication technologies on teaching and learning in developing countries. The program is now an independent nongovernmental organization. As of 2004, World Links was operating in more than 35 countries, reaching over 400,000 teachers and students. The program introduces students and teachers to the vast educational resources available on the Internet, the possibilities for information sharing and networking among learners and educators, and the potential for the creation of new knowledge and learning resources in electronic format. Much of the World Links pedagogy for professional development programs for teachers centers on the use of technology for international collaborative project-based learning. Teachers develop curriculum-based projects ranging from a study of local flora and fauna to an examination of myths having to do with the traditional role of women in society. Each project involves interaction with one or more classrooms outside the teacher's city or country.

An important finding from the implementation of the program is that although individual teachers were enthusiastic about engaging in innovative pedagogy in the classroom, there were no incentives for doing so. The collaborative project work was not a formal part of the curriculum and was not measured by any examinations. Many of the projects, therefore, were developed and implemented as extracurricular activities outside normal school hours. The lesson is that if teachers and students are to gain from the use of ICTs in the classroom, a broader commitment must be made at the policy level to ensure full integration of technology into education systems through, for example, appropriate curricular integration and associated professional development for teachers.

Sources: World Bank staff; World Links program data, 2004.

---

own countries and around the world on collaborative learning projects. Such projects can expose students to the personal stories, expertise, resources, and authentic feedback necessary for in-depth analysis of other cultures and can give them opportunities for interaction and collaboration they would not otherwise have had (Spector 1999).

Controlled studies of cross-classroom collaboration have shown an increase in students' writing skills and motivation to read, write, investigate, and explore science and social science topics (Riel 1996). Teachers have also benefited from electronic communication, which enables them to form new working relationships with educators throughout the world and to learn from one another.

Challenges and Risks

As noted above, despite all the evidence about the positive impact of the use of computers and the Internet on student learning, some studies show no significant effects or even negative effects. Certain limitations in these studies need to be taken into account when comparing findings on the effects of computer-based instruction. The first limitation is the wide variety of computer-based instructional arrangements contemplated in the studies, as well as the multiplicity of subject areas involved and the grade level of students.[2] The second is the wide variation in the duration of the implementation of the instruction. The third is the inherent technical difficulty of measuring the skills these studies attempt to assess, such as motivation, student attitudes, self-directed learning, and teamwork (Sinko and Lehtinen 1999).

Several reasons have been given for limited and even negative effects on student learning: (a) the transition to computer-based instruction is disruptive; (b) real change and lasting results take time to appear, and the evaluation does not always cover the necessary duration; (c) computer-based programs were not implemented appropriately or as intended (too short implementation periods, failure to integrate the programs into the curriculum, inadequate teacher knowledge about the program, and so on); and (d) computer-based instruction may have consumed school resources or displaced educational activities that would have been in place otherwise (Angrist and Lavy 2002; Honey 2001; Van Dusen and Worthen 1995).

An extreme example comes from a study of two high schools in California's Silicon Valley, where new technologies were made lavishly available to teachers and students and where there was indisputably great encouragement to use computers in classroom instruction. Yet according to the study, the use of computers and the Internet in classrooms yielded no clear and significant effects on student learning achievement (Cuban 2001). Moreover, there were some unexpected findings: fewer than 5 percent of high school students had intense "tech-heavy" experience in school, and only a tiny percentage of teachers used the new technologies to accelerate student-centered and project-based teaching practices.

Conclusion: Options for Change

The mere availability of computers and the Internet in the classroom provides no guarantee that the quality and relevance of education and student learning will improve. Changes in teaching and learning or in school organization and management are difficult to bring about because a school is a complex system—socially, culturally, and politically. In order for change to take place, a comprehensive reform in the overall school context is needed (Cuban 2001). Some recommendations for policy makers and practitioners seeking to optimize the potential and the impact of the use of computers and the Internet in classrooms are summarized below (Cuban 2001; Earle 2002; Hepp et al. 2004; Honey 2001).

Program design and planning

- Understand teachers' expertise and perspectives on classroom work and engage teachers fully in deliberations about the design, deployment, and implementation of technology plans.
- Involve principals, parents, and the community in designing the program, using democratic processes, and provide them with access to ICT resources.
- Start small, with a pilot, and build on experience (step-by-step project development).
- Incorporate lessons learned from other programs.
- Focus on sustained and intensive teacher training and professional development as the central focus of the project.
- Include evaluations—preferably by an external body—in the original program design evaluations to increase program transparency; make certain that school leaders and teachers are informed about the impacts of the programs.

Organization

- ICT should be an integrated part of the existing education system, not a stand-alone project; it should be a vehicle for change and should be anchored in solid educational objectives. Accordingly, plan for fundamental changes in how secondary schools are organized, time is allocated, and teachers are prepared.
- Reduce the structural constraints that limit teacher choices in secondary schools and implement a more relaxed schedule with large chunks of uninterrupted time for joint planning, crossing of departmental boundaries, and sustained attention to different forms of learning.

Technical dimension

- Hardware manufacturers, software firms, and telecommunication companies need to develop software and equipment specifically designed for teachers and students.
- These suppliers must improve product reliability to limit the defects in their wares, increase technical support to teachers, and test software on consumers before marketing it to district and state administrators.

- The infrastructure for technical support and professional development needs to be redesigned and made responsive to the organizational incentives and workplace constraints that teachers face.

Whether the use of ICT is aimed at expanding access or at improving the quality and relevance of secondary education, the program needs to be cost-effective and financially sustainable. It is important that the forecasts of fixed and variable costs and the financing options be well thought out during the planning stage. Low- and middle-income countries face serious challenges with respect to the availability of supporting infrastructure, connectivity, and appropriate hardware and software. Countries may want to explore, in light of their particular educational needs and infrastructure availability, the new technologies available: solar energy, wireless solutions, digital satellite radio, and so on. The key decision should focus on the educational objective for which ICT is to be used, and this decision should lead to the right choice of technologies and modalities of use (Haddad and Draxler 2002).

Notes

1. By 2000 over 90 percent of students in 14 OECD countries surveyed—Belgium (Flanders), Denmark, Finland, France, Hungary, Ireland, Italy, the Republic of Korea, Mexico, Norway, Portugal, Spain, Sweden, and Switzerland—attended upper secondary schools where standard computer applications such as word processing, spreadsheets, and graphics programs were available. By 2001 the Internet was accessible in practically all schools in all these countries, with the exception of Mexico, a middle-income country.

2. Among the computer-based programs used in the studies were computer-assisted instruction (CAI), computer-enriched instruction (CEI), computer simulation in instruction (CSI), drill, computer tutorials, and microcomputer-based laboratories (MBLs).

7

Financing Secondary Education

This chapter explores options for improved secondary education financing, and attempts to address some of the issues and tensions highlighted in previous chapters. The anecdotal excerpt in box 7.1 serves as a humbling reminder that secondary education reform issues are not purely, or even mostly, technical. This chapter examines the features of secondary education that make its financing a somewhat different problem from financing primary or tertiary education. The focus is more (than is traditional) on financing per se—that is, more on how funds are moved between secondary education actors and the incentives this generates than on the amount of funding needed. Suggestions are made as to how countries can balance the financing approach between more funding and more efficient use of funding. An attempt is made to emphasize areas of financing that have not yet been covered in what is already an extensive, high-quality, and widely available literature. To sum up, the chapter seeks to add value to what is already known and available and to provide some suggestions for innovative operational and decision-making techniques.

The chapter does not offer a calculation of the amounts likely to be needed for global or regional expansion of secondary education. The reason is that there is no consensus on a benchmark such as exists for primary education in the form of the 100 percent completion rate. Accordingly, goals have to be set country by country. Furthermore, the secondary education subsector is extremely heterogeneous in its "supply" options. Binder (2004) provides a useful start in quantifying total cost, and Mingat (2004) makes some calculations for West African countries. A summary and discussion of the estimates are presented in this chapter.

The chapter does not make recommendations regarding the financial returns to various models of secondary education; these issues require resolution on a case-by-case basis. Nor does it recommend ideal technical ratios, delivery models, or parameters for the efficient running of secondary education from a financial viewpoint because of the significant within-country and between-country heterogeneity in how secondary education is conceptualized, defined, and delivered.

The discussion begins with a summary of the fiscal magnitude of expansion of secondary education. There follows a stocktaking of the existing knowledge base: a simple classification scheme for how to approach the problem of financing secondary education is set out, and suggestions in the

Box 7.1 Excerpt from a Debate in the British House of Commons, July 9, 1999

Mr. Blunkett (Secretary of State for Education and Employment): I am being heckled, but just for once I shall not rise to the bait. What about the golden legacy of no basic curriculum for teacher training, no new deal for schools, none of the investment that we are making in transforming the environment for schools and no learning grid?

I was interested to learn tonight that there have been grumbles from St. Joseph's primary school about the way in which the learning grid resources are being allocated. I thought that we were supposed to rely on the diversity of local government to arrange that allocation with schools. I thought that we were being chided for being too centralist and for running everything from Sanctuary buildings, and we are told that we should let county councils and schools run everything. However, on every scheme that we are not running from Sanctuary buildings, we are chided for what is happening at local level, which is the fault of the county council.

Here is another conundrum: every time we have formula funding, we are criticised, as we were criticised tonight in respect of St. Joseph's, and when we do not have formula funding, we are criticised for making the funding too specific. What do the Opposition want? Do they want formula funding, or do they want funding to be specifically provided to schools? Do they want the local authority or the Department of the Environment, Transport and the Regions to determine that funding? Do they want a literacy hour and a numeracy hour, or would they like to leave two out of five children languishing without a decent education, as they were before?

Dr. Julian Lewis (New Forest, East): I have a positive suggestion to make, and I want to know whether the Secretary of State will subscribe to it. Given, as he rightly says, that the key problem is that by the time children move on, at age 11, to secondary school, too much damage has been done by insufficient levels of literacy and numeracy, does he accept that it would be in everybody's interest if national performance tables were published, showing the results of the tests at age seven, so that one could find out which schools were succeeding and which were failing? Would it not be helpful also if the tables contained a register of how much cash was being spent per pupil at each school and the average class size at each school? We would not then be having these debates in a vacuum; we would have solid data and people would know what was working and what was not.

Mr. Blunkett: I thought that we were being criticised for taking too much time and spending too much money on measures that are not directly

(Continued)

Box 7.1 Continued

related to teaching in the classroom. We are criticised for collecting too much information, for asking too much of schools and teachers and for giving them too many forms to fill in, so that too much information is coming out of Sanctuary buildings. We have been so hurt by that criticism that I have asked the Under-Secretary, my hon. Friend the Member for Norwich, South (Mr. Clarke), to spend a great deal of his time unravelling that process and making sure that we do not place greater demands on schools. The Conservatives sent out 80 separate documents when they organised the national curriculum, but we have reduced that to one document.

We are doing our utmost to respond to the needs of teachers and schools. I am hurt by the terrible fact that whatever we do, we cannot get it right.

Source: http://www.parliament.the-stationery-office.co.uk/pa/cm199899/ cmhansrd/vo990707/debtext/90707-44.htm (accessed February 27, 2005).

literature as to key nodes of the classification scheme are summarized. Specific topics on which the existing literature does not make many operational recommendations are then analyzed in some detail to develop suggested operational and decision-making guidelines. The chapter ends by examining how various financial tools can be applied to expansion of access, or enhancement of quality, or both. This emphasis is important because these tools are likely to be useful in different ways for various purposes.

This chapter makes explicit use of the discussion in chapter 1 of characteristics specific to secondary education. These characteristics affect the range of options that are optimal for financing this level of education.

Fiscal Magnitude of Trends in the Expansion of Secondary Education

Developing firm estimates of the likely fiscal cost of expanding secondary education is an enormous task that is beyond the scope of this report. Under the authorizing policy environment of the Education for All Fast-Track Initiative (EFA-FTI), the World Bank has made a considerable investment in developing estimates of the cost of achieving universal primary education and of the resulting financing gap. But the investment needed to calculate with any degree of accuracy the likely cost of expanding secondary schooling would be much higher than what was needed for calculating such costs for primary schooling, and the results would never be conclusive because of the significantly greater number of policy options. The world community has not developed the same sense of urgency and legitimacy concerning secondary education as it did for primary education in the EFA-FTI authorizing environment, and investment in a conclusive costing exercise has never been on the global agenda in international education forums. Nonetheless, various analysts have attempted to develop some preliminary estimates. This section reports on those estimates, noting why they may be more important than is normally thought.

There appears to be a common perception that the pressure created by secondary enrollment is a problem that can be deferred to the future. True, the pressure is likely to grow in the future—but it exists already. Taking income group averages, secondary enrollment is already growing faster than primary enrollment, even in the poorer (low-income) regions of the world. Table 7.1 shows the trends during select periods (1998–2001) for key country groupings and for large low-income countries for which data were available and were considered to be reasonably reliable.[1] Secondary enrollment growth rates in Sub-Saharan Africa are similar to those for

Table 7.1 Rates of Growth of Primary and Secondary Enrollment, Selected Countries and Periods
(percent)

Country	Primary			Secondary		
	1998–2001	1992–2001	1970–1990	1998–2001	1992–2001	1970–1990
Bangladesh	0.1	0.1	3.4	5.1	5.1	3.0
Ethiopia	11.3	15.1	6.9	17.0	9.8	9.6
Kenya	2.4	0.2	6.3	4.7	4.7	8.4
Nepal	4.5	2.3	10.3	9.8	7.4	5.5
Myanmar	0.2	−2.7	2.7	4.4	5.6	2.5
Vietnam	−3.1	−0.1	1.1	5.6	5.6	—
10 percent trimmed mean for all low-income countries	3.9	3.6	5.0	7.3	6.4	7.9
10 percent trimmed mean for all lower-middle-income countries	−0.4	−0.4	1.6	2.6	4.5	4.5
10 percent trimmed mean for all upper-middle-income countries	−0.5	−0.6	1.0	2.5	3.8	3.2

Source: Authors' calculation based on EdStats data.

Note: —, Not available.

low-income countries in general: 6.4 percent for secondary and 3.8 percent for primary education during the period 1998 to 2001. In short, overall, secondary enrollment is already growing 50 to 100 percent faster than primary enrollment, albeit from a smaller base.

The present and future impact of differential growth rates cannot be ignored. A simple analysis illustrates the point. If secondary enrollment is currently one-half the size of primary enrollment (which is approximately appropriate for the median developing country and even for the median low-income country), and if unit costs (per-pupil costs) at the secondary level are twice as high as at the primary level (again, a reasonable round-number approximation), then the fact that primary education in all low-income countries is growing at only 3.9 percent, whereas secondary education is growing at 7.3 percent means that the real unit cost of primary and secondary education as a whole will grow at approximately 0.5 percent per year, just from the change in the composition of enrollment. The real problem, therefore, is not just the absolute cost of meeting a demand that seems to be growing quite rapidly. Because demand for secondary education is growing so much faster than that for primary education, the composition of enrollment is changing dramatically and must be putting severe pressure on the weighted average of unit costs. It should be noted that this concern is not simply the result of pressures from the success of EFA-FTI. Those pressures may exacerbate the problem, but it is clear from the data in table 7.1 that this is an exogenous ongoing trend, and that it responds to both demographic pressure and the pressure from changes in the transition from primary to secondary schooling.

Given these trends, it is important to carry out further analysis on the cost implications. Binder (2004) explores costs for all developing countries. Using a unit-cost approach and looking at only one of the estimates she presents, it can be concluded that to reach a 90 percent net secondary enrollment rate by 2015, low-income countries will have to spend, by that date, an extra 3.4 percent of GDP on secondary education beyond what they currently spend (Binder 2004, 30, table 9). Low-income countries currently spend about 3.3 percent of GDP on education as a whole, so according to these scenarios, reaching universal secondary education would imply a doubling of total education expenditure as a share of GDP by 2015, just to accommodate the expansion of secondary education. Based on a more detailed exercise but for a limited set of low-income African countries, Mingat (2004) calculates that if primary completion increases to 100 percent by 2015, if the transition from primary to the first phase of secondary also reaches 100 percent, and if the transition rate to upper secondary stays fixed, total expenditure on secondary education would reach 4.7 percent of GDP (Mingat 2004, 16, table 8).[2] If the countries included in the simulation are spending on secondary education at the low-income average of 1.1 percent of GDP, the extra expenditure required is about 3.6 percent of GDP, not far from Binder's result. Another way of looking at the issue, using Mingat's analysis, is to note that financing the expansion of secondary education would imply using about 43 percent of state revenues for education—approximately a doubling from current levels, and clearly not feasible.

The problems with making firm forecasts using these sorts of analysis, especially for secondary education, are illustrated by the fact that both authors present a wide range of estimates. Even avoiding the most extreme estimates, Binder shows extra expenditure ranging from 2.9 to 4.2 percent of GDP for low-income countries. Similarly, if the transition rate from primary to secondary stayed as low as it is today, according to Mingat's work total spending on secondary education could be as low as about 2 percent of GDP.[3] That would imply an extra cost (above today's cost) of only about 1 percent of GDP—but it would still mean a doubling of expenditure on secondary education as a share of GDP. In absolute terms, these numbers imply that just for the 10 countries in Mingat's exercise, the financing need is about $3 billion per year for secondary education. A reasonable assumption about resource availability suggests that about $0.5 billion (2001 dollars) would be available, leaving a financing gap, just for these 10 countries, of $2.5 billion per year. Even under fairly favorable assumptions regarding unit-cost reduction (achieving 100 percent transition to lower secondary education but keeping transition to upper at current levels), the financing gap for secondary education would exceed the projected financing gap for primary education (Mingat 2004, 21). Options for further savings to the public purse would almost certainly have to include recourse to private or community financing and reduction of the unit costs of the first phase of secondary education so that they become similar to those in primary education.

As noted above, the pressures created by expansion of secondary education are already present, and they seem to be exogenous to EFA-FTI policies because the trends predate the policies. These trends are already putting pressure on the unit costs of the entire basic education system. Thus, improved financing mechanisms for secondary education, including incentives for cost control, most likely would have been needed with or without EFA-FTI and are needed now—not after EFA-FTI starts to have a knock-on effect on secondary enrollment.

Approaches to Improving the Financing of Secondary Education

The basic approaches toward funding secondary education are well known. For example, the International Institute for Educational Planning (IIEP)–UNESCO has carried out a thorough assessment of financing for the expansion of secondary education (Lewin and Caillods 2001). Over the decades, international organizations have produced various studies on the financing of education in developing countries (for example, Bray 1996;

Patrinos and Ariasingam 1997; Psacharopoulos and Woodhall 1984; Psacharopoulos, Tan, and Jimenez 1986). Some of the studies may be literally dated in a chronological sense, but their recommendations are mostly as valid today as when they were written. For purposes of stocktaking, the best baseline is provided by Lewin and Caillods (2001), which is recent and comprehensive.

Several options, and combinations of options and pathways, are available for improving the financing of secondary education—so many options that the landscape can be confusing. For organizing policy makers' thinking about all these options and pathways, a classification scheme is useful. Figure 7.1 shows possible approaches. The scheme can be used to summarize and discuss the options proposed in Lewin and Caillods (2001), supplemented by other literature (see table 7.2).

The following discussion takes some of the key nodes in the classification scheme, and presents criteria for deciding which strategies might be most promising in particular cases. Given the plentiful literature that already exists, the discussion attempts to add value by concentrating on a few aspects that are not already widely covered.

Simple Benchmarks for Determining the Adequacy of Investment in Secondary Education

In the classification scheme presented in table 7.2, an important analytical node is whether to try to obtain more funding for education in general, and for secondary as opposed to other levels, or to concentrate on increasing efficiency. The criteria for making this decision would be (a) whether education, and secondary education in particular, have credibility as efficient spenders with finance authorities, cabinet members, and other high-level decision makers and (b) whether the education sector and the secondary education subsector spend reasonable amounts as measured against some defensible benchmarks.

Making the case for additional resources for education as a whole. If central authorities (ministry of finance, civil service management) have the impression that the education sector is using resources inefficiently, arguments about the intrinsic merits of secondary education (in terms, for example, of social and economic impacts) would not be well received. In the case of primary education, international pressure can help elicit a positive response from finance ministries. Where secondary education is concerned, policy makers cannot depend on such support alone to defend the request for budget increases. Most ministries of finance agree that education is potentially an important investment, but they often consider education authorities to be poor investment managers. It is incumbent on education policy makers to make the appropriate case for support for additional budget requests to expand secondary education and improve its quality.

Figure 7.1 Decision Pathways for Financing Secondary Education

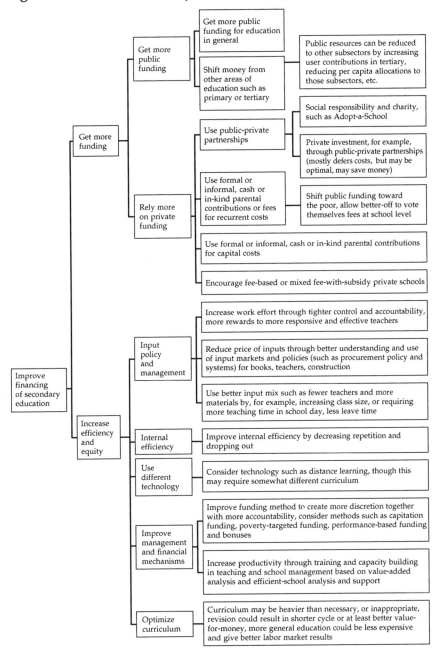

Source: Adapted from Tsang (1996).

Table 7.2 Options for Funding Secondary Schools

	Approaches	Specifics, pros and cons, and related issues
Obtain more funding. — *Obtain more public funding.*	Obtain more public funding for education in general.	Increasing funding of education to about 5–6 percent of GDP could create more scope for secondary spending. If spending is already at that level or higher, arguing for further increases will tend not to be fruitful. Ability to actually increase funding may be constrained by the size of the tax base. If access to primary education is very low or university lobbies are very powerful, it would be difficult to ensure that increases in overall finance are used for secondary education.
	Obtain more public funding for secondary education via reallocation within education expenditure.	Countries with low secondary enrollment do not typically allocate very low shares of resources to the secondary sector. There are exceptions, and the matter should be examined case by case, but the real problem often lies in the unit cost of secondary education or in total spending and not in the subsectoral share of total education resources.
Obtain more private funding.	Use public-private partnerships (defined here as excluding fee-based private schooling). → Corporate social responsibility and charity, or self-interest in a trained labor force.	Not discussed extensively in Lewin and Caillods (2001). Could be of some use at the margin. The issue of whether ministries are willing to relinquish some control as a quid-pro-quo is often not considered.
	Formal public-private partnerships.	Not discussed extensively in Lewin and Caillods (2001). Still a somewhat experimental technique restricted to developed or middle-income countries. Likely to be useful mostly in middle-income countries with well-developed financial markets and formal sectors; may be worth considering in those cases.
	Use formal or informal, cash or in-kind parental contributions or fees for recurrent costs and shift public funding toward the poor, either by encouraging private provision or by charging fees in public schools.	Could have deleterious effects on access and equity without necessarily adding much accountability. Careful consideration should be given to this issue to avoid various dangers. The text contains a detailed checklist of issues to be considered in structuring a fees or contributions framework.

Use formal or informal, cash or in-kind parental or community contributions for capital funding; if formal, can be public-community partnership.	Feasible and has often been tried with some success but may be more difficult at the secondary than at primary level because "the community" is not as clearly defined in the case of secondary education. Reliance on community efforts may be more logical in areas where communities are more identifiable, but these may be poorer areas. This method could thus be seen as a form of regressive taxation.
Encourage fee-based or fee-with-subsidy private schools.	If not planned or analyzed properly, may encourage socially inefficient provision. Total cost of provision, not simply cost to the state, needs to be considered. Private schools for poor or lower-middle-class children can be efficient in use of total (public and private) funds, but some are not.
Increase work effort through tighter control and accountability, rewarding more responsive and effective teachers, eliminating "ghost" teachers, and so on.	Audits often show significant absenteeism, teachers on payroll who are not at school, schools that do not exist, substandard work effort deployed, and the like. In some cases eliminating these problems could produce savings of between 5 and 20 percent of the budget, but it is not easy.
Reduce price of inputs through better understanding and use of input markets and policies (for example, procurement policy and systems, labor relations) for books, teachers, and construction.	Input prices, particularly teacher salaries but also textbooks and school construction, may sometimes be higher than is necessary to recruit or procure good-quality inputs. Methods for reducing teacher costs have been tried more at the primary than the secondary level. The impact on learning is only now beginning to be assessed. When *exactly* the same inputs could be had (or could be made equivalent, for example, through in-service training) for a lower price if the procurement, management, and market structure could be improved, the prima facie case for reform is clear. This is less likely to be valid for teachers than for other inputs because teacher quality is inherently difficult to observe and adverse selection can become a problem.

Improve input policy and management.

Improve efficiency and equity.

(Continues on the following page.)

Table 7.2 Continued

	Approaches	Specifics, pros and cons, and related issues
Improve efficiency and equity. Improve input policy and management.	Use better input mix, such as fewer teachers and more materials by, for example, increasing class size, requiring more teaching time in the school day, and giving less leave time.	Difficult to generalize because input mix depends so much on curricular options. But if the ratio of salary to nonsalary costs deviates by more than about 10 points from about 75 percent, the mix is probably not optimal. Increasing the supply of services from the existing stock of teachers may be considered if class-period loads are light, leave policies are effectively unmanaged, and so on. Excessive leave for further studies may have a direct impact on learning, as well as on cost. The literature on class size and student-teacher ratios is well known, and the evidence strongly suggests that if properly managed, fairly high ratios do not have much of a negative impact on learning (or, the negative impact is extremely small compared with the cost savings). A common source of inefficiency is the existence of very small schools. School consolidation should be considered, while taking care not to damage community support. Attention should be paid to whether students in smaller schools are performing worse or better than students in larger schools in a given country's actual situation. If small schools tend to perform better, consolidation is less attractive.
	Improve internal efficiency by reducing repetition and dropout, through norms and policy, with or without specific quality interventions.	Some positive impact on access if repeaters are taking up space; some impact on cost per graduate if dropouts can be reduced. Dropping out is often caused by excessive repetition.
	Use improved technology such as distance learning (may require a somewhat different curriculum).	Some success with use of distance technology is documented, although success is uneven. Alternative technologies often lack strong lobbies. Start-up costs are high, and organizational talent is required to get systems going. Nonetheless, successful cases exist, and the option is worth considering.

Improve management and financing mechanisms.	Improve funding method to create more discretion together with more accountability; consider methods such as capitation or other formula funding, poverty-targeted funding, performance-based funding, and bonuses.	Not discussed extensively in Lewin and Caillods (2001). This approach is being tried in several countries. (Case studies are provided in the text.) Whether such methods—whatever their other merits, such as greater transparency in funding—can lead to efficiency improvements largely remains to be seen and will generally be very difficult to evaluate. The option should still be considered on its equity and transparency merits.
	Increase productivity through training and capacity building in teaching and school management based on value added analysis and efficient-school analysis and support.	Some discussion in Lewin and Caillods (2001) related to pupil-teacher ratios and the analysis of schools that perform well in spite of high pupil-teacher ratios. Elsewhere, there is evidence of widely disparate learning results across schools with similar resource endowments catering to students with similar socioeconomic backgrounds. This suggests that the scope for cost saving through improved management is high, perhaps 15 percent or so of budget.
	Optimize curriculum and structure.	Discussed extensively in Lewin and Caillods (2001). When the secondary cycle is very long, and if secondary education is more expensive than primary for largely definitional reasons, reforms that shift grades back toward primary or lower secondary could be cost saving. Curricula are often overloaded or inappropriate and may lead to higher absolute costs or to lower effectiveness relative to cost. These issues are discussed extensively in other chapters of this report.

Comparative analysis could help assess the efficiency parameters of the education sector and assist authorities in understanding whether the sector is generally efficient or inefficient. This would involve simple comparisons across countries of enrollment ratios, completion ratios, level of student learning (if appropriate, on the basis of an international assessment), and education spending as a share of GDP or of government budget. Other, more sophisticated analyses could also be carried out. If the results show that spending on education, and on secondary education in particular, is relatively efficient in comparison with other countries, policy makers could develop arguments and marketing materials to make additional budget requests and to change attitudes and impressions, as part of the strategy. If education and secondary education spending are found to be inefficient, there is a high likelihood that the ministry of finance and the cabinet have already been made aware of this, either through analyses commissioned in-house or through reports by international organizations. Under these circumstances, marketing and persuasion techniques to bolster the request for additional budget, or attempts to gloss over inefficiencies, are not likely to elicit the required support. Rather, education policy makers would need to focus on identifying the sources of inefficiencies and on formulating plans to reduce or eliminate them.

Making the case for additional expenditure for secondary education. Another important aspect to consider is whether the secondary education subsector objectively uses few resources in an absolute sense; that is, without an explicit sense of efficiency but with some benchmarked sense of "need." This could be assessed in two ways: via simple international benchmarks of spending itself, where the spending benchmark provides the sense of "need," or via comparisons of spending and enrollment benchmarks, where the enrollment benchmark provides the sense of "need."

Simple international benchmarking of ratios of spending on education as a proportion of GDP or by level can be useful. This method is covered extensively in Lewin and Caillods (2001). It is important to note that spending levels for secondary education as a share of the education budget do not vary dramatically across countries. The median secondary education expenditure level in the late 1990s as a proportion of total education spending for 72 countries for which data were readily available was 32 percent, but only 6 countries were below two-thirds of the median. In fact, the median spending share in the quartile with the lowest secondary enrollment was 30 percent, and for those in the highest enrollment quartile it was 34 percent—neither of which is very different from the median for all countries. Using these criteria, perhaps only a few countries can be singled out as being constrained by the share of secondary spending in total education spending. These countries enroll few students and devote a noticeably small share of education spending to secondary education. Since not many countries are in this category, the approach is not likely to be very useful in most countries, although it should be considered. In general, low prioritization of secondary education within education spending does not seem to be a problem.

Another point is whether more private funding should be brought to bear in subsectors such as tertiary or vocational education, and this in turn depends on equity, efficiency, and political economy considerations. If tertiary education has high private returns but lower social returns than other levels such as secondary, and is benefiting mostly the wealthy, then economic rationality would suggest that funding be redistributed toward the lower levels. But the political economy reality is that such redistribution may be difficult, given the political power (both "street power" and political connections) of university students and their parents. Ministries attempting to redistribute funding from tertiary to secondary education need to carry out adequate market analysis, consultation, and public relations.

International benchmarking relative to enrollment or educational "need" and trends, rather than spending per se. In a country where the enrollment pyramid is "too narrow" at the secondary level relative to the primary or tertiary levels (using relevant comparator countries), spending benchmarks can be compared with the enrollment benchmarks as a simple way of gauging the relative merits of spending more on secondary education or of determining the financial constraints on expanding secondary education. This is a more fruitful, but more complicated, approach to benchmarking. Using cross-country analysis that compares the normal or standard response of secondary enrollment to primary enrollment "push" or tertiary enrollment "pull," one can single out countries that do not fit the norm—countries where secondary enrollments appear to be too small. The data in table 7.3 show the central tendencies for groupings of the 12 or so fastest- or slowest-growing developing economies in the selected periods.

Even though there is some evidence linking educational development to economic growth, no causality is implied here. The enrollment patterns are seen only as a useful way to benchmark. If benchmarking is to be used,

Table 7.3 Mean Gross Enrollment Rates by Subsequent Economic Growth Record

	Primary	*Secondary*	*Tertiary*
GER in 1970 in slowest-growing economies in the period 1970–2000	53	11	1.3
GER in 1980 in slowest-growing economies in the period 1980–2000	72	19	3.4
GER in 1970 in fastest-growing economies in the period 1970–2000	92	34	4.3
GER in 1980 in fastest-growing economies in the period 1980–2000	100	46	7.1

Source: Authors' calculation using EdStats.

Note: GER, gross enrollment rate. Differences between country groups are statistically significant at least at the 5 percent level.

then benchmarking according to patterns associated with fast economic growth is a logical approach.

The implicit ratios in table 7.3 can be used as a rough guideline to assess whether expansion plans are consistent with international experience. For example, in economies that experienced high growth during the period 1980–2000, the secondary GER at the beginning of the period tended to be approximately 46 percent of the primary GER, and the tertiary GER tended to be 15 percent of the secondary GER, whereas in the slow-growth economies

Figure 7.2 Gross Enrollment Rates for the Countries with the Lowest and Highest GDP per Capita Growth Rates, 1970–2000 and 1980–2000

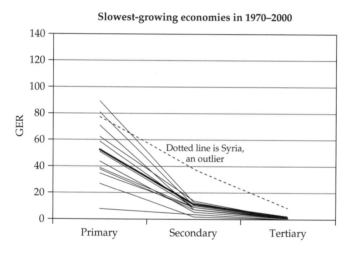

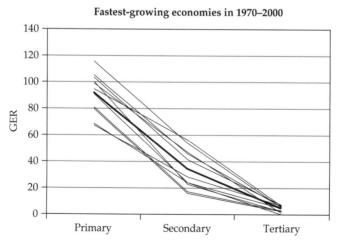

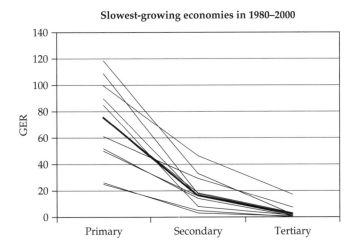

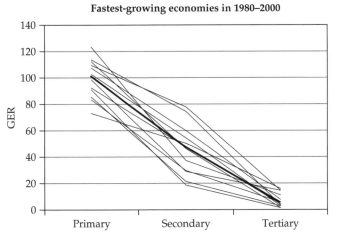

Source: Authors' compilation.

Note: GDP, gross domestic product; GER, gross enrollment rate. The heavy line in each panel links the median points.

these proportions were 26 and 18 percent, respectively. This suggests that fast-growth economies placed a higher proportionate emphasis on secondary than on tertiary enrollment as a basis for growth. Two noteworthy points are that (a) the fast-growing economies placed a great absolute emphasis on primary education and (b) in the less successful economies tertiary education tended to expand faster than in the fast-growing economies and faster than any of their other education subsectors, in relative terms.

Figure 7.2 shows the same information and provides an impression of central trends and the spread or variation. In this figure, traditional enrollment pyramids have been turned on their side, and total enrollment as opposed to enrollment by gender, is shown. The horizontal axis shows the levels of schooling system, and the vertical axis shows the GER. The line showing the median country at every level is shown in bold. The fast-growing countries were generally characterized not just by different central tendencies but also by much less spread or variation among countries. The figure clearly shows that countries with high growth between 1970 and 2000 already had education systems that were fairly well balanced in 1970; the lines linking the median points are nearly straight. Countries with high growth between 1980 and 2000 had, in effect, nearly perfectly balanced systems in that the median lines are almost perfectly straight. Some of the panels exhibit what de Ferranti et al. (2003) term a diamond shape (although their analysis refers to labor force education pyramids rather than enrollment pyramids). The countries that grew slowly have kinked median lines, indicating that secondary enrollments are too low in relation to primary or tertiary levels. They also have low primary enrollments, suggesting that the kink arises from too high tertiary enrollments rather than too high primary enrollments. Finally, they show more dispersion around the median for primary enrollment, whereas the fast-growing countries were uniformly closer to universal primary schooling, although some had not achieved universal primary schooling even as late as 1980.

Analysis of social demand. Another useful approach to benchmarking relates to the analysis of push and pull factors between levels of education that create pressure on growth of secondary education enrollment as primary or tertiary enrollments expand. These factors can be assessed somewhat independently from patterns of economic growth, and they seem to have some demographic or social inertia. Table 7.4 shows the patterns. For example, when countries have a primary GER of 50 percent, the corresponding secondary GER, 10 years later, tends to be 25 percent. The table shows the change in the GER at each level (secondary and tertiary) associated with a change of 10 points in the GER of the previous level. A country going from, say, a primary GER of 70 percent to a primary GER of 80 percent will typically expand its secondary GER by 9 points. A country going from a secondary GER of 70 to one of 80 percent will face a subsequent expansion of 7 points in tertiary GER. The pattern accelerates: 10 is larger than 9, which is larger than 7. The higher the GER at one level, the larger the response of the GER at the next higher level. The impact of the primary GER on the secondary GER seems to be higher than the impact of the secondary GER on the tertiary GER.[4]

Although this is not shown in the table, the patterns also differ by geography. For example, the response of tertiary GER to secondary GER is lower in the former Soviet Union countries of Central Asia than the median trend suggests. (This result does not hold in Eastern Europe.) Thus, although

Table 7.4 Stylized Patterns of Response in Gross Enrollment Rates to an Increase in the Next-Lower Educational Level, after 10 Years

	Primary or secondary GER	Corresponding secondary or tertiary GER after 10 years	Change in secondary or tertiary GER for every 10 percentage point change in primary or secondary GER
Primary impact	50	25	7
on secondary	75	45	9
	100	69	10
Secondary impact	50	17	5
on tertiary	75	30	6
	100	47	7

Source: Authors' calculation from a median regression of the logarithm of the gross enrollment rate (GER) at one level on the logarithm of the GER at the previous level lagged 10 years, using EdStats data.

Note: The first column shows a hypothesized level of primary or secondary GER; the second column shows the median GER associated with the next-higher level, 10 years later; and the third column shows the change in the GER at the next-higher level around the hypothesized level in the first column.

countries with secondary GERs of around 100 percent tend to have a tertiary GER around 47 percent, using a worldwide average, in the late 1990s Tajikistan, Kazakhstan, and the Kyrgyz Republic had tertiary GERs of 14, 28, and 35 percent, respectively, according to EdStats data. In the early 1990s the respective secondary GERs were 77, 84, and 88 percent.

Economic Analysis: In addition to social-demand and stylized economic benchmarks, such as those discussed above, more detailed economic benchmarks should be brought into the policy-making process. Information on relative labor supply scarcity at various levels of education should be analyzed; if secondary education appears relatively or absolutely scarce, the case for investment and expansion of secondary education appears stronger. One approach to the analysis of relative demand is covered elsewhere in this report or in de Ferranti et al. (2003). To illustrate, according to such analyses, in Latin America the relative demand for workers with tertiary education has clearly increased, whereas there is some ambiguity as to whether relative demand for workers with secondary education has increased. The call is for a generally balanced approach to expansion of education, along the lines of the rapidly growing economies in figure 7.2. (Analyses for other countries, outside Latin America, are presented in "Demand for More Educated Workers" in chapter 2 of this volume.) Relative demand approaches should be complemented by an assessment of the cost of producing different levels of education.

A simple and traditional approach to considering both the labor market benefits and the production costs of education is to use rates of return to education, by level. (See Psacharopoulos and Patrinos 2002 for a recent example of rates of return across a large number of countries.) In these analyses, secondary education generally tends to have lower returns than primary schooling, but returns are still above reasonable benchmarks for profitability of investment (for example, a 13 percent social rate of return for secondary education and 17 percent for primary education in Latin America, and 18 and 25 percent in Sub-Saharan Africa). These returns can change considerably over time and should not be taken as fixed. Most important, returns analyses need to be done for the specific country in question, and done frequently; stylized results across many countries should not be a guide to action in any particular country, and old analyses, even of a specific country, are dangerous, since labor market conditions respond to past expansion in supply. Considerable debate surrounds the interpretation and use of rates of return (see Psacharopoulos 1996), but, if such analysis is used judiciously and if the information produced is broadly consistent with that from other analyses such as relative scarcity analysis and social demand pressure, the case for an expansion of secondary education might begin to appear clear.

Grouping the various analyses together with cost patterns can help in understanding how rapid an expansion of secondary enrollment is justified in particular cases. More important, the analyses can aid understanding of whether such expansion is being constrained by unit costs at the secondary education level or by a combination of high unit costs and unbalanced growth at other levels (primary or tertiary), resulting in too much spending at other levels.

Tables 7.5 and 7.6 highlight some spending norms that are useful when compared with enrollment norms. The data refer to spending patterns

Table 7.5 Per-Student Spending as a Proportion of GDP per Capita by Country Group, Late 1990s

(percent)

	Primary level	Secondary level	Tertiary level
Fast-growing economies	11	18	55
Slow-growing economies	13	24	265

Source: Authors' calculation using EdStats data.

Note: The figures are based on an average of data from 1998, 1999, and 2000. The sample consists of 15 developing countries (using a 1970 per capita income cutoff of $1,000).

Table 7.6 Typical Per-Student Cost Patterns by Educational Level, Economic Growth Record, and Growth Pattern of Education System

| | Economic growth | | Education system growth | |
| | | | Countries succeeding in expanding | Countries not succeeding in expanding |
	Fast-growing economies	Slow-growing economies	secondary enrollment	secondary enrollment
Per-student spending on secondary students as a ratio of per-student spending on primary students	1.4	2.2	1.4	2.6
Per-student spending on tertiary students as a ratio of per-student spending on secondary students	3.0	11.0	3.2	9.3

Source: Authors' calculation from EdStats data.

Note: The figures are based on an average of data from 1998, 1999, and 2000. The sample consists of 15 developing countries (using a 1970 per capita income cutoff of $1,000).

typical in the late 1990s. Fifteen developing countries were selected for their fast or slow economic growth and for having achieved, or failed to achieve, significant expansion of secondary education enrollment by the late 1990s.[5]

The tables show that fast-growing economies and countries that had succeeded in expanding secondary enrollment had much more balanced per-student spending. In fast-growing economies, expenditure per secondary student was only about 40 percent higher than per primary student; in slow-growing economies, it was 120 percent. Expenditure per tertiary student was only about 3 times that per secondary student in fast-growing economies, as against 11 times in slow-growing economies. Developed economies are typically even more balanced. The absolute numbers in table 7.5 make it clear that the divergence in patterns is created by divergence at levels higher than primary. In other words, it is spending on secondary and tertiary students that is unbalanced and too high in slow-growing economies. But the relative numbers in table 7.6 clearly show that slow-growing economies and education systems had much less balanced spending than the fast-growing ones. Costs per secondary student were very high compared with costs per primary student, which means that funding did not go very far, and spending on tertiary students was also very high. In such a case, less funding is available for secondary students even if tertiary enrollment is balanced in terms of international benchmarks. Box 7.2 provides a demonstration of how analysis can assist with decisions about whether levels of finance are appropriate and can illuminate the relationship between finance and simple measures of efficiency such as unit cost per student as a proportion of GDP per capita.

Private or Community Funding Options

Another key analytical node is whether to use more private or community funding for secondary education. Some options worth exploring are discussed next; the case of school fees or direct contributions is taken up in a separate section.

1. *Community-based finance.* Because secondary education has a more heterogeneous clientele than primary education, there may be fewer possibilities for private or community funding based on community solidarity such as those involved in in-kind efforts. Furthermore, social benefits for secondary education are more likely to accrue over a dispersed area, such as a large region, than is the case for primary education. Those with secondary education may be more likely to sell their labor in a larger market (for example, by migrating) than those with only primary education. In this situation, community-based funding of a more formal sort, such as local taxation, or even use of block grants from higher levels of government for secondary education, seems less likely to be either forthcoming or socially optimal. There may simply be more free riders, and more problems of collective action, involved in the funding of secondary education from highly localized sources in a poor country. To complicate matters, secondary education is likely to be more expensive, and buildings more elaborate, than is the case for primary education. The collective-action problems may appear even worse in comparison with the absolute cost of running secondary education. For these reasons, reliance on fees (or fee-like contributions), on central government subsidies, or on a combination of the two is more likely to generate the needed resources than reliance on totally voluntary or in-kind contributions or on relatively narrow local taxation (if the tax districts are small relative to the labor market for graduates of secondary schools).

2. *Reliance on local private enterprise* to support education, motivated by corporate social responsibility or by the need for trained labor. Secondary schools are more likely to be readily associated with private enterprise than primary schools, both because of their location (they are more likely to be in areas of concentrated and large-scale economic activity rather than dispersed in rural areas) and for output reasons (a greater proportion of secondary schools' output goes directly into the labor force). Private

---

Box 7.2 Analyzing the Distribution of Education Expenditures: A Case Study of Lesotho

Lesotho's primary, secondary, and tertiary GERs are 113, 31, and 3, respectively. Using the conclusions of the analysis in the text, if Lesotho has median enrollment patterns, the secondary enrollment ratio should be about 47 percent (about 16 percentage points) higher than it actually is. It may be that the country has calculated rates of returns, or has assessed market demand, and has concluded that expanding secondary education is not a good idea. Or it may be that this constrained access to secondary education is attributable instead to high unit costs at the secondary or tertiary level. Comparison of spending with enrollment in Lesotho and against international norms is revealing. Lesotho fits squarely in the bottom row of table 7.5. This is not to say that it is a slow-growing economy but simply that its enrollment and cost patterns are typical of slow growth and slow secondary expansion; in fact its spending is more unbalanced than in the pattern typical of slow growth. Spending per secondary student is about 2.5 times spending per primary student, and spending per tertiary student is about 15 times spending per secondary student. As can be seen from the data in table 7.4, tertiary education enrollment is not excessive compared with that in high-growth economies more than a decade ago. Primary enrollment does appear to embody inefficiencies, in that the primary GER is considerably above 100 percent. Finally, cost per student at the primary level is a large percentage of GDP per capita, and the unbalanced cost structure at the higher levels amplifies this problem. In both slow-growing and fast-growing economies, cost per student at the primary level is not much higher than 10 percent of GDP per capita, but in Lesotho it seems to be around 30 percent. The costs then increase for secondary and tertiary education—tertiary education costs about 900 percent of GDP per capita.

The conclusions that can be derived from this type of benchmarking are that Lesotho's secondary expansion is possibly being blocked by excessive unit costs overall, an unbalanced cost structure that makes costs at secondary and tertiary levels even higher, and excessive enrollment at the primary level, probably due to uncontrolled repetition. Expansion of secondary education is not constrained by excessive enrollment but by excessive per-student cost at the tertiary level.

This type of analysis is only indicative. It is offered strictly as a likely example of how benchmarking could be used in a particular country, not as a real analysis of Lesotho's situation.

Source: Authors' analysis.

corporate funding for secondary schools may take a traditional charitable form or a more modern corporate social responsibility form, or it may simply stem from private self-interest in skilled labor.[6] Exercising this option may mean giving schools much more discretion in the type of output they generate, so that this output can meet localized business needs, and also giving them more incentives to be entrepreneurial in their fund-raising. It may also mean giving businesses a more formal say in defining their interests and holding schools accountable at the local or national level.

Although ministries of education may welcome private funding, they are sometimes less willing to make the policy changes in accountability and governance needed to make the funding possible. There is no doubt that private funding will tend to mean more private control of some sort and more "functionalization" of schools to match the needs of the private sector. If the authorities are not willing to accept these changes and to create an appropriate regulatory framework that not only encourages collaboration but also ensures that it happens efficiently and transparently, large amounts of private funding might not be forthcoming. Before devoting time, attention, and political capital to pursuing this option, an important step for a ministry of education is self-examination regarding its willingness to make the policy changes needed for this sort of funding to flow. It is important that the analysis be careful and detailed, as some of the objections to functionalization of schools to meet the needs of private enterprise may be valid (for example, concern that functionalization may result in excessively narrow training that is not in the public interest) but others may be rooted in relatively shallow positions and emotions rather than analysis. (For example, the objection may be that the public sector should not "help" the private sector but that the private sector should "help" the public sector.)

The degree of formalization of such relations with the private sector needs to be weighed carefully. Formalization offers the benefits of transparency, clarity of mutual expectations, and the replication of successful cases. But there is a cost, in that attempting to create formal regulatory frameworks early in the process may slow progress through bureaucratization or may stimulate opposition. A logical compromise might be to encourage informal efforts and then formalize only when such efforts begin to pay off.

3. *Public-private partnerships.* The options in this area range from the better-known arrangement of simply increasing private provision of education in various ways to more innovative formal partnerships between the public and private sectors—for example, in building schools.

A vast literature exists on increasing private provision of education, so not much need be said about this option. Some salient elements are, however, worth mentioning. It is often reasoned that private provision reduces fiscal pressure and improves educational effectiveness; that is, private schools deliver more or better cognitive achievement than public schools, even when peer effects and self-selection are controlled for. In addition to fiscal cash flow and educational effectiveness analyses, it is necessary to perform an assessment of whether the specific types of private schools proposed are more efficient in the use of public *and* private funding than public schools. Another dimension is whether the load-shedding to the private sector increases inequality. Ideally, the focus ought to be more on whether private provision policies increase inequality of opportunity and results than on whether input provision is unequal. Generic international evidence is insufficient, although it can be used to justify decisions about taking initial steps for subsequent analysis or to create motivation for local analyses. It is important to note that even if private schools are more efficient in the use of total (public and private) funds, and even if stimulation of private sector participation does not increase inequality, these schools might still not be a fiscal panacea. The reason is that, in principle, the efficiency of private schools may imply that they ought to receive some degree of public subsidy. In that case the optimal fiscal savings would not be as high as in a simple, but suboptimal, sharing of responsibility with the private sector (see box 7.3).

A strategy worth considering, but only in countries that have reasonably well-developed private financial sectors and are giving expansion of secondary education a high priority, is the notion of public-private partnerships for school building and maintenance or in services such as ICT. The term public-private partnership is often used very loosely to refer to any sort of arrangement whereby private energies are deployed in favor of education. In some countries public-private partnerships are developed much more formally, as is described in more detail in appendix G.

Fees or Cost Recovery

An important analytical or policy option is the use of school fees or direct charges. In many countries secondary education, especially upper secondary education, is neither compulsory nor free, as a matter of constitutional or legal right or political promise. This means that there may be scope for charging fees. Taking into consideration the heterogeneity of the secondary education clientele and the fact that this level of education is less likely to have a community base and be able to rely on very localized taxation or in-kind contributions, individuals may be required to make private contributions. Structuring a proper fee regime is a complicated matter and generally faces criticism (some of which is justified). The idea is to craft, where fees already exist, a more appropriate (efficient and equitable) fee structure or contribution regime that protects the poor in some effective way, rather than to

---

Box 7.3 Expanding Access through the Use of Private Sector Capacity: The Case of the Republic of Korea

In the 1970s Korea was faced with increasing demand for lower secondary education resulting from rapid expansion of primary education. The government responded by eliminating entrance examinations for lower secondary schools and substituting a lottery system that directs students to schools on the basis of residence rather than performance on a test and by tapping private sector capacity through public financing mechanisms. On the financing side, the government introduced subsidies and tax exemptions to induce private providers, in the short term, to utilize their existing capacity fully and, in the medium term, to increase capacity as demand increased. The subsidy amount is usually determined by the difference between the school's own budget and a standard budget for a public school of the same enrollment size and type.

Private providers responded to the incentives by quickly scaling up their capacity. The government began providing direct financial assistance to private secondary schools only in the early 1970s, when the admissions policy was reformed. Private lower secondary schools began to receive government subsidies in 1971, and private upper secondary schools, in 1979. As of 2000, the share of private sector enrollment had reached 20 percent for middle schools and 55 percent for high schools.

Source: Authors' compilation.

---

introduce fees or contributions where none currently exist. Some options are explored below.

There is a considerable literature on fees and community contributions—for example, Bentaouet Kattan and Burnett (2004); Bray (1996); and Penrose (1998). Most of the literature concentrates on the pros and cons of fees and various forms of cost-sharing and community-based finance. Most conclude that if fees or community contributions are implemented badly (and in some cases even if they are implemented well), they can be counterproductive to access or equity objectives. As in many matters of public policy, the emphasis in this discussion is more on whether things are done well than on what is done. The literature tends to be short on concrete suggestions on how to implement a fee regime properly or modify an existing one so as to maximize the positive and minimize the negative. Fees and other forms of cost-sharing in secondary education may be an option, but only if analyses of the kind outlined in table 7.7 are carried out. Box 7.4 summarizes secondary education fee issues in selected countries.

Table 7.7 Suggested Criteria for Analyzing a School Fees or Contributions Regime

If most of the following conditions apply, fees and contributions are more likely to further the attainment of efficiency, quality, and equity objectives.	*If more than just a few of the following apply, contributions or fees are likely to hinder the attainment of efficiency, quality, and equity objectives. If most of them apply, fees are likely to cause serious problems.*
Payments are applied to improve quality at the margin (books, library, extra teachers, and so on).	Payments fund core delivery.
The poor receive sufficient public funding so that they can receive a basic education package without making payments.	The poor do not receive sufficient public funding so that payments by them are in fact unnecessary.
The crucial issue is quality, not access; demand for schooling is already high. (GER is at the appropriate level, 100 percent or higher.)	Access is still a crucial issue. (GER is well under 100 percent.)
Payments are decided by the community.	Payments are decided by a central agency or by private bodies, even nongovernmental organizations, or are decided (or unduly influenced) by the principal or teachers.
If the community is responsible for the decision on fees, at least a 67 percent majority must approve.	If the community is responsible for the decision on fees, a simple majority is sufficient.
Other forms of localized community financial ownership such as local government taxation have been considered and analyzed but are viewed as not as administratively feasible as payments.	Other options have simply not been considered or have been considered too lightly to lead to a solid conclusion as to their viability.
Clear sliding scales and exemptions exist.	Payments are flat both between and within communities.
The voting community is defined as all parents at the school, not simply the PTA or the governing body.	The community is defined as only the PTA or the governing body.
Funds generated by payments stay at the school level.	Payments flow to a bureaucracy or tax system.

(Continues on the following page.)

Table 7.7 Continued

If most of the following conditions apply, fees and contributions are more likely to further the attainment of efficiency, quality, and equity objectives.	*If more than just a few of the following apply, contributions or fees are likely to hinder the attainment of efficiency, quality, and equity objectives. If most of them apply, fees are likely to cause serious problems.*
Payments are not considered part of the country's tax revenue fund. Thus, there is no substitution of public funding through individual payments. (This is a separate condition from the preceding one.)	Payment generation may result in withdrawal of public funding if payments are considered part of the tax revenue fund.
Informal payments would tend to exist anyway and would be more random and even harder to regulate than allowed but regulated formal payments would be.	It is unlikely that informal payments would exist in any case.
Core funding is pro-poor; payments are used more by the middle class to top up, generating middle-class support of public schools and allowing public schools to compete with private schools; empirically, payments hardly exist among the poor.	Core funding is not pro-poor or not sufficiently pro-poor. The poor therefore have to assess themselves payments to make up for the state deficit.
Children cannot be prevented from enrolling in school even if parents have not paid and no matter what the level of parental income; clear exemption processes exist.	Payments are used to exclude certain children; no exemption processes exist.
The payment regime is regulated, and regulation is effectively implemented; parents in PTAs or governing councils are effectively trained in school finances as part of the overall system of financial decentralization.	Regulations do not exist, or if they exist, they are not implemented.
Education delivery has a strong rights orientation with regard to actual learning, and spending is efficient.	There is no right to education as such; education is inefficient; children are not seen as having a right to actually learn (schooling rather than education is the operational right); parents may end up paying for schooling in systems with no quality control.

Payments apply less to the basic levels of schooling; the secondary and higher levels are more payment based.	Payments apply more to the basic levels of schooling; and the higher levels are less payment based.
Payments have been studied in the context of broader issues such as tax policy and progressive favoring of the poor in fiscal policy.	Payments have not been analyzed in the context of other fiscal taxes and benefits.
Payments are explicitly used in a strategy to help the public sector compete with the private sector.	Payments are seen simply as another source of revenue.
The impact of the payments regime has been assessed specifically for AIDS-affected families and orphans and with specific reference to gender and ethnic considerations.	No particular care has been taken to deal with special populations.
Payments in education have been analyzed in the specific context of educational delivery, not just as part of a general (economic) framework on payments; that is, educational interests have vetted the approach.	Payments have not been analyzed with specificity to education.

Source: Authors' compilation.
Note: GER, gross enrollment rate; PTA, parent-teacher association.

Box 7.4 Fees and Contributions in Secondary Education: Examples from Africa and Chile

Many countries treat fees in secondary education differently from fees in primary education. Education at the secondary level may not be compulsory, in which case fees are less likely to be thought of as a regressive tax. Furthermore, free education at the secondary level may simply not be the subject of important political promises or rights-oriented commitments. In most countries much secondary education is provided by private schools, and they are almost always allowed to charge fees.

Among the African countries that have made major changes in fee regimes at the primary level (in order of policy change, Malawi, Uganda, Tanzania, and Kenya), all maintain fees at the secondary level. The reality is that in spite of the notion of free education, some types of fee often remain and tend to reassert themselves, even at the primary level (Bentaouet Kattan and Burnett 2004). At the secondary level, acceptance that education may not be free is much more widespread and explicit. And if the government has had to increase public funding for primary education to respond to the surge in demand and the decrease in private funding via fees, making primary education free may have a knock-on effect that makes secondary education even more expensive to parents. This may well be both efficient and equitable, but it has to be noted as a complication.

Malawi was the first country (at least in the recent wave of interest in free education) to make primary education free, in 1994. Its secondary schools still charge fees for enrollment and for a revolving textbook fund and other inputs. Uganda introduced free primary education starting in 1997. Some types of fee persist in some public primary schools (urban schools may charge fees, and there are fees for school funds). In secondary education fees are allowed and are common. They are, however, controlled, and increases beyond a certain level have to be cleared with the Ministry of Education. In 2001 Tanzania became the third country to announce free primary education. Secondary education in Tanzania is considered more an economic good than a basic right or public good, and therefore fees are allowed. Some attempt is made to secure at least some access for the poor via bursaries or scholarships and using gender and geography as targeting criteria. Finally, in 2002 Kenya instituted free public primary education. Secondary education continues to rely on fees, usually determined at the school level by head teachers or principals.

Whereas in the African countries fees were simply retained at the secondary level when primary education became free, in Chile fees in

Box 7.4 Continued

public secondary education were actively introduced rather recently. Under Chile's funding formula, private schools may receive subsidies if they keep their fees within certain parameters. Initially, and as late as the early 1990s, even private schools could not charge fees if they received subsidies. Starting in the mid-1990s, fees were allowed in subsidized private schools and in public secondary schools. The Chilean system forces schools charging fees to exempt a proportion of parents from fee payment and to use some of their income to set up internal cross-subsidies from fee-paying parents to non-fee-paying parents. In addition, some public funding is withdrawn from schools charging fees, although at a less than 1-for-1 ratio. (Otherwise, schools would not make their own fee effort.) Private schools charging fees above a certain level forfeit public subsidies.

Source: Compiled by the authors, with inputs from country-based consultants, officials, and analysts.

Formula Funding

Formula funding is often recommended for many levels of education. A summary of relevant considerations is provided here; for more details and discussion, see Ross and Levacic (1998) and Lang (2003). Appendix H provides country examples of the use of formula funding at the secondary level.

Most education systems, even in many developed countries, do not fund schools. Rather, schools are usually provided with inputs through teacher placement, provision of books and materials, and so on. For example, in most school districts in the United States schools have real discretionary funding for only about 10 to 20 percent of their total resource use; the balance comes in the form of direct inputs. The objectives of formula funding are to provide schools with money (not inputs) to help them purchase inputs and to set funding according to known rules rather than on an ad hoc, traditional (incremental), or negotiated (budget-driven) basis. Formula funding differs from other budget-oriented innovations such as zero-based or performance-based budgeting in that it is not based on the notion of a school budget but is more akin to the notion of an entitlement based on, say, enrollment. In this sense formula funding is compatible with a strong rights-oriented funding regime. A further distinction is whether the formula funding flows on a block basis, giving schools a great deal of discretion about what to purchase with the funds, or on an earmarked basis, with more or less stringent restrictions on what may be purchased. Finally, formula funding may be applied as a way of financing districts, or as a way for districts to finance schools, or both. In some cases, the money flows to districts on a formula basis, but districts then directly manage the provision of inputs to schools in a fairly centralist or nonformula fashion. Both approaches have advantages, but the most distinct advantages are likely to flow from direct funding of schools. If districts are funded on an innovative or formula basis but they in turn resource schools in a very centralist and traditional way, the advantages of formula funding are likely to be greatly diminished.

In thinking about the advantages and disadvantages of a formula, it is important to note that some of the advantages follow from the formula itself, while others follow from the fact that schools are being financed rather than provided with inputs. Even if schools were not financed on a formula basis, the fact that they are financed (for example, on a budget or negotiated basis) instead of being physically provided with inputs, still allows them to buy their own inputs, which can improve timing and could save costs (where there are no economies of scale). Other advantages follow from block funding. Nearly infinite variations are possible. A formula can be applied to provide physical inputs such as books or teachers on the basis of transparent ratios, as opposed to ad hoc or incremental allocations. This method could also be applied to true funding, as opposed to physical inputs. Furthermore, even if driven by a formula, the funding need not be on a block basis. The formula could transfer actual funds restricted as separate earmarks. It is also possible to use combinations—for example, physically providing teachers (on a formula basis or otherwise) but providing funding for other labor and nonlabor inputs. An example is the practice in Ireland and South Africa, where teachers are paid by the education department but other recurrent costs are covered through a capitation grant—that is, a simple per-student formula (see Murray, Smith, and Birthistle 2003).

Finally, in principle it is possible to have combinations of direct input provisions and provision of funding for the same inputs; that is, schools are provided in such a way that the inputs equal the value that would be predicted by a formula. This can be done by providing inputs to schools against a budget through a procurement and distribution system that can keep track, in real time, of the value of provisions against the budget. This approach would require considerable accounting and budget tracking skills and systems, and if the system is requisition based instead of being formula based, things can get even more complicated. In most countries even physical allocations to individual schools are not reported, much less their total value; at best, they might be recreated after the fact from files. The attempt to track, in real time and on an individual school basis, physical allocations against a monetary budget to make sure that the physical allocations match the funding formula would overwhelm most low-income or even middle-income education systems.

Formula funding has advantages over ad hoc or budgetary or negotiated provision, but there are also potential disadvantages. It is likely that the conceptual advantages outweigh the conceptual disadvantages in most cases, so a good ex ante position is that formula funding is a worthwhile idea to at least consider in almost any situation. Most donor proponents of formula funding stop at this point and do not consider the many practical difficulties that would need to be overcome if formula-based funding is to work. In many cases it will be worthwhile paying the cost of overcoming these difficulties. But the costs and practical problems cannot simply be ignored; they are serious considerations. We next review the conceptual advantages and disadvantages of formulas and outline some of the practical issues that arise.

Advantages of formula funding

- Formulas can allow schools to follow an autonomy-with-accountability organizational model that might be more efficient than the traditional centralist school organization, or its opposite, chaotic individualism with support unrelated to performance, particularly in dealing with populations with heterogeneous needs (see Ouchi, Cooper, and Segal 2003).
- Formulas can allow for more predictable funding, permitting better planning. Because formulas automatically adapt to certain forms of change, they might make funding less dependent on financial planning and budget negotiation and allow educators and principals to concentrate on educational rather than financial planning. (Note, however, that although formulas reduce the need for financial planning and budget negotiation, they increase the need for *current* financial management relative to an input-based model that has neither budgeting nor management requirements.)
- Formulas can allow for more transparency and accountability, since the amounts to be transferred are known. This can also assist in developing a culture of rights.
- If formulas support block grants, they can add flexibility, allowing managers to allocate resources to specific problems and as needs arise, without having to constantly seek permission from a higher level.
- If funding is accompanied by latitude to procure inputs, principals and schools are more likely to be able to use a just-in-time procurement mode, a flexibility that is not feasible if items have to be requisitioned from or provided by a central ministry.

- In systems that allow fees for certain types of goods, the school's own funds and public funds can be merged (if the accountability system allows it) to provide even more flexibility. The funding sources can then leverage one another when purchases are made, allowing, for example, negotiation of better bulk discounts.
- Because a formula makes the amount of funding clearly dependent on its explicit "drivers" (enrollment, graduation rates, and so on), it tends to send clear messages about what the government values and to reward schools that deliver. If schools' average costs for the drivers in the formula are lower than the "price" of the drivers in the formula, and if the school is allowed to keep the "profit" thus generated, this can be an incentive to deliver what the government wants.

Disadvantages of formula funding

- The automatic nature of a formula means that if there is a small but significant decrease in enrollment, there may be a corresponding decline in funding (unless the school is small and there is a fixed-cost component to the formula). This can make planning unpredictable. Safeguards can be created to mitigate this problem by funding on a moving-average basis, but this requires more systems and skill.
- There is considerable debate and confusion about the degree to which formula variables should send signals about inherent value (for example, about the value of science and technology training for society) by rewarding schools beyond the average cost of providing that kind of training, as opposed to simply reflecting the costs of what is valued and including what is valued in the formula.
- During the initial planning phase, countries often do not distinguish between the two major elements of formula funding. If formula-based funding is applied at the district level rather than the school level, the approach may be more effective, since calculating average infrastructure needs is more cost-effective for a group of schools than for individual schools. In any case, at the most basic level, it is not possible to fund a school on a formula basis if the school does not exist, so formula funding of construction costs at the school (rather than district or higher) level is not really possible.
- It is difficult to carry out funding of capital or infrastructure needs on a formula basis except for relatively large aggregates. Even then, the formula is more likely to be one that responds to measured need rather than to enrollment or even enrollment growth, except in countries where current inequalities are low.
- Formulas that depend only on enrollment without allowing for fixed costs create disadvantages for small schools. (Note that this is a different

issue from that of input indivisibility, discussed below.) Given the evidence that small schools can be effective, care should be taken to create a foundation fixed cost per school and to recognize this in the formula.

- If schools overspend and receive additional infusions of funding to bridge the funding gap, the formula has little effect, and schools that do manage resources wisely are penalized. But few education systems can resist the pressure to provide additional funds to schools in financial trouble.

- Many inputs, particularly teachers, are not easily divisible. Unless schools can hire teachers by the hour or adjust their salaries, it is difficult to match the personnel budget to a funding level that is calculated using a formula. But permitting schools to make such adjustments can infringe collective bargaining agreements or labor codes, which are often inflexible. Research suggests that the overall advantages of the formula approach are likely to make unions more amenable to the approach. This is especially true from the point of view of the professional interests of teachers, even if the approach implies more labor flexibility. For example, formula funding can make principals more accountable—a move many teachers might welcome. The indivisibility of teacher costs, particularly in small schools, is one reason why many systems simply provide teachers physically and restrict funding formulas to nonpersonnel costs.

- Formula-based funding may represent a double innovation—the formula aspect and the funding aspect—for most schools in most countries. Schools would have to become accustomed to being funded rather than being provided directly with inputs. This means taking on the responsibility for procurement while adhering to a budget constraint and, at the same time, having to acquire and develop new and relatively complex sets of skills. If the schools prefer to keep their profits as an incentive, they will also have to absorb losses.

Governance issues

- Misused funds may be difficult to track. If, however, petty corruption takes place at the school level, principals could be held accountable, and this might be easier than holding higher-level authorities accountable.

- In some systems the probability of local corruption and capture by special interests (leading to a suboptimal input mix) may be higher than at the central level. Thus, if the funding is not matched by capacity to procure locally (which maximizes the advantage of formula funding), funds may be misused. This hazard is relatively difficult to guard against if it does not involve outright fraud but simply what might appear to a central bureaucracy as unwise decision making—for example, spending on the wrong inputs, such as too much sports equipment. It must be assumed that principals and schools know what inputs should be given priority, or they must be trained so they know. In general, the system would lose some control over the input mix. But the input mix is hardly optimal when procurement is central, so the alternative is a better option. Reporting on the input mix used is not eliminated; only direct central control over the input mix is relinquished. The center can maintain some control over the input mix if the funding is more or less earmarked, but that would destroy some of the very advantages of formula funding. This is particularly the case when a formula is applied at the school level (rather than, say, at the district level) and when needs vary greatly among schools.

Moral hazard issues

- If the formula design is developed in too simplistic a manner (say, too much emphasis on graduation rates or progression rates), schools could engage in perverse behavior, such as trying to select the better learners from other schools, and other forms of zero-sum behavior that add no value to society but add value to those schools that are good at selecting the appropriate students. A poorly designed formula could then become an entry barrier and result in inequalities.

Procurement issues

- For formula-based funding to be advantageous, procurement should ideally be done by the schools themselves. In this regard, at least two problems emerge. First, principals might complain about conversion from being professional educators in charge of an education mission to becoming business managers, for which they were not trained and perhaps have no inclination. This complaint would typically be related to managing, for example, the procurement function, to making appropriate decisions, and to the need for more reporting. Second, local schools may not have the capacity to follow generally accepted procurement principles. But central procurement may be just as inefficient and corrupt.
- Suppliers might be uncomfortable with having schools procure every item. Suppliers of utilities (electricity, telephone, gas, and so on) might prefer to deal directly with a ministry focusing on conducting bulk procurement rather than with several decision-making points (schools). This is particularly germane if suppliers have prior knowledge that the ministry of education does not rescue schools that run into financial trouble because of overspending.

- Economies of scale in bulk procurement may be lost. If, however, legislation and regulations are progressive and well designed, schools can act as contractual agents and can form purchasing clubs. Alternatively, funding can be decoupled from procurement, but then some of the advantage of the block funding approach is lost.

Tension between funding formulas and other mandates

- Formulas can conflict with other mandates. If the decision is to use formula funding on a per-student basis and there are also regulations regarding teacher provision or student-teacher ratios, these two criteria may not match. The requirement that funds be calibrated to match spending in relation to student-teacher ratio mandates could lead to fiscal crisis for schools (or for municipalities, if the formula is applied at that level).

Formula funding applied to secondary schools

- Secondary schools require autonomy and are more capable of handling it than are primary schools. Formula funding would thus be applicable to them.
- Because secondary schools are larger than primary schools, some of the practical difficulties with teacher indivisibility mentioned above are not as applicable. For example, if a school has 15 teachers based on guidelines issued for formula funding, having to pay for a part-time additional teacher would make less difference to the budget than if the school had only 4 teachers. Under similar guidelines or conditions, having less of a teacher's time would do limited pedagogical damage.
- Since secondary schools are more heterogeneous than primary schools, there is greater need for purchasing flexibility. A funding formula (if the chosen option is block funding) can respond to such specific needs.

Despite the issues discussed above, formula funding is well worth exploring. Suggestions on how to prevent some of the problems that arise in formula funding are implicit in the caveats.

Since in some cases implementation problems are a fundamental aspect of formula funding, an option is to carry out some form of asymmetric decentralization based on formula funding. Asymmetric decentralization refers to a situation in which schools or districts are given different levels of duties and powers depending on some (ideally, formal and transparent) means of evaluating their capacities. A frequent conundrum that discourages decentralization is the belief that decentralization depends on the prior existence of capacity. But local talent in centralized situations is typically only latent, and does not appear until decentralization puts real management tasks at the local level. Thus, it is difficult to identify who to train prior to decentralization.

Furthermore, local actors tend not to take training seriously until they have to perform real tasks for which training is required. There are, however, valid concerns about local capacity to manage. One way out of this impasse is to decentralize selectively. This sends the message to localities where talent has not yet emerged or been tapped that decentralization is a real possibility and that there are incentives for talented people at the local level to assume organizational responsibilities. At the same time, this type of decentralization can force higher-level government authorities to lay out the requirements for decentralization explicitly and transparently via, for example, checklists, which can then constitute a self-development or capacity-building agenda. Schools or localities not meeting the requirements can be referred for further training. The training needs are explicit and clear because they will be in the areas where the school or locality failed, as identified in the checklist. Examples of asymmetric decentralization efforts in Colombia and South Africa are reviewed in appendix I.

Conclusion

Table 7.8 illustrates how the financing options that have been discussed in this chapter apply to the goals of expanding secondary education and enhancing quality. In short, expansion requires additional funding, for which relatively simple financing mechanisms can be designed. Improving quality and increasing equality require more sophisticated funding mechanisms.

Financing secondary education expansion and quality improvement is one dimension of the enabling environment. The other critical element is the governance aspect, including the political economy of secondary education. Chapter 8 explores the subject and examines alternative forms for governing secondary education.

Notes

1. Large countries are defined somewhat arbitrarily as those with primary enrollment in 2001 of more than 3 million. The selected countries in table 7.1 are all those low-income countries that had a primary enrollment larger than 3 million, and had complete and credible data in EdStats for both primary and secondary levels for the period 1998–2001.

2. The 10 countries in Mingat's sample are Benin, Cameroon, Madagascar, Mali, Mauritania, Mozambique, Niger, Rwanda, Senegal, and Togo. It is difficult to say whether Mingat's estimate approximates a net enrollment rate of 90 percent that would equate it to Binder's assumptions. The estimate for total spending as a share of GDP is derived by adding columns 4 and 10 in Mingat (2004), table 8.

3. Calculated from Mingat (2004), table 8, totals in columns 2 and 8.

4. The table suggests the median trend, but there is actually a fair amount of dispersion around the median. Thus, for example, according to the median trend,

Table 7.8 Application of Financing Tools and Options to Access, Quality, and Equity Goals

		Effect on access and quantity	Effect on quality	Effect on equity
Improve financing of secondary education.				
Obtain more funding.				
Obtain more public funding.	Obtain more public funding for education in general.	Easiest way to increase access; increasing access typically requires more spending unless efficiencies can be increased significantly.	Increase in quality may or may not require increased expenditure; evidence is weak that increasing expenditure leads to improvements in quality.	Increasing expenditure on secondary education, particularly on access; if primary education is already at or near universal access, can improve equity (marginal benefit incidence), as those already served are typically the better off.
	Obtain more public funding for secondary education.	Same as above, care needs to be taken not to underspend on other sectors, as discussed in the text.	Same as above.	Same as above, but care is needed because shifting funding from a more equitable sector (say, primary) to a less equitable one (secondary) could reduce the overall degree of pro-poor spending.

(Continues on the following page.)

Table 7.8 Continued

Improve financing of secondary education.

Obtain more funding.

Obtain more private funding.			Effect on access and quantity	Effect on quality	Effect on equity
	Use public-private partnerships.	Corporate social responsibility and charity.	Likely minor increase in access and quantity.	Could have strong demonstration effect on quality, as is the case with all pilot projects.	Could have small positive effect on equity if spending is targeted on the poor.
		Formal public-private partnerships.	Potentially large impact.	Unlikely to have a major impact on quality except in possible cases of outsourced technical assistance; outsourced teaching as such is likely to be problematic.	Potentially positive effect, in that access could be brought forward in time.
	Use formal or informal, cash or in-kind parental contributions or fees for recurrent costs and shift public funding toward the poor.		Minor or no positive impact, could have a negative impact if the purpose is revenue seeking rather than equity and shifting of resources to the poor.	Possible positive impact on quality if middle-class individuals are thereby more likely to reengage in or stay engaged in public education.	If the purpose is to shift public funding to the poor, impact on equity could be positive. If the motivation is to simply seek revenue, impact on equity could be negative.

Improve efficiency and equity.	Input policy and management.	Use formal or informal, cash or in-kind parental or community contributions for capital funding; if formal, can be public-community partnership.	Some positive impact if schools would otherwise not be built.	None or minor.	None or minor.
		Increase work effort through tighter control and accountability and more rewards for more responsive and effective teachers.	Could generate some savings that could be used to expand access.	Could generate some savings that could be used to purchase quality-enhancing inputs normally crowded out by excessive salary expenditure. Could have a direct impact on quality if more work effort is deployed.	Possible positive impact, since the poor are usually the most underserved by poor work effort.
		Reduce price of inputs through better understanding and use of input markets and policies (such as procurement policy and systems) for books, teachers, and construction.	Could generate some savings that could be used to expand access.	Could lead to more affordability of key quality-enhancing inputs such as books and stationery.	The poor are often most affected by lack of such materials, so the impact on equity of results could be positive.
		Use better input mix, such as fewer teachers and more materials, by, for example, increasing class size, requiring more teaching time in the school day, or granting less leave time.	None.	Could lead to more use of quality-enhancing inputs and thus have a positive impact on quality.	Same as above.

(Continues on the following page.)

Table 7.8 Continued

Improve financing of secondary education.
Improve efficiency and equity.

		Effect on access and quantity	Effect on quality	Effect on equity
	Improve internal efficiency by reducing repetition and dropout through norming and policy, with or without specific quality interventions.	Some positive impact on access if repeaters are taking up space.	Some impact on quality if age heterogeneity can be reduced. Automatic promotion may reduce quality.	The poor are often most affected by unnecessary repetition, so improvements in age-grade management could improve equity.
	Use improved technology such as distance learning (may require a somewhat different curriculum).	Could have a positive impact on access, but most distance learning requires that children already be at school.	Significant and low-cost impact on learning has been reported, but numbers have to be large, and some technologies are more effective than others.	Ability of distance learning to improve learning has been mostly demonstrated with poor populations. Distance learning could have a positive effect on the equity of results.
Improved management and financing mechanisms.	Improve funding method to create more discretion together with more accountability; consider methods such as capitation or other formula funding, poverty-targeted funding, performance-based funding, and bonuses.	Minor or none.	Formula funding that increases school discretion could help improve quality, if accompanied by other measures.	Formula funding could powerfully affect equity if poverty is an important driver in the formula. It may be the clearest way to affect input distribution so as to favor the poor. Whether this leads to improved equity of learning results has more to do with how the funding is managed.

Increase productivity through training and capacity building in teaching and through school management based on value-added analysis and efficient-school analysis and support.	Minor or none.	Potentially very large. Well-managed schools using the same level of resources and targeting similar populations often have results 20 to 30 percent better than badly managed schools.	The poor are more often affected by poor management than the rich. Improved management can improve results for the poor and bring about more equality of results.
Optimize curriculum.	Some, if an optimized curriculum leads to cost savings that are then used to improve access.	Some, depending on how much the curriculum is truly improved and whether it is actually applied.	Some, if the current curriculum is not favorable to the poor, by requiring teaching techniques and skills or subjects likely to be unavailable in rural areas.

Source: Authors' compilation.

when the secondary GER is at 75, the expected tertiary GER will be at 30, but the values predicted by quantile regressions at the 25th and 75th quantiles would be 18 and 41, respectively. Thus, in half of the countries, when the secondary GER is at 75, the tertiary GER will tend to be between 18 and 41.

5. The differences among the groups with varying economic growth records are statistically significant, albeit only at the 10 percent level for secondary education because of insufficient case numbers, as countries tend to report these data in a very haphazard manner. (The differences are significant at the 1 percent level for tertiary education.) The differences among groups with different secondary expansion records are not statistically significant and are helpful only as broad characterizations.

6. A motivation for involvement on social-responsibility grounds may be, for example, that multinational enterprises are facing public relations pressures to meet triple-bottom-line accountability, formal or informal.

8

Governance in Secondary Education: Managing Expansion and Quality Improvement

None will doubt that the legislator should direct his attention above all to the education of youth; for the neglect of education does harm to the constitution. The citizen should be molded to suit the form of government under which he lives. For each government has a peculiar character which originally formed and which continues to preserve it. The character of democracy creates democracy, and the character of oligarchy creates oligarchy; and always the better the character, the better the government.

—Aristotle, *Politics*, B.VIII

Management of the twin challenges of secondary education—expansion of its coverage (in particular to those excluded because of poverty, ethnicity, gender, and disability) and improvement of its quality and relevance— entails the identification of the most appropriate arrangements for governing secondary education systems. This poses a difficult task for policy makers, given the lack of agreed solutions backed by consensus. A review of the literature on schooling and governance (Lindblad and Popkewitz 2001) revealed no explicit agreement on how to define education governance. There is an implicit assumption, however, that governance refers to the "machinery" of government—that is, what the ministry of education and education offices do, which involves the rational process of planning and evaluating outcomes, as well as the exercise of power by these authorities.

For the purposes of this report, governance is defined as the set of processes, goal-setting and steering mechanisms, and institutions (rules and regulations) through which the social action of providing secondary education takes place in a society (Kettl 2002). Key dimensions of governance in education are regulations regarding curriculum, standards, admission policies, and certification; the procedures used to assess student achievement and monitor the state of the system; the mechanisms used to steer the operation of schools and the provision of educational services; and the instruments used for resource allocation and funding. The past decades have witnessed significant changes in the way legislation has been used to regulate education—changes in resource control and utilization, and movement toward the devolution and decentralization of school administration. New management practices at the central and local levels have been introduced to support the implementation of these changes.

Although there is no single model of effective governance in secondary education, the analysis of governing practices across countries reveals four common basic elements in countries that have a long tradition of state provision of compulsory secondary education and, at the same time, have had reasonable success in providing most of their young people with good secondary education:

- transparent, well-known regulations
- a sharp definition of responsibilities, including the responsibilities of citizens and of different levels of government
- strong public management
- precise definition of outcomes and measurement of results

The type of governance resulting from the combination of these four core elements is closely associated with the broad sociocultural and economic characteristics of the society.

This chapter examines the governance of secondary education from two angles. First, it analyzes from a macro perspective questions relating to the institutions and mechanisms used to steer the system. Special attention is given to exploring how the relationships between the center and localities are being redefined to respond to the twin challenges of expanding access to secondary education and improving quality, and how admission and selection policies can ease or restrict opportunities. Second, it focuses on the micro dimension of secondary schools as organizations and examines the main organizational characteristics of effective secondary schools.

Steering Secondary Education

Secondary education has specific characteristics that shape the institutional arrangements used to steer the system and that are not found in primary education. One is the relationship of secondary education to labor markets and to higher education institutions, which enables secondary school graduates to obtain employment or attend tertiary education institutions in places far away from their secondary schools. Secondary education thus has spillover effects across localities that justify a stronger role of central government in financing and in standard setting and curriculum policy. The second difference involves a curriculum organized around discrete disciplines, with a multiplicity of education paths and teaching by specialists.

The curriculum has a strong influence on decisions about the optimum size of schools and about the establishment of catchment areas that more often than not take in two or more local jurisdictions. This in turn affects the composition and definition of local education boundaries and authorities, leading to a weakening of the linkages between parents and schools and, in many cases, with the local business community.

Central policy making and administration has been the dominant governing paradigm during periods of educational expansion (Lundgren 2002). Centrally controlled reform has been the main instrument used to define and help achieve the goal of increasing access. As the focus of policy making began to shift from expansion to issues of equity, quality, and relevance, the micro aspects of efficiency, productivity, and school organization received increasing attention. The traditional role of state institutions in providing secondary education was questioned, and clarification of the state–market–civil society relationship moved to center stage in the debate on education reform. The issue of what types of problems and decisions are best handled at the school, subnational, and national levels is now open to ample scrutiny in most countries. By 1998, 85 countries were moving toward some form of decentralization. For example, 38 of 40 countries in Asia (Adams 1998) and 20 of 35 countries in Latin America and the Caribbean (Winkler and Greshberg 2000) are reported to have some form of educational decentralization either under way or in the planning stage.

Obviously, there is no unique and straightforward answer regarding the role of the nation-state in providing secondary education; the ability of central and state governments to deal with issues of access, quality, equity, and efficiency and to make decisions that address these issues largely depends on their institutional and management capacity. Nevertheless, there is ample evidence of a global shift in the role of the nation-state in education, from a model of governance based on rules supported by a centralized normative framework toward new forms of governing that rely on steering mechanisms based on agreed goals and clearly defined outputs, supported by a national outcome-monitoring system. This also means a shift away from large government bureaucracies charged with the provision of services and toward smaller administrative bodies that are responsible for developing the capacity of schools and of government at various levels and that are complemented by a wide and diverse network of service providers.

It is important to keep in mind that the state does not "go away" in the decentralization process. Its continuing role as the overwhelmingly most important financier and regulator of education enables it to remain very much in the driver's seat (see table 8.1). "True, the nature of the work it does has changed, very broadly speaking, from carrying out most of the work of the coordination of education itself to determining where the work will be done and by whom. This devolution and detachment demonstrate strength rather than weakness" (Dale 1997, 274).

Table 8.1 Direction of Change in the Role of the National Government in Education

Old role	New role
Design the development of education.	Create national vision.
Design education plans and manage implementation.	Steer by goals; define standards and manage national student assessment.
Administer all details.	Monitor results by assessing student and system performance; support educational research and development.
Provide all services.	Coordinate equalization of services; facilitate provision of services of good quality; create pilot programs and provide resources to help targeted populations achieve agreed-on educational outcomes; manage partnerships between central and local government and with service providers.
Distribute public services.	Mobilize and coordinate interest groups.
Act as main or sole financier of educational development.	Act as important financier, with complementary role as catalyst of partnerships with local bodies and the private sector.

Source: Adapted from Adams (2001).

The transformation of the central government from direct provider of secondary education services to indirect manager of other actors through a complex system of regulations and incentives has led to a diversification of providers of educational services. It has also created a host of "fuzzy boundaries" (Kettl 2002) that central and local government bureaucracies, as well as the private sector, must learn to manage in order to ensure that educational services are provided to all at an appropriate level of quality.

It is generally assumed that the trend toward devolution to local governing bodies has promoted a generalized move toward decentralization. A closer examination of national practices reveals, however, that the decentralization trend does not apply to all aspects of secondary education. For example, in both the United Kingdom and the United States some important aspects of education policy have shifted toward a more active role by the central government. In the United States the establishment of standards can be viewed as a means of steering from the center, guided by the definition of national outcomes. In the United Kingdom the central government now plays a more direct role in steering education through the development of curriculum norms (setting a national curriculum,

Figure 8.1 The Governance of Education

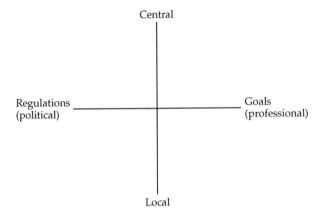

which had never existed before) and by strengthening the school inspection system and local control.

Both Finland and Korea have implemented important changes toward decentralizing their education systems, but their practices differ significantly in some ways. For example, in Finland the authority to hire and fire teachers is located at the school level, where principals can make the decision. In Korea, although many functions have been transferred to lower levels of government, the central authority retains the ultimate decision power over personnel, since hiring and firing teachers, who in most cases belong to and are identified with the community, is a culturally sensitive matter.

Lundgren (2002) has developed a useful scheme for understanding what is involved in the shift from a normative model of governing education to a goal-oriented model (figure 8.1). The *central-local* axis describes the creative tension that governs the process for defining the roles and responsibilities of institutional actors such as the national government, at one pole, and the local government and the community, at the other. Since education is a vehicle for the reproduction of culture from one generation to the next, the state will always have a significant role. What needs to be defined at any given moment is the degree of decentralization.

The *regulations-goals* axis refers to the tension that arises in defining the locus of control of educational processes ("who has the power") and the mechanisms used for steering the system. The political establishment may control the definition of educational content and the learning methods and may use normative mechanisms (regulations) to exercise that control, or control can be located in the professional sphere and be exercised through outcome-oriented devices (goals).

These two axes are in constant interaction. As an education system moves along the central-local axis toward more local involvement, the professional dimension becomes more relevant because there is a greater need for highly qualified and more responsive principals and teachers who can take control of key educational processes. Professionalism and responsibility for results take center stage. Movement along the central-local axis brings with it a shift toward governing by goals and outcomes, increasing the need for and value of timely and reliable information, which, in turn, demands new forms of administration and new qualifications of local education authorities, principals, and teachers. The renewed attention to school management, school leadership, and the professional role of teachers can be considered a by-product of the trend toward governing by goals and outcomes.

These shifts have brought about significant changes in education planning and management. On the one hand, there is a trend toward more centralized planning and management of changes in curriculum and assessment, which can be interpreted as a strengthening of central bureaucratic control. On the other, there is a trend toward decentralizing the budget and the day-to-day implementation of changes to the local or district level and even directly to schools. The simultaneous movement toward centralized control and decentralized professional empowerment is creating a need for education bureaucracies and professionals that are more responsive to demands from localities and schools, as well as for stronger and better-prepared school professionals and education administrators.

Where a country ends up in the quadrants generated by the intersection of these two axes will depend on its political history and culture, the state of development of its education system, and its institutional capacity to propose and implement changes (see box 8.1). The specific country arrangement will represent a balance between central and local governance and between political and professional power and accountability (Lundgren 2002).

Center-Locality Relationships

Various approaches have been taken toward describing the center-locality and political-professional relationships in education (Colclough 1993; Cummings and Riddell 1994; Green, Wolf, and Leney 1999; James 1994; McGinn and Welsh 1999; Prawda 1992; Weiler 1990; Winkler 1989). Here, we are interested in how the locus of decision making affects, on the one hand, the financing and management of schools and, on the other, curricular and pedagogical decisions at the classroom level. We make use of the typology developed by Green, Wolf, and Leney in their comparative study on education governance in OECD countries. The authors identify four main models: the centralized system with some devolution, the regional

---

Box 8.1 Decentralization in India: Kerala State

With a literacy rate of nearly 91 percent and almost universal basic education, Kerala, in southwest India, is among the Indian states with the highest numbers of educated people. During the 1997–2002 five-year plan, administrative responsibility for Kerala's approximately 11,000 government-sponsored schools was transferred from the state government to local self-government, or *panchayati raj*, institutions. Primary education became the responsibility of the village *panchayats* (elected councils). The transfer of responsibility was supported by a revision of the school curriculum and the introduction of a comprehensive education program that was to serve as a general guideline.

An evaluation after six years revealed that despite good intentions and sporadic support, few local initiatives have been implemented, and state-level regulations continue to dominate the day-to-day operation of the school system. The main reasons for poor local engagement were lack of understanding by village authorities of the new tasks devolved to them, lack of expertise for carrying them out, and resistance by teachers to what they considered political incursions into their professional domain. Although village *panchayats* were responsible for monitoring and evaluating teaching and learning, they lacked the professional resources and legitimacy to perform this task effectively. The few localities that showed some success in carrying out the new responsibilities had local leaders with experience in education and some legitimacy among their peers. State-level authorities, meanwhile, have been concerned about inequalities that might arise from a full implementation of decentralization and have been extremely cautious in moving forward on this initiative.

Source: Bray and Mukundan 2003.

---

devolution system, the local control system, and institutional autonomy through quasi-markets.

Centralized system with elements of devolution. France provides a good example of the evolution of governing practices within this model. (See box 8.2 for the characteristics of this type of system.) Since the early 1980s, France has been experimenting with various forms of devolution and deconcentration. Some power has been deconcentrated to local offices of the Ministry of Education—for example, development of local curricula; shared responsibility for school supervision between the local, regional, and central levels; and transfer of legal ownership of school buildings to local elected governments. Schools themselves have acquired some autonomy with

---

Box 8.2 Characteristics of a Centralized Education System with Elements of Devolution

- Strong central control is exercised over various aspects of secondary education (structure, curriculum, forms of examination and assessment, management, allocation of resources, teacher recruitment and training).
- The political rationale is that of the traditional welfare state, with an emphasis on solving social problems.
- Education governance is conducted through a professional bureaucracy organized in a highly structured and hierarchical manner.
- The ministry of education has strong control over the design and implementation of the curriculum through detailed regulations on course content, course sequencing, and examinations and through approval of textbooks and teaching materials.
- The ministry of education, through its central office or via regional outposts, has full responsibility for funding, maintaining, inspecting, and staffing schools.
- Schools have very little autonomy over issues pertaining to curriculum, budget, and personnel.
- The driving force is egalitarian ideals (equality of education provision).
- A strong state presence is seen as the most appropriate way of dealing with inequalities in access and quality.
- The evolution of the model is toward one in which regional levels (territorial tiers of the center) have limited powers to select textbooks and administer small discretionary budgets but strong central control is maintained over all other aspects of education.

---

respect to curriculum issues, and school specialization has been encouraged. The introduction of elements of competition through the relaxation of rules for allocating places in public secondary schools has increased parental choice by allowing students to apply to schools outside their home zone.

The experience of China demonstrates the importance of well-developed capacity at the local level as a prerequisite for successful transfer of responsibility from the center to local authorities. Educational decentralization was initiated in China in 1985 with the aim of mobilizing local resources and stimulating local initiatives so as to achieve the goal of nine years of compulsory education. Although decentralization led to more choices in curriculum and increased the availability of a wider variety of textbooks, the transfer of authority for the management of primary and secondary schools to the township had to be reversed because of lack of capacity and staff at the township level. Inadequate understanding of education issues led to poor decisions on allocation of funds and on the hiring and selection of school principals. Consequently, the national government decided to move educational responsibilities and authority up one level, to the county, where offices of education were in full operation. Decentralization has had the side effect of increasing the disparity between poor and wealthy counties because poor communities often find it difficult to generate additional resources and attract good teachers; even teachers' salaries are not guaranteed.

In Mexico the central government plays a key role in financing education through transfers to the states, while decision-making authority for primary and secondary schools and for recruitment and hiring of teachers is situated at the regional (state) level. An exception is that to ensure equality of educational opportunities for children living in remote and indigenous areas, the central government directly operates a system of rural schools through the National Council of Education Development (CONAFE).

Simultaneous implementation of changes that entail both devolution and deconcentration carries the risk that deconcentration will thwart devolution to some degree. Whereas devolution empowers local governing bodies that are subject to local election and accountability, deconcentration to lower-level offices of central ministries has the opposite effect; it extends the effective reach of the center and thus imposes constraints on the scope of local authorities for self-regulation and self-management (Green, Wolf, and Leney 1999).

Regional devolution system. The U.S. education system shares some of the characteristics outlined in box 8.3. The federal government exerts influence over state governments and local authorities indirectly through incentives in the form of grants and the promotion of scientific and academic research. Local school districts and schools have significant control over curriculum, teaching practices, and allocation of resources, making the U.S. system a classic example of local control.

In Brazil most authority over education matters lies with the state government. The 1988 constitution guarantees the states and municipalities autonomy in carrying out their educational responsibilities. States play a central role in secondary education, and municipalities have the primary responsibility for delivering primary and preschool education. The main role of the federal government is to provide financial and technical assistance to the states and municipalities so as to guarantee equality of educational opportunities and minimum quality standards (see box 8.4).

Local control system. The features of this model are captured in box 8.5. From the early 1990s to early 2000, the United Kingdom introduced significant changes in its local control system (pattern 1 in box 8.5) by

---

Box 8.3 Characteristics of a Regional Devolution System

Power and responsibilities rest at an intermediate level of political authority, below the central government but above the level of the municipality or local district. Although the federal government retains relatively few powers, the strong control and power devolved to the state or regional level can make this model a very centralized one indeed. Germany provides a good illustration.

- The states are responsible for most legislation and regulations concerning the school system.
- The federal government can participate in the fulfillment of the states' educational duties through education grants and by funding academic research and projects of supranational scale.
- The federal government oversees regulations on teacher salaries, benefits, and pensions.

Within each state the organization of education may be highly hierarchical.

- The state ministry of education may be responsible for regulations on curriculum content, assessment, textbook approval, recruitment of teachers, payment of teachers' salaries, and so on.
- Local school authorities may be responsible for organizing, administering, and funding schools. Schools have some autonomy with respect to curriculum and assessment, but they are still controlled by tight guidelines handed down by the state.
- There is parental choice regarding the type of school children can attend, but stringent entry requirements imposed by the system limit the choice.

---

promoting consumer choice, the removal of state subsidies, and deregulation. It has been argued, as a reason to favor pattern 2, that the traditional organizations established to handle the political governance of state institutions in a modern industrial society are no longer suitable for dealing with the same institutions operating in postmodern, knowledge-based societies. A strong center supported by reactive local institutions becomes an obstacle to innovation, organizational change, and agility in responding to new challenges. When the volume and structure of knowledge are changing rapidly, it becomes more and more difficult and unproductive to plan the content of education centrally. Yet decentralized management of education content requires professional capacity evenly distributed across

---

Box 8.4 School Report Card in Paraná, Brazil

In 2002, for the second consecutive year, the Paraná State Secretariat of Education issued a school report card (SRC) to provide the community with relevant information about the performance of schools. The SRC, which was introduced by the State Secretariat in its drive to promote quality education, is designed to bring the community closer to its schools. The idea is that student achievement can be improved when parents and schools work together in an informed way toward the same set of objectives: if parents know what is happening in their schools and in neighboring ones, they will put pressure on the school and local authorities to improve education.

The SRC contains three kinds of information: (a) student scores in association with family background (the "school effect"); (b) student flow (promotion, retention, and dropout) and school characteristics (teachers' qualifications, class size) compared with data for all schools in the municipality; and (c) information from parents, students, and school administrators. This third category includes parents' views about teaching quality, parents' involvement, exchange of information, safety of the school, and parent profile. Student input includes information on parents' involvement in supporting school activities, the family's economic status, students' opinions about the teaching, students' attitudes, and their difficulties in learning. The survey of principals focuses on the principal's leadership in bringing parents and the school council into the education process and in spending time with teachers analyzing and discussing ways to improve student learning.

Source: Authors' compilation, http://www.pr.gov.br/cie.

---

levels of administration (see box 8.6). Solving this dilemma becomes a major challenge for developing countries where professional expertise is highly concentrated in central-urban areas (see box 8.7).

Under pattern 2 of the local control model (pattern 2 in box 8.5) the center plays a modest role through a governing modality called "steering by goals" (Aho and Pitkänen 2004; Lundgren and Román 2003). The main role of the center is to provide a framework, based on clearly defined goals and steering principles, for the operation of the system. Local authorities and education professionals enjoy a large degree of autonomy and are given ample managerial and organizational roles, while school professionals are vested with autonomy and power to organize the teaching and learning process

Box 8.5 Characteristics of a Local Control System

- Central regulations are light, providing a framework for the operation of the school system with limited control from the center.
- Locally elected authorities have significant control of schooling within their boundaries.
- Schools enjoy different levels of autonomy depending on the sociocultural realities of each country.

There are two patterns of local authority control:

1. Educational localism based on historical traditions, as in the British system
   - Local education authorities are heavily involved in the organization and steering of the school system.
   - Schools enjoy considerable independence based on professional trust and a high level of professional autonomy of teachers, especially with respect to curriculum implementation and student assessment.
2. Educational localism based on the "Nordic local control" model
   - Local communities play a strong role in the management and provision of education.
   - Professional autonomy is much less prominent.

Box 8.6 Transfer of Responsibilities and Power to the Local Level in Sweden

In the early 1990s the Swedish government launched a decentralization reform. The bill regulating this effort, "Responsibility for School," gives municipalities large responsibilities and wide autonomy in interpreting national goals and curriculum, translating them into local objectives, and organizing their own schools in terms of structure and type of providers, as long as the schools and the students attain national goals and general regulations and directions are followed. The reform was meant to close the gap between decisions regarding school policies made at the center and school practices. Decentralization has allowed increased choices for students in terms of school options, programs, and courses. But since small municipalities have been able to offer only a limited number of programs compared with what large and wealthy municipalities can do, children from families living in larger towns have been given more opportunities than those from families living in small and less affluent places.

Source: Lundgren and Román 2003.

Box 8.7 A Well-Structured but Not-So-Effective System: The Case of Bangladesh

There are two sides to the story of secondary education in Bangladesh. On the one hand, the country has recorded remarkable achievements: over the past decade enrollments have more than doubled, and female enrollment has increased from 33 to 50 percent. This progress is attributable to the effectiveness of the government's incentive policies that provide food and female stipends for disadvantaged families and for girls from poor and rural families. It is also the result of a well-developed public-private partnership under which 95 percent of private schools receive public financing (90 percent of teachers' salaries in all recognized schools). In addition, the management structure of secondary schools strengthens their capacity to make decisions that are aligned with local needs. A school management committee (SMC) is the main governing body of secondary schools. It has authority to appoint, suspend, and remove teachers and to set teachers' salaries and monitor school performance and teachers' and students' attendance. Education stipends (scholarships for girls from poor areas and food programs for all children from poor families) and tight regulations allow students to go to schools of their choice.

The system, however, suffers from deteriorating quality of education. Some crucial elements of effective governance appear to be absent. First, there is a lack of accountability in the system. The government provides large subsidies to private schools, but there is no mechanism linking subsidies to school performance. Second, a decentralized management system has not resulted in a real shift of authority or to improved capacity at lower levels of government. The Ministry of Education is skeletal, with few staff at the zonal and district levels to monitor, evaluate, and inspect privately managed schools that are not under direct government administration. Third, while there is an institutional mechanism for community involvement through SMCs, quality assurance procedures to enable SMCs to function well do not exist. The lack of regulations and the limited capacity of SMCs have resulted in the hiring of unqualified teachers and poor student achievement.

Source: World Bank 2004c.

---

according to their best professional judgment. The empirical support for this governing model is derived in part from research on school effectiveness that shows the importance of qualified leadership and a developed school culture.

**Box 8.8 Characteristics of Institutional Autonomy
through Quasi-Markets**

The institutional autonomy through quasi-markets approach embraces
various schemes for promoting parental and student choice in secondary
education. In most of these schemes

- Central authorities retain control over funding and remuneration of
  teachers, creating a quasi-market for state schooling. The main
  underlying assumption of the policy is that forcing schools into a
  competitive market will lead to improved quality of schooling.
- School choice can assume different modalities, ranging from allowing
  parents to choose among a limited group of existing public schools to
  giving vouchers directly to families to pay tuition in a private school of
  their preference.

The main policy decisions involved in designing a school choice
program are: who is entitled to provide schooling, who decides what
school a child will attend, and how schools are paid for their services.

A big risk of steering by goals is that measurement of goals in the form
of outcomes could itself become the de facto way of steering the system,
resulting in "governing by evaluation" instead of governing by goals. Central
control of educational processes would then begin to dominate again, cur-
tailing flexibility and severely restraining the scope for local professional
responses and initiatives.

Institutional autonomy through quasi-markets. To stimulate the diversification of schooling provision, many governments, especially in OECD countries, have introduced schemes to promote parental and student choice in
secondary education (see box 8.8).

Pure school vouchers are the extreme form of choice: the government
does nothing toward school provision and gives money directly to families, leaving to them the decision as to where to send their children. This
model is being implemented in only a few places, mostly in states and counties in the United States.

Regulated voucher programs are a more common form of school choice.
Schools are funded through lump sums on the basis of enrollment numbers (capitation grants). The difference from the pure voucher scheme is
that "money follows the student," and the government is directly involved
in paying schools. (The Netherlands and Chile are examples.) The government sometimes intervenes in regulating the entry of new schools, either
by restricting the establishment of new schools or through licensing. In

other cases, such as Chile, the government encourages the establishment of new, subsidized private schools.

Under some of these schemes, secondary schools are allowed to "opt out" of local authority control after gaining majority support from parents (as in England and Wales), but they continue to receive direct funding from the central government, becoming grant-maintained schools. So far, a relatively small number of schools has opted out of local authority control. A similar scheme has been introduced in the United States in the form of "charter schools"; parents are allowed to choose among publicly funded schools that are run by independent not-for-profit groups formed by teachers and parents.

In 2000 the Colombian government launched an experimental program whereby private schools and other organizations and groups could take over the management of one or more public schools (Rodríguez and Hovde 2002). The program, which is concentrated in low-income areas, has two different models: (a) a one-to-one relationship in which one private school takes over the management of one public school and (b) multiple-school relationships in which one organization or private group takes over the management of several schools. In both models the managing institutions or schools have a contract with the district secretary of education to provide educational services to poor children in return for remuneration on a per-student basis. The contract specifies standards such as hours of instruction, the quality of nutritional provisions, and the establishment of a single shift. Management has full autonomy and is evaluated on the basis of results. If the school does not reach preestablished targets on standardized tests and dropout rates for two consecutive years, the secretary has the right to end the contract. The contract is set for 15 years to ensure continuity in management and to encourage the long-term sustainability of efforts and investments. The education secretary ensures that a private firm carries out school inspection, that pedagogical norms and standards are followed, and that academic objectives are met. Initial evaluation of this program indicates some success as measured by expansion of access, but the quality of services is uneven.

In the United Kingdom the involvement of private for-profit institutions in partnerships with the public sector to provide education services has fallen far short of achieving the expected results. A five-year, £100 million contract signed in 2001 between WS Atkins, one of the world's leading providers of technologically based consultancy and support services, and the London borough of Southwark was ended after two years. Atkins believed that it was not benefiting from the arrangements and decided to walk out of them before the five-year period ended. The local government had no clear exit strategy and was left with the problem of finding another contractor (*The Economist*, May 1, 2003). It appears that one of the main reasons for the collapse was that neither organization understood how the other worked. Local authorities blamed Atkins for working under pressure to meet the company's targets instead of the education targets agreed on at the beginning of the contract.

In many English-speaking countries, including Australia, Canada, New Zealand, and the United Kingdom, devolution of power to institutions has been accompanied by an increase of central control in areas such as curriculum, assessment, and accreditation. Furthermore, the central government has increased the monitoring of outcomes—not only those related to performance of schools and teachers but also those bearing on the functioning of the overall system. Thus, parents, policy makers, and the general public have additional information that, in principle, families could use in deciding where to send their children and policy makers could use in deciding which schools to support and which to close.

Studies on the benefits and perils of school choice are inconclusive (Lamdin and Mintrom 1997; McEwan 2000a). A few show that under certain conditions choice could lead to gains in student learning, especially for minority and disadvantaged children, if the school choice programs are well targeted. A comparison of learning achievement of U.S. students who attend choice schools with that of similar students attending public schools showed that the former do not always learn at a dramatically higher rate (Teske and Schneider 2001). In New Zealand Fiske and Ladd (2000) found that choice could lead to worse education for low-income children because the schools where they end up have instructional resources of much lower quality.

Regulations Affecting Access and Parental Decisions

In chapter 1 various institutional arrangements for secondary education were examined to trace how they generate secondary education structures with various degrees of internal differentiation, from fully comprehensive schools to selective schools that screen students into educational tracks at a very early age. In this section we examine how some key regulations regarding admission affect parental decisions and opportunities for children to gain access to secondary education institutions.

Regulations on admission can be grouped into two types: (a) those that concern the rights of families to select schools and the mechanisms used to assign children to schools, and (b) those related to the transition between levels. The latter primarily have to do with the existence or absence of screening mechanisms, and they have a direct impact on access. This classification helps in identifying four main types of access policies for secondary schooling: zoned—selective admission, zoned—open admission, choice—selective admission, and choice—open admission (see box 8.9).

Box 8.9 Models and Features of Policies on Access to Secondary Education

Access models may be classified according to how much choice families have in selecting schools and on how students move between primary and secondary school.

Right of families to select schools

- *Zoned models* are based on a strict definition of geographic boundaries for each school. Children are obliged to go to a designated school within a given geographic area, which is generally established in relation to feeder primary schools. One variation of allocation by zoning is busing, whereby children are moved (bused) across zones to achieve social balance or other related policy objectives.
- *Choice models* offer families total freedom to select where to send their children. These models require funding mechanisms based on student enrollments, daily attendance, or similar forms of tracking family preferences and behaviors.

Transition between primary and secondary education

- In *selective admission models* students are selected on the basis of academic ability or aptitude. To determine these attributes, government authorities use ranking procedures to gauge students' past academic performance. These procedures may make use of entrance examinations, school-leaving certificates, and letters of recommendation issued by primary school teachers or other school professionals such as school counselors. These models tend to be predominant in school systems with highly differentiated curricula and mechanisms for early tracking of students into academic, vocational, and technical tracks and in developing countries where the supply of secondary education is limited and is often concentrated in urban areas.

  Other forms of selection include quotas based on criteria such as ability mix, ethnicity, or any other personal or social attributes that can be targeted for social policy (engineering) purposes. A local government agency or someone acting on behalf of the government is given the responsibility for applying the screening criteria.
- In *open admission models* all children are offered the opportunity to continue secondary education on completion of primary or basic education. There is no exit examination to certify graduation from primary education. Open admission policies are common in countries where the supply of school places is not constrained, where most schools

(Continued)

Box 8.9 Continued

offer a comprehensive curriculum, and where tracking is delayed or nonexistent. Most schools offer a broad curriculum combining the liberal arts with some technical/vocational components or orientation.

Four general types of access policies can be identified.

Zoned—selective admission model

The *zoned—selective admission model* is found in countries such as Germany where students from families living within a predefined catchment area are screened at an early stage into specializations offered by schools operating within that area. It is also found in countries where demand for secondary school places outstrips the capacity of established schools. It can be anticipated that many countries where Education for All succeeds could end up with this type of structure, not by policy design but because governments are not able to invest in secondary school expansion now. This situation could be particularly conspicuous in urban areas, but rural areas would also be affected—although in a different manner, since the population is more dispersed, opportunity costs are higher, and transport can be an additional obstacle. Developing countries could expand real access opportunities to lower secondary education by delaying selection until the upper secondary level and by simultaneously extending the duration of compulsory education to include both primary and lower secondary in basic education.

Zoned—open admission model

The *zoned—open admission model* is the typical arrangement found when families must send their children to schools located within a given jurisdiction but there is no constraint on the supply of school places. Schools operating under this type of arrangement offer comprehensive education, and education authorities have a strong policy commitment to maximize equity by balancing the social intake of schools. Countries where local governments run the school system and there is no problem of supply, such as the United States, tend to operate under this model.

Choice—open admission model

The *choice—open admission model* does away with all types of restriction and is based on school-funding mechanisms such as grant-maintained schools, capitation grants, assisted place schemes, and vouchers that fund schools on the basis of enrollment and the "money follows the student" principle. In order for open admission to exist, the school system must offer comprehensive education or be able to satisfy a

Box 8.9 Continued

multiplicity of demands. The U.K. assisted place scheme provides financial support so that children from families below a certain income level can attend private schools. In some U.S. states and localities vouchers are issued to give parents from targeted families the possibility of sending their children to private schools. (An example is the Milwaukee Parental Choice Program.) Under a similar program in Chile the government, through a "paperless" voucher program, allows families to select service providers (municipalities or operators of private schools).

Some countries initially operating under the choice—open admission model could end up, in practice, with a selective admission situation because a few very popular schools are oversubscribed and there is limited capacity or political will for expansion. This situation is seen in some Eastern European countries such as Bulgaria, Lithuania, and Poland.

Choice—selective admission model

The *choice—selective admission model* is a social engineering attempt to balance preference (parental choice) with predefined public goals or social objectives. Parents are asked to list schools in order of preference, and a public official takes these preferences into account when assigning children to schools.

The government, working through partnerships to provide financial support, could greatly influence access to quality secondary schooling. Table 8.2 shows supply-side, demand-side, and other financing options.

In their study of changes in governance and admission to lower secondary education in OECD countries during the 1970s and 1990s, Kivirauma, Rinne, and Seppänen (2003) found two main trends: on the one hand, movement toward comprehensive education systems with open enrollment and, on the other, a trend away from centralized systems toward local control (see figure 8.2). Only in England and Wales have the conditions for operating the system under quasi-market conditions been created.

An interesting finding of the research is that as countries moved away from central steering of the system and toward various degrees of autonomy, they began creating more sophisticated forms of control through either indirect accountability mechanisms or direct monitoring. Among developing countries, Chile is perhaps the one that has moved farthest toward a quasi-market situation. There, the central government has kept strong control over most of the key levers of the system, such as curriculum design, student assessment, and teachers' professional development. Municipalities' managerial responsibilities are limited to staffing of municipal schools and

Table 8.2 Government-Initiated Partnerships Using Various Financial Support Schemes

	Supply-side financing	Demand-side financing	Shared financing	Market-based financing
Country example	Argentina	Colombia	Chile	China
Purpose	Increase access by encouraging private school development.	Alleviate the space constraints that prevent poor primary school graduates from enrolling in secondary school.	Increase enrollment and competition.	Provide diversified services.
Incentives	Subsidize the salaries of teachers and principals.	Provide vouchers to students from poor communities.	Subsidize schools according to the number of students enrolled.	Make available to fully private schools government loans or free land in the initial years but no financial subsidies.
Regulations	Subsidies vary from 30 to 100 percent, depending on tuition charged, socioeconomic conditions of students, and educational needs of the community, minimum class size is required to avoid having excessive number of teachers.	Students must enter grade 6, reside in low-income neighborhoods, and have previously attended public school. Vouchers can be renewed each year until graduation from secondary school. When demand exceeds supply, vouchers are allocated through a lottery. Schools must be private, nonprofit institutions.	Private schools are allowed to charge limited tuition, and the level of voucher payment is tied to the tuition charged. Students can enroll in any participating private school. Schools must comply with norms governing curriculum and infrastructure established by the ministry of education.	Schools must be accredited by the government and be regularly evaluated by the government for quality.

| Benefits and impact | Steady growth of private school enrollment, but a decline of students in the public system would not imply a need to reduce personnel and cut subsidies. | Within the first five years the program provided 100,000 vouchers to students from poor communities. | Private enrollment increased by 20 percent. There is no solid evidence that unrestricted choice has improved test scores, repetition rates, or years of schooling. | Students who failed to attain admission to public schools or who wish to attend boarding schools gain opportunities to study in private secondary schools. |

Sources: Delannoy 2000; Hsieh and Urquiola 2003; King et al. 1997; McEwan 2000b; Wang 2004.

Note: Countries in parentheses have similar financial support schemes.

Figure 8.2 Evolution of Models of Education Governance in Relation to Admission Models, Europe, Late 1970s to Present

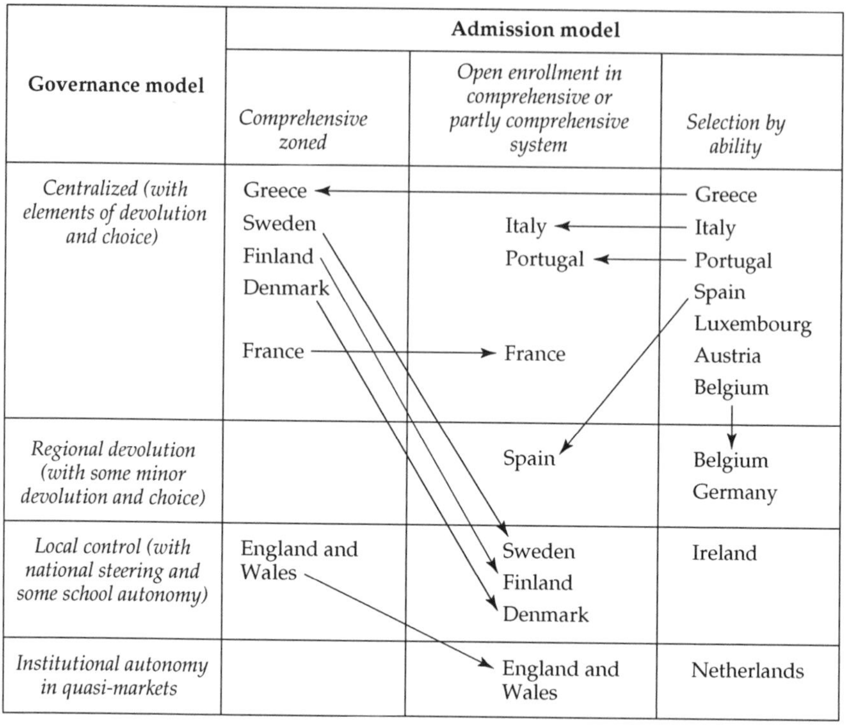

Governance model	Admission model		
	Comprehensive zoned	Open enrollment in comprehensive or partly comprehensive system	Selection by ability
Centralized (with elements of devolution and choice)	Greece, Sweden, Finland, Denmark, France	Italy, Portugal, France	Greece, Italy, Portugal, Spain, Luxembourg, Austria, Belgium
Regional devolution (with some minor devolution and choice)		Spain	Belgium, Germany
Local control (with national steering and some school autonomy)	England and Wales	Sweden, Finland, Denmark	Ireland
Institutional autonomy in quasi-markets		England and Wales	Netherlands

Sources: Green, Wolf, and Leney 1999; Hirvenoja 1999.

Note: Several countries experienced no change in governance or admission policy.

distribution of capitation grants, and schools' decision-making authority is restricted to the selection of pedagogical approaches and noncore curriculum areas (Delannoy 2000).

Managing the Political-Professional and Central-Local Tensions

One of the biggest challenges in moving from governing by rules administered by strong central authorities toward governing by objectives through local bodies and school empowerment is how to preserve an equivalent education nationwide and maintain quality standards. Governing by goals requires strong management capacity at the central, local, and school levels, to follow up on progress toward the goals, and a well-functioning system for monitoring and evaluation. Most important, it must be supported by a transparent process for formulating clear goals that are widely accepted and can be evaluated.

As experience with secondary education reform in Sweden demonstrates, at least three main conditions are necessary for the long-term success of these changes. First, those who are responsible for implementing the goals must understand why it is important to pursue a given goal, must agree on its desirability, and must have the skills and competencies required for reaching the goal. If this condition is not fulfilled, the stated goal will become mere rules. Second, education professionals must be held accountable for goals that they know and understand well. They should have a strong knowledge base, to interpret the goals and formulate them in a concrete way appropriate to students' needs and capabilities (Lundgren and Román 2003). Third, there should be a clear division of responsibilities among system and school actors, or between politicians and administrators and teachers and principals (Lindblad, Ozga, and Zambeta 2002), so that there is total clarity on who is accountable for what (see box 8.10).

We have used the two-axis framework (central-local and political-professional) to show that decentralization in secondary education must be seen as a balance between central and local governing, and between

---

Box 8.10 Engagement of Stakeholders in Policy Dialogue: Chile

In 1990 the government of Chile embarked on reform of the secondary education system. In order to define a common agenda that could gain wide support, the government initiated a broad research program to help identify needed changes in curriculum, pedagogy, teacher training, and supervision. A wide consultation process involving political parties, national ministries, schools, universities, businesses, churches, teachers, and community and grassroots organizations complemented the research effort. Universities and research centers became involved in identifying not only the strengths and weaknesses of the education system but also the way schools were responding to the demands of a changing labor market and the integration of the country into the global market. A central objective of this two-prong approach was to seek consensus on a common set of problems and principles that would serve as the basis for identifying policy options for reforming secondary education. The process was not devoid of conflicts and contradictions, but the end result was a program of reform that has been under implementation for the past 10 years.

Source: Cox 2004.

political and professional power and accountability (Lundgren 2002). In this sense, centralization and decentralization are not two poles of a continuum but complementary terms that need to be balanced. Countries can find the right balance by defining clear goals that are compatible with educational institutions' institutional and professional capacity to achieve them. Changes in the production structure of a country imply new demands and, inevitably, new education goals.

A review of national efforts to "modernize" governance makes it apparent that centralization-decentralization is a creative tension that countries have managed in very different ways, depending on how the competing political ideologies are negotiated within each country. In some cases centralization is pursued to create the conditions in which market forces can operate and different forms of competition and mixed forms of service provision can emerge. Central steering through target setting, monitoring, and evaluation requires the development of new management capacities at the center and at the local and school levels, as well as informed and active citizens. A condition for success is having the capacity to be receptive to information and to make responsible and informed decisions and choices. Raising the low levels of education found in many developing countries is a precondition for the successful introduction of self-managed, competition-based forms of governance. Inequalities resulting from the uneven distribution of these capacities and resources must be dealt with from the center.

The Organizational Challenges of Managing Secondary Schools

For an organization to prosper, its rate of learning must be at least equal to the rate of change in the external environment.
—David Hargreaves (2003), 17

Traditional Organizing Principles of Secondary Schools

Secondary schools as institutions have been reluctant to change, showing little responsiveness to the rapid transformations taking place around them in society and the workplace. Although the literature on school effectiveness is full of examples of how changes in school culture and leadership have led to improvements in student performance, such changes have had little effect on the core organizing principles of secondary schools, which can be summarized as follows:

- Teaching is organized around individual subjects, leading teachers to work in isolation. (In some schools, however, the establishment of subject-based departments has helped foster collaboration among teachers in the same department.)

- Teaching is framed by school schedules in which classes are broken into short intervals that are not necessarily related to each other.[1]
- A central assumption is that all students can learn at a similar pace on the same schedule.
- One consequence of subject teaching is large schools. This contributes to creating an environment experienced by students as uncaring.
- Catchment areas are larger than for primary schools. As a consequence, secondary schools may be governed by higher-level political-administrative units at a higher level than for primary schools.
- Management structures are more complex, reflecting the need to coordinate a larger body of staff and more complex schedules.
- There is not much lateral contact among secondary schools, even when they are under the same local authority. Schools therefore find it difficult to judge how they are faring in comparison with other schools, reducing the possibilities for sharing good practices.

Key Factors in Secondary School Effectiveness

Within these constraints, the capacity of schools to succeed and to produce excellent educational outcomes is the result of the interplay of several factors related to the intellectual assets of the school, the school working environment, and the deployment and utilization of resources. Hargreaves (2001) presents these factors as three forms of capital: intellectual, social, and organizational. The intellectual capital of a school is related to the skills, competencies, capabilities, talents, expertise, and practices of the staff, students, families, and communities. Social capital refers to cultural and social aspects that permeate the relationship among individuals inside the school and with the community. It is related to the trust that exists among all stakeholders involved with the school and to the sense of community, collaboration, and sharing that encourages the creation of strong networks both inside the school and with the surrounding community. Organizational capital refers to the capacity of the school as an institution to perform its primary function—to deploy, mobilize, make good use of, and continuously increase its human and social capital. Box 8.11 summarizes the effective-school literature using Hargreaves's framework, highlighting the findings that are most pertinent for secondary education.

An obvious conclusion emerging from the literature on school effectiveness is that in order to produce good educational outcomes, secondary schools need to move away from the "factory model," in which young adolescents are put on a conveyor belt and move from one individual teacher to the next to be doused with disconnected content on lessons administered

Box 8.11 Characteristics of Effective Secondary Schools

Intellectual capital

- Teachers have the knowledge, skills, and competencies to help all students learn and to accept responsibility for their own learning.
- School staffs believe that they have the capability to help all students achieve and reach their potential.
- The principal provides education leadership and supports continuous professional development to increase the competencies and involvement of staff.
- School staff has the know-how to decide "what goes and what stays" in the curriculum on the basis of a good professional understanding of how young adolescents learn.
- Teaching staff can design and deliver a curriculum that responds to the demands of accountability and is responsive to the social and developmental needs of students. Staff members are skilled at interdisciplinary curriculum.
- Parents and the school community understand and support the school's basic mission.
- The role of parents in the education of their children is clear, helping to forge real partnerships between home and school.

Social capital

- Teachers master the technology of teamwork; they do not work alone in isolated classrooms.
- There is a consistent practice of cooperative learning among students.
- All have high expectations for success; there is a generalized belief that all students can master essential knowledge, competencies, and skills.
- There is respect for human diversity and appreciation of democratic values.
- Leadership is a dispersed concept that includes all teaching staff. Teachers are empowered, so that the principal is not the only one providing leadership.

Organizational capital

- The school climate is positive, with a clearly articulated school mission and agreed goals.
- The school has a purposeful, safe, and orderly environment.
- The principal's leadership is focused on achievement of the agreed goals and the promotion of a school ethos oriented toward teaching and learning.

Box 8.11 Continued

- The principal is a leader of leaders rather than a leader of followers.
- There are appropriate structures and opportunities for collaboration.
- There is a proactive organizational response when students do not learn.
- The school exercises its power to abandon some less important content.
- Students' progress is monitored frequently. Assessment for learning receives central attention; less attention is given to assessment for grading purposes.
- The school has organizational structures that make it possible to pursue and take advantage of external support and community involvement.

Sources: Association for Effective Schools 1996; Bellei et al. 2004; A. Hargreaves 2003; Hill 2001; Lezotte 1991.

---

to them six or more times a day. Creating a teaching and learning environment that breaks away from this pattern is the real challenge of secondary school management. Primary schools, in comparison, have the advantage of smaller environments with a much more integrated curriculum and stronger culture of teamwork.

Over the past few decades educators and school administrators have been experimenting with organizational arrangements in secondary schools with the explicit aim of aligning teaching and learning with lessons learned from effective-school studies. One special concern has been to create learning spaces that are more responsive to the needs of individual students. There is significant research evidence showing that students attending small schools are more satisfied, better behaved, and more committed to academic achievement than students attending large schools (Gladden 1998; V. Lee 2000). These findings have called into question the traditional way of thinking about the optimum size of secondary schools, turning policy makers and education administrators slowly away from the efficiency-of-scale considerations that have dominated secondary school organization design for so long. The focus on student learning and accountability has revitalized the idea that "small is better" when it comes to the organization of secondary schools.

The downscaling idea is by no means new. It has, for example a long tradition in the United Kingdom in the form of "houses" and in the United States in the form of "minischools" or "schools-within-schools," which have existed in Texas since 1919 (Raywid 1996). What is new in current proposals is the focus on a broad concept of school effectiveness that encompasses both student learning and social, affective, and noncognitive outcomes such as students' attitude toward school, school attendance, truancy, and level of participation in nonacademic activities. A pressing need of secondary education in today's world is to keep young people committed to education by making schools a place where they want to spend more of their time (Gray 2004). Smaller learning environments seem to work well in furthering this goal (Gladden 1998; V. Lee 2000).

The idea of small schools does not necessarily mean small buildings; on the contrary, in urban areas where land is at a premium, it is difficult to avoid having large school buildings. The establishment of smaller learning environments that reduce the *experience size* of schools is the defining concept, rather than the size of the building. A more appropriate term for this idea is perhaps schools-within-schools, with variants that include house plans, minischools, and learning communities (Raywid 1996). Box 8.12 summarizes some of the similarities and differences between these types of small school.

Box 8.12 Main Characteristics of Different Types of Small School

Similarities

- The "organic" or "communal" organizational form is facilitated by the small, manageable size, ranging from 300 to 900 students.
- There is a clearly defined school identity and mission and an emphasis on faculty sharing the same philosophy.
- Autonomous entities control key decisions on curriculum, personnel, students, budget, and organization.
- The focus is on personalized education; teachers know their students well.
- Teachers are expected to assume multiple roles, increasing their involvement in decision making and empowering them.
- Governance relies on school-based teams, teacher-teaming, or teacher-based decision-making processes.
- The curriculum is interdisciplinary, sometimes organized around themes.
- Interest-based grouping (rather than tracking by ability levels) facilitates grouping students by their own choice.

Differences

Schools-within-schools

- Multiple school units are housed within a school building, with a host school as an anchor.

Box 8.12 Continued

- A building principal decides on issues related to building operation, but individual schools report to the local education officer.
- Each school is an autonomous entity with its own program, staff, and students and its own separate budget.

Minischools

- Schools are independent from each other; each has its own program, which is most of the time different from that of the larger school or the coschools.
- Although the minischools do not have a status separate from the larger school, each enjoys school autonomy, with its own teachers and students.
- Each minischool depends on a single principal and the budget and staff of the larger school.

House plans

- Students across grades are organized in houses within a school.
- Teachers are assigned to houses.
- Students take most of their coursework with their housemates and the same house teachers.
- Houses share in extracurricular activities.
- Houses can change every year or can be organized on a multiyear basis.
- Each house has its own plan, which is overlaid on school departments.

Learning communities

- Students are organized in houses or focus areas to provide them with a sense of belonging and give focus to the curriculum.
- The houses and focus areas operate within a larger, comprehensive, buildingwide program structure, under one principal.
- Teams of teachers share common groups of students and follow them for several years in order to know students better and create more personalized learning experiences for them.
- Use of alternative scheduling allows teachers to develop lessons that are more compatible with learning objectives and to facilitate work-based learning opportunities, integrating business and community volunteers into the curriculum.

Sources: Cotton 2001; Dewees 1999; D. Hargreaves 2001; Irmsher 1997; Raywid 1996; Rissman 2000.

The primary challenge in creating smaller learning environments is to identify the core programmatic elements that will define the identity and mission of the school. The main design aspects to take into consideration when designing these environments are (a) how much autonomy each subunit will have and what will be done to ensure collaboration, (b) what type of program each subunit will offer and how separate the subunits will be from each other and from the larger institution, and (c) what organizational structure they will adopt individually and collectively. The challenge is to create conditions that enable schools to maximize their human, social, and organizational capital. As Andy Hargreaves (2003) points out, through collaboration and networking, an education institution increases its social capital, and by increasing its social capital the school also increases its intellectual and human capital.

Research on small schools suggests that positive impacts on students include greater self-esteem and satisfaction with school (V. Lee 2000; Raywid 1996; Robinson-Lewis 1991; Tompkins 1988), less likelihood of dropping out, and increased commitment by students to one another and to their teachers. Positive impacts on teachers are reflected in increased job satisfaction and motivation (Robinson-Lewis 1991). Evidence related to improvement of students' academic achievement is less conclusive. Some studies find that small schools do contribute to increased educational achievement (Crain, Heebner, and Si 1992; Robinson-Lewis 1991), while others indicate that these schools produce modest or mixed gains (Morriseau 1975). A problem with the operation of small schools is that they can be divisive and lead to conflict by weakening preexisting relationships (Raywid 1996). There is also the potential for inequitable tracking if students are grouped by criteria unrelated to their interests.

One clear advantage of smaller schools is that students have opportunities to choose programs and to move without losing their reference group of peers. In addition, schools have more opportunities to collaborate, to gauge how well they are doing in comparison with other schools, and to actively exchange good practices. All this should lead to gains in the social, organizational, and intellectual capital of the school.

From a cost perspective, there is concern that small schools could be more expensive than large ones. On a cost-per-student-enrolled basis, smaller schools are somewhat more expensive, but if cost-effectiveness is factored in and cost is examined on the basis of the number of students graduating, small schools are clearly less expensive than medium-size or large high schools (Raywid 1996).

A different approach to improving school performance is school-based management (SBM), a managerially inspired policy initiative aimed at improving school performance by transferring to schools key managerial responsibilities such as power (authority) over budget, personnel, and curriculum. Although there is scant evidence that school-based management initiatives have improved school effectiveness and student achievement across the board (Wohlstetter and Mohrman 1996), there is clear accumulated evidence that under certain conditions SBM could lead to improvement in teaching and learning conditions in schools. These conditions are as follows:[2]

- SBM is part of an overall strategy of school improvement encompassing all levels, from school to regional authorities. Schools are empowered with knowledge and information, and rewards are contingent on performance and contribution. The new role of local and regional education authorities is one of support and encouragement through incentives.
- The main task of principals is to ensure constant school improvement. This implies a continuous focus on educational change, active educational leadership, and delegation of other leadership and managerial tasks to administrative staff. Principals must receive continuous support to "learn" their new role through formal training and mentoring.
- Since group management is not always the most effective means of school management, there must be a balance between group empowerment and empowerment of the school principal. Decision-making power is shared by a multimember, teacher-led team with clearly defined accountability (see box 8.13) and resources.
- The role of teachers changes—from being responsible for managing their own classroom to actively participating in shaping the school environment, working with other stakeholders, and taking responsibility for resource allocation and use.
- There must be continuous investment in schoolwide training in functional and process skills and in areas related to curriculum and instruction.
- Rewards should include both extrinsic motivators, such as pay and opportunities for professional development, and intrinsic ones, such as an environment of collaborative work with peers.

The Evolving Role of Principals

As more decision-making power and responsibilities move down to schools, the figure of the principal comes to center stage. Principals must lead and manage the change in the mission of the school from delivering stable, centrally defined educational content to devising learning strategies that are responsive to the characteristics and needs of young adolescents and to the continuous transformation of the workplace. Furthermore, they have the responsibility for developing solid and permanent partnerships with families and communities in order to create ownership and encourage investment by the local community in their school. This is particularly important in developing countries, where self-generated resources are an important funding source for school operation.

Box 8.13 Teacher-Led Decision-Making Teams

The establishment of teacher-led decision-making teams that cut across the school both horizontally and vertically allows the involvement of teachers and parents in the school's decision-making processes. Their creation facilitates interaction across the traditional boundaries of departments and grade levels. Some of these teams include subcommittees of school councils that are open to both teachers and parents. The most effective school councils are those dedicated to coordinating and integrating the activities of the various decision-making groups operating throughout the school. The role of the councils is to focus on the needs of the school as a whole rather than on the needs of individual academic departments or teaching teams by providing leadership and direction for the changes taking place in the school and by allocating resources to support these changes.

Other teams are formed exclusively by teachers and are incorporated in the consensus-building process for school decisions. These groups are concerned with topics such as curriculum, assessment, and professional development. They help address day-to-day professional and management issues, thus facilitating communication and promoting reflective dialogue around specific tasks. By widening faculty involvement in the decision-making process beyond the select few on the school council, the teams help reduce the workload on individual teachers, promote participation, and deepen the commitment to change.

Source: Wohlstetter and Mohrman 1996.

Table 8.3 is a stylized presentation of the main changes that are taking place in the principal's role. What is interesting is that as schools are given more autonomy, the new roles are added to the traditional ones, which would imply that principals should be receiving extra support until the new organizational culture is firmly established.

In reviewing experience with school-based management, Cotton (1992) observes that the role of principals is subject to the greatest degree of change.

- The change is sometimes expressed as reconceptualizing the principal's role from that of "boss" to that of chief executive officer with a strong educational leadership mandate.
- Instead of enforcing policies made elsewhere, which inevitably sets the principal apart from the staff, the principal works collegially with staff, sharing authority with them.

Table 8.3 Changing Roles of School Principals

Traditional roles	New roles
Maintaining administrative control	Problem solving, crisis management, and decision making
Ordering supplies	Physical facilities management
Ensuring teacher supply and assignments	Instructional leadership
Performing bureaucratic routines	Performance accountability
Basic record keeping	Resource management and generation
Maintaining communications between school and ministry	Management of communications with higher levels and surrounding communities

Source: Authors' compilation, 2004.

- The principal typically moves closer to the educational process, serving as an instructional manager.
- The principal moves higher in the district chain of command because of the increased authority and accountability that shift to the school.

Roles and expectations of principals may vary among and within counties. In the French system, for example, principals are expected to focus on administration, while the British system emphasizes the role of principals or head teachers as leaders in pedagogy. The small-school and school-based management models, however, require that principals have instructional knowledge and leadership skills. Thus, the new role of the principal entails being a motivator, instructional leader, team coordinator, and facilitator in order to fulfill the expectations for the school.

A typical day for secondary school principals is often filled with administrative responsibilities such as managing personnel and budgeting, organizing teaching activities, dealing with crises and conflicts between teachers and students, and handling relations with parents and the community. Most principals tend to gravitate toward the inevitable administrative duties, and few act as instructional leaders for teaching and learning improvement.

If, however, the goal is to build a learning community in which all students acquire the full range of knowledge and skills necessary for their future, the principal's role as instructional leader is vital. In this context, an instructional leader needs to be able to motivate teachers and improve teaching practices. These tasks require a great deal of knowledge about the details of the curriculum, teaching methods, and student learning. In this capacity, the principal needs to be a resource provider, instructional resource, and communicator and to have a visible presence. Table 8.4 illustrates this with four models for instructional leaders at the secondary level.

Table 8.4 Secondary Principals' Behavior as Instructional Leaders: Four Composite Portraits

Model	Resource provider	Instructional resource	Communicator	Visible presence
A	• Uses lottery, observations • Regularly distributes educational articles to update staff • Departmental meetings used to develop curriculum • Seen as an aggressive fund-raiser	• Models teaming • Feedback sought by teachers as they prepared for a presentation for a board meeting	• Communicates "I care" by being a good listener • Articulate spokesperson for not labeling students	• Always seen in rooms, hallways, at school events; "ever present" • Accessible—always seen as having time for everyone • Everybody seems to know what this person stands for
B	• Invests in the improvement of department heads through special training • Taps businesses and political leaders for school support • Uses staff talent in budget development through faculty senate	• Pushes teachers to expand into new ways of teaching to improve instruction • Shares data and helps staff interpret meaning of data for their school	• Lets staff know that everyone can grow professionally • Regularly gives staff members feedback concerning their performance • Regularly gives department heads feedback • Shares decision making through use of senate	• Hall walker • Strategically selection of office in order to be visible • Master consensus builder • Always seems to be where the action is taking place

C	• Provides released time for staff to learn to work as a team • Staff ideas used as a resource • Much teacher-to-teacher observation and peer coaching	• Spends a great deal of time observing teachers in classrooms • Inspires teachers with knowledge of curriculum • Provides data concerning the school's performance to both teachers and staff	• Staff members know they must keep their feet to the fire • Accountability is prized and expected • Inspires others with understanding of how students learn	• Bob's businesslike tone is ever present in the school • Seems to be everywhere • Parent coffee hours are used to discuss school matters
D	• Uses team concept with common planning period to help teachers grow • Astute allocator of budget; gets a bang out of every dollar	• Demonstrates good teaching by taking over classrooms • Inspires teachers with knowledge of innovations	• Developed a program improvement council to spread ideas • Communicates the importance of students and parents through involvement	• Knows all kids in the school • No matter what is going on, always seems accessible

Source: Smith and Andrews 1989.

How can such school leaders be developed? Fink and Resnick (2001) note that even in the United States, few principals come to their position fully skilled in all the elements of instructional knowledge and leadership skills; even those with substantial capacities will need sustained support from the district level. Drawing on the success of an 11-year program of school improvement in New York's District 2, the authors outline effective organizational support measures at the district level for building principals' instructional leadership skills and so promoting student achievement. Such support could include:

- *Principals' conferences and institutes:* a daylong conference every month to discuss new instructional initiatives, revisit and evaluate old initiatives, explore approaches for improving learning, and find out how to use test scores as a guide to effective practice.
- *Support group and study group:* new principals' group that focuses on how to develop effective teaching strategies and techniques for assessing student learning, evaluation methods for teacher instructional performance, and skills for designing and carrying out in-school teacher conferences. Study group guide focuses on content area or problems of practice.
- *Peer learning:* visits by a principal to another principal's school to observe specific practice, or frequent informal meetings of small groups of principals to share problems and strategies of professional development and leadership.
- *Individualized coaching:* activities organized by the district superintendent and deputy superintendent to provide individual coaching for principals needing help in setting objectives or in matching the school budget with instructional and professional development plans. Such coaching also takes place between principals: those judged to be expert work with those who need help.

The principal's role as instructional leader may be crucial in developed and developing countries alike, yet in developing countries in particular, this role can be limited by additional responsibilities. In addition to all their administrative duties, principals in many African countries have to deal with issues relating to the loss of teachers resulting from HIV/AIDS. Within the context of education decentralization, many principals, especially in developing countries, are responsible for raising funds for schools. In countries where school principals' responsibilities mainly consist of fund-raising, principals can rarely focus on teaching and learning, and their role as instructional leaders will be substantially reduced. To support principals' instructional leadership, a good education system must provide resources so that principals can focus on teaching and learning.

Involving Parents and Communities

When students enter the adolescent years, parents may become less able to influence their behavior and increasingly lose touch with schools. Parents' participation in secondary schools is also hindered by the fact that young people tend not to share their school experiences with parents. Moreover, many parents do not live in the neighborhood where the schools are located. Yet parental and family involvement is considered crucial in the overall development of youths and in crisis resolution. A UNESCO (Ohsako 1997) study reveals that among the main causes of school violence are lack of parental supervision, punitive parents with unclear disciplinary orientation, family breakup, and lack of strong, supportive family values.

Dynamic principals and teachers nevertheless find ways to engage parents. Experience from an effective secondary school in a high-poverty, low-performance school in New York indicates that holding educational meetings and courses for parents, involving parents in school committees, and drawing parents into the discussion of issues that matter to them are effective ways of influencing students (Langer 2004). Other innovative examples include providing parents with regular updates on the curriculum, assessment plans, school profiles, and school programs. Some principals buy space in local newspapers to share school events and report student successes (Brown and Anfara 2002). In some Latin American countries opportunities were offered, through community centers, churches, mosques, youth clubs, and professional associations, for parents to learn how to understand, care for, discipline, and educate youths (Mayorga Salas 1997).

With the growing recognition that involvement of parents is crucial for school effectiveness, parent participation in school governance increasingly takes place through formal organizations. South Africa has moved farther among Sub-Saharan African countries in introducing countrywide, school-based governance, where parents serve as majority members of governing bodies. The South African School Act provides for the election of school governing bodies (SGBs) by students, parents, and staff. The SGBs' functions include determination of school admission policy, setting language policy, recommending teaching and nonteaching appointments, managing finance, determining school fees, and conducting fund-raising. Principals and teachers, however, do not necessarily value parent participation, and so such participation is often little more than information sharing or limited consultation decided on by principals and teachers to make their work easier. This kind of participation does not stimulate substantial organizational change; rather, it reinforces existing patterns of power and privilege in schools and in the broader society (Grant Lewis and Naidoo 2004). Similarly, in Indonesia parent involvement through parent-teacher associations (PTAs) mainly consists of setting and helping to collect PTA fees; parents have a minimal role in monitoring school activities (Alatas and Filmer 2004).

Although many countries have recognized the value of involving students in school governing boards, participation often has not developed into real decision making. One of the most important lessons from the experiences in South Africa and other countries is that if parents and students are to be engaged in a meaningful way, not only policy makers but also principals and teachers must acknowledge the value of parents and the community in school management. To achieve effective participation, principals should understand and listen to parents and act on their views concerning school improvement.

Conclusion

The industrial-age type of school that produced "standard outputs" through uniform teaching processes centered on individual teachers and a subject-fractured curriculum is no longer relevant in a global information society where knowledge, innovation, and the introduction of technology are the drivers of improvement in productivity and economic growth. The traditional mode of organizing education allowed secondary mass education to flourish and to dramatically increase its output, but it also created rigid structures and processes that hampered educational institutions and organizations from responding quickly to the twin challenges of rapidly expanding access to secondary education and improving quality and relevance while reducing inequality in education.

Education decision-making structures have undergone accelerated transformation since the late 1960s. Although the articulation of relationships between decision-making levels and actors has become more flexible, this flexibility has introduced increased complexity as new actors and new modes of power distribution and linkage among levels emerge. The long-established form of governance based on a system of publicly authorized, publicly funded, and publicly operated schools supported by centrally defined norms and regulations is being replaced by an array of governance arrangements in which the central government continues to play a central role in steering and monitoring the system but lower-level governments and the private sector share in the funding and operation of schools. Hybridization of education governance is taking place as the environment within which educational institutions operate evolves.

- The hierarchical chain of command is becoming less important than the relationships among the various players within the education system.
- Division of responsibilities between central authorities and schools is developing into a balanced set of arrangements. Central or regional authorities not only define the steering document that guides the work

of schools but also provide technical support and resources to ensure that schools succeed. Schools, for their part, have autonomy to develop their own curricula to fit the demands of their students within the framework provided by the steering document.

- A system of evaluation and quality assurance, operating in harmony with a system of incentives, technical support, and advice, is becoming a key instrument for central governance.
- Evaluation and quality assurance mechanisms are evolving on the basis of an agreed division of responsibilities among the system's managerial levels, with each level taking full responsibility for monitoring processes and outcomes within its area of competence.
- Schools are building active exchange and strong two-way relationships with the communities they serve.

From an organizational standpoint, the operation of schools should rest on a new set of principles that reflect the need for flexibility, adaptation, responsiveness, and continuous learning. If the appropriate metaphor for describing the industrial model of schooling is the *mechanical system*, a useful metaphor for visualizing the operation of schools in an information-dense environment is *living systems;* that is, organizations structured around relationships, with built-in capacity to continually evolve and renew themselves. Thus, the most important gauges of success for schools are the capacity to respond to diversity and change and the readiness of individual members to balance their particular self-interest with the interest of the larger whole and to form partnerships and collaboration. Schools of this type have several salient features:

- The principal plays a pivotal leadership role in the operation of the school by facilitating and coordinating the work of teachers individually and in teams and by nurturing relationships among school players and fostering change. The managerial role, although important, is subordinated to the responsibility for leadership.
- Schools work in collaboration, not in isolation. Cooperation among principals is the keystone of this collaboration.
- Teachers are motivated to work in teams. There is a real community of learners, formed by teaching staff, administrators, and students engaged in the pursuit of knowledge and the promotion of critical thinking. The organization of the school allows all staff to take advantage of the "collective competence" embedded within its boundaries. In other words, social capital stimulates the growth of intellectual capital.

These features, which summarize the main directions for the transformation of secondary education, have a solid empirical basis (Sharan, Shachar, and Levine 1999) derived from the examination of real experiences of "successful" schools. This is, however, by no means an exhaustive list, and it does not pretend to be an agenda for change that should be applied everywhere. The direction, features, and content of the transformed system should be specific to the socioeconomic situation of each country and the capacity of the education system to generate and assimilate change. The final shape of the transformed system will depend on the implementation capacity of the parties involved, the degree of acceptance of or resistance to change, and how the initiatives are implemented.

Notes

1. It is not uncommon to find that secondary school schedules call for six classes per day five times a week. Some variations of this pattern include block scheduling, in which some part of the daily schedule is organized into larger blocks of time.

2. This section is adapted from the assessment of school-based management conducted by Wohlstetter and Mohrman (1996).

Epilogue
Rethinking Secondary Education

Ignorant nations are always enslaved, superficially educated ones are ungovernable, truly educated ones are free.

—Angel Ganivet, *Cartas Finlandesas* (1898)

... the answer does not lie in designing better reform strategies. No amount of sophistication in strategizing for particular innovations or policies will ever work. It is simply unrealistic to expect that introducing reforms one by one ... in a situation which is basically not organized to engage in change will do anything but give reform a bad name.

—Michael Fullan, *Change Forces* (1993), 3

Strong political leadership, consistency, and transparency will be needed if reform of secondary education is to enjoy legitimacy and long-term sustainability. This is the main lesson emerging from the background papers commissioned for this report, which reviewed secondary education reforms in countries and places as different as Brazil, Chile, Finland, Hong Kong (China), the Republic of Korea, and Sweden.[1] The biggest challenge faced by all reforms is to change the deeply rooted mental models of schooling and education governance that dominate current thinking and policy practices both inside and outside the education community. These models and archetypes are powerful obstacles to much-needed innovation in the organization of secondary education systems and in the structuring of learning.

The widespread institutional model that proved so successful in supporting the expansion of primary and basic education and even of secondary schooling in many countries during the 1980s and 1990s is no longer suitable for the emerging educational needs of fast-changing societies. The task before today's societies is to transform secondary education institutions and current schooling practices to align them better with the needs and demands of a dense, overloaded, information environment.

Are the challenges surrounding the immediate future of secondary education the same for low-, middle-, and high-income countries? A first response might be, no. As discussed in chapter 4, the assumption that it is possible to find uniform and orthodox solutions that are applicable to every country's situation is highly questionable. Most developing countries will need to face more complex challenges than will developed ones. This is because developing countries have to deal simultaneously with problems of provision and quality and, more important, to do so under serious financial and institutional constraints. But the question might also, on the basis of the same evidence, be answered with an unqualified yes. Developing countries, like developed ones, are affected by the speed of new scientific discoveries and by technological and organizational innovations that transcend frontiers, and the impetus in this direction is unlikely to diminish. Consequently, education systems everywhere will need to be reorganized to be more flexible and more responsive to local needs and global demands.

The effort to expand access and improve the quality of secondary education demands transformation of the approach to policy making and of institutional practice in general. Given the new pressures resulting from globalization and the need to accelerate the expansion of secondary education opportunities, policies that fail to target the core characteristics of prevailing systems of secondary schooling have a limited chance of success. In other words, doing *more of the same* is not the way to meet the challenges facing secondary education.

Is It Just *More of the Same?* The Case for Transforming Secondary Education Policy and Practice

Will the model for expanding secondary education follow, in structural terms, the one used for primary and basic education? Are policies aimed at expanding access to secondary education and improving its quality and relevance fundamentally a matter of providing more of the same? The answer is a resounding no, for numerous reasons having to do with the peculiarities of the secondary education structure—its organization, delivery modes, curriculum, governance, and financial arrangements. Some examples will illustrate the difficulties for policy stemming from the distinctive features of secondary education.

- *Financial arrangements.* Past lessons from the drive to improve participation rates at the primary level are not applicable to secondary education. To begin with, the availability of lower secondary schools in no way approaches the ubiquity of primary schools in many countries, even given that many primary schools do not have a full complement of grades. Several studies (for example, ADE-KAPE 2003) have pointed out that direct and opportunity costs are greater inhibitors of secondary school than of primary school enrollments. These costs are estimated to be 10 times higher for secondary education than for the primary level. The effort to accelerate participation rates at the lower secondary school level will likely require a combination of supply-side and demand-side interventions.

- *Structural peculiarities of the secondary sector.* Structural differences between primary and secondary education manifest themselves, for example, in recruitment and assignment of teachers for the rural areas where the great majority of students in developing countries live. Research findings suggest that whereas many primary school teachers are native to the localities where they teach, this is not generally so for secondary school teachers. Teacher shortages at the secondary school level have therefore tended to be much more severe, leading to high rates of absenteeism, overcrowding of classrooms, and, in some cases, teacher incompetence. These problems are of a decidedly supply-side nature.

- *Curriculum differentiation in secondary education.* A diversified curriculum is one of the keys to retaining students in the secondary education system, preventing dropout, and ensuring relevant and meaningful certification and accreditation leading to job market entry and to further educational and training opportunities. Curriculum differentiation as a basic and essential trait of secondary education has important financial implications and calls for more complex governance and managerial arrangements, for more efficient and varied external support to schools and teachers, and for more sophisticated counseling and guidance services to support students.

- *Methodological and pedagogical issues.* Especially in low-income countries, expansion of access to secondary education must be accompanied by major changes in the way education services are delivered. The choice of delivery mode has inescapable quality and equity implications peculiar to secondary education.

- *Political considerations.* Building political consensus for secondary education reform has proved to be a much more difficult task than it was or is for expansion and reform of primary and tertiary education. Moreover, unlike those levels of education, secondary education suffers from a lack of national champions and strong international lobbies.

For all these reasons, the established policy framework of education—the sequence of first ensuring access and then focusing on quality—is not viable for secondary education. It is not enough to "open the doors" of the system if poor-quality, irrelevant schooling eventually leads a majority of youngsters to drop out of secondary school. The "open doors" become "revolving doors" as young people, their rising expectations of the education system disappointed, vote with their feet. This failure would lead to a serious crisis of legitimacy for the entire education system, especially since it would mean that a subsector with a mandate to be inclusive was becoming de facto exclusionary.

Regardless of whether more of the same would be financially viable for any country, policies in that direction are unlikely to bridge the growing quality gap between education-rich and education-poor countries. What is needed now is to find new ways to address old problems. New approaches can include combining structural reforms aimed at changing how schooling is organized and instruction is delivered with targeted interventions to ensure that real opportunities are opened to the poor and the excluded and that these groups are in a position to take full advantage of the benefits.

Trade-Offs in Secondary Education Policy: The Old and the New

Secondary education has traditionally been framed by perennial policy trade-offs that have informed and shaped policy discourse and mental maps worldwide. This report has examined in more or less depth the most critical ones: quality and equity, efficiency and equity, the general-vocational balance, and centralization and decentralization. Traditional frameworks are being reformulated and have been superseded in many countries. They reflect cultural and political molds that it has been necessary to break in an environment of soaring demand and massive participation in secondary education. This section looks at the state of the long-standing trade-offs and at the new alternatives that education policy makers confront.

Quality and equity. Traditionally, debate on education policy has emphasized access issues in primary education and quality issues in tertiary education. For secondary education, equity issues are the central ones. Equity can be understood as the policy area at the intersection of access and quality, and this area has the greatest implications for secondary education. It is at the secondary level that students begin to be tracked or streamed into different programs and groups and have to face high-stakes examinations that condition the terms of certification and transition to the labor market or to further education. This is also the time when students are required to make the first important decisions about their intellectual affiliations, when schools are expected to both counsel and sort students, and when parents all over the world are ready to invest heavily in private tutoring to help their children succeed (Bray 1999).

In many countries the big equity divide lies between lower and upper secondary. For example, in China data for 2003 reveal that enrollment was 88.7 percent in lower secondary education and decreased sharply, to 43.0 percent, in upper secondary. It does not come as a surprise that the equity debate on education is centered at just that level of schooling.

Efficiency and equity. Progress toward mass secondary education systems requires efficient allocation and use of scarce financial and human resources. As a general rule, inefficiency in the provision of social services harms the poor and the vulnerable (World Bank 2003f). The agenda for democratizing secondary education therefore needs to be based on careful and detailed analysis of efficient resource deployment and maximization of efficiency gains.

General-vocational balance. In a rapidly changing environment driven by the application of knowledge and innovation, competencies and skills tend to depreciate and become irrelevant much faster than in the immediate past. As a result, the once sharp divide between general and vocational skills in secondary education is shifting and fading as demand for knowledge and information-intensive skills grows.

Centralization and decentralization. Efficient and responsive delivery of educational services calls for decision making that is closer to the students. Flexible and adaptable delivery of services can be promoted by competent and professional staff through school-based decision making. At the same time, to ensure that service provision is also responsive to and aligned with country needs, a strong central or national steering system is indispensable, together with monitoring capacity, professional support, and political consensus on clear and transparent rules and regulations. In short, as progress is made toward decentralization, the active role of the state becomes more important than ever.

In sharp contrast to old trade-offs that are no longer so relevant, a number of relatively new and emerging policy dilemmas are implicit in contemporary approaches to thinking and decision making in secondary education. Some important ones are summarized here.

Competitiveness and inclusiveness. Increased emphasis on education as the key to national competitiveness reinforces the selective and sorting functions of secondary schooling, thus potentially taking a huge toll on the inclusiveness of a system. This dilemma emerges at a time when secondary school inclusiveness is crucial to building citizenship and to the very sustainability of an education system.

Curriculum modernization and teachers' professional identity. Growing consensus on the need to modernize curricula around the new competencies of an information-dense society has to accommodate secondary teachers' professional identity, which is still being defined and shaped by traditional disciplines.

Trend toward smaller schools and a broader curriculum. Consistent evidence about the beneficial effects of smaller secondary schools on student achievement and well-being is difficult to balance with the imperative to be responsive to students' needs through a broader and increasingly diverse curriculum.

Local, classroom-based assessment and national and public examinations. The tension between competitiveness and inclusiveness is reflected in contrasting views about evaluating student achievement. While classroom-based assessment is being promoted as an education-oriented, learner-centered form of student assessment, national high-stakes examinations persist as a governing tool for steering the system by means of signals and incentives that affect the behavior of students, parents, teachers, and administrators.

Emphasis on outputs and impact. The battle to improve the quality of secondary education has recently shifted from an inputs-based policy approach to an output-based one. Many countries are placing heavy emphasis on standardized test results as the only available proxy for educational quality. But the stress on outputs will lead to a new transition that will highlight the pressure to evaluate the impact of secondary schooling on critical elements of well-being such as health, income, citizenship, productivity, employability, empowerment, community development, and strengthening of democracy.

Low-tech and high-tech solutions to teaching and learning materials. In low-income countries especially, there is a mounting tension between the need to provide basic teaching and learning aids, particularly textbooks, and growing pressure to close the technology gap, in the context of national strategies for the information society and e-development alternatives and of a perceived urgency about not being left behind. Doubts about the leapfrogging potential of ICTs are mounting, even as decision makers are primed to embark on major investments in this area.

The Political Dimension of Change in Secondary Education

The deeply entrenched structure of the institution of secondary education, which evolved in a relatively information-poor society (Lundgren 2002), cannot be transformed within the four or five years of an elected administration's term. Change will take much longer and can only be the result of a powerful combination of forces inside and outside the education system.

Established education policies have conceived of expansion of secondary education as a gradual and orderly process and have treated the education needs of youngsters as a closed system by presenting them with linear paths of learning experiences to be followed in a prescribed sequence. These policies give little or no consideration to the explosive rate of growth in demand for secondary education or the wide diversity in young peoples' interests, attitudes, social backgrounds, and aptitudes. Such policies have de facto limited expansion of educational opportunities beyond primary education. Innovative policies should focus on making secondary education a diversified and flexible system that provides young people with wide-ranging options to enter and leave secondary education institutions at different points and that is able to use diversified instruments to assess and certify skills and competencies (OECD 1999). This general vision of the system would help guide the transformation process;

it does not pretend to be an all-encompassing, universally valid policy statement.

Reviews of recent secondary education reform initiatives conducted for this study[1] have helped identify the following key strategic policy orientations for decision makers to bear in mind when designing and implementing systemwide policies for transforming secondary education institutions and practices:

1. There is more than one way of proceeding with improvements; no general formulas or "magic bullets" exist for transforming secondary education. In other words, there are no ready-made, off-the-shelf solutions or best practices that can be applied regardless of country-specific conditions and challenges. Nevertheless, some lessons have been learned in the process of expanding secondary education and improving its quality, and these are helpful in framing the policy debate and dialogue in a country.

2. Energy should be directed toward a number of levers found inside and outside the education system. When agents inside and outside the system push together, each working on different aspects of the transformation process, the chances of real and lasting improvement become significantly higher. For instance, both the contemporary push for accountability from outside the school system and the matching drive for autonomy from inside the school underline the need for highly skilled, competent education professionals.

3. Transformation is a continuous process requiring leadership, political support, consensus building, energy, and resources. Since frequent turnovers in top political and administrative positions disrupt changes that are under way, the continuity and success of the change effort can be ensured only by continual consensus-building exercises and the deep commitment of school leadership to a shared vision.

4. The transformation process must be continuously informed by relevant regional, local, school, and student data. On the one hand, monitoring and evaluation systems are needed as system improvement tools, permitting the identification of strengths and weaknesses. On the other hand, capacity building must be reinforced so that decision makers, school leaders, and practitioners are empowered to effectively use the data and evidence available to them to design the best possible services for students.

5. Schools operate in different contexts, and so they react in different ways to similar policies. External support to schools must be targeted, diverse, and flexible. Education reform must combine efforts to improve the best schools even more (moving ahead) with efforts to close the gap between the least effective and the most effective schools (leveling up). This is exactly the way schools and classroom teachers should function, especially given the increasing diversity of secondary students.

6. An important management strategy for successfully implementing new policies is a concerted focus on improving teaching and learning at the classroom level. The primary vehicle for this effort is well-defined, sustained, and coordinated professional development of teachers.

Countries seek to increase the number of secondary school graduates with the skills to identify and solve problems and make contributions to society throughout their lives. A fundamental tenet of modern learning theory is that different learning goals require different instructional approaches. New goals for education require changes in opportunities to learn. From a micro policy or school perspective, the core principles of transformation can be articulated as follows:

- *The learner-centered principle.* Make the learner the center of all decisions. That is, every effort to transform the schooling environment where learning takes place must be oriented to the concerns, interests, and needs of youths. Focusing on students as learners can be a catalyst for the practical transformation of teaching and learning in schools.
- *The inclusiveness principle.* Act in the interests of all students, but pay special attention to offering equal education opportunities to all youngsters by implementing targeted programs aimed at reaching low-income students, girls, and minorities.
- *The flexibility and customization principle.* Ensure that content delivery is flexible and customized to the students' concrete situation and needs.
- *The contextualization principle.* Focus special attention on the context in which the transformation will take place by forging strong connections between the school system and local communities and by linking teachers with youths.

Policy makers, experts, and research-based policy advisers matter and are much needed. But the final content of transformation should be community centered to ensure continuity and sustainability. This means a transformation driven by local problems based on local research capacity and local governance structures that facilitate change and citizens' engagement.

The overall change effort is never explicit in its fullness; rather, it operates as a "hidden education policy" (Kivirauma, Rinne, and Seppänen 2003) in which a succession of small but interconnected changes in curriculum, resource allocation, funding, and governance arrangements result in an entirely new course of action. The most important ingredient of a transformation strategy is the process of generating a shared vision through the promotion of active policy debate among all stakeholders. Experience from other countries and findings from research can contribute to the debate. This policy report is intended to be just such a contribution.

The report provides strategic directions for reconstituting external aid for secondary education in developing countries. Appendix J outlines the World Bank's strategy and support for secondary education projects and programs to date. Looking ahead, steps could be taken to strategically align projects and programs toward addressing the recommendations contained in the report.

Note

1. The background papers are by Aho and Pitkänen (2003); Cox (2004); Kim (2002); Lundgren and Román (2003); and Souza (2003).

Appendix A
Structure of Education Systems and Compulsory Education

Most-common organizations of secondary cycles

All / first stage	Second stage	Third stage	Predominant region
Preparatory, complementary	General secondary		Middle East and North Africa
Basic secondary	Middle / diversified secondary		Central America, Andes
Middle school	Secondary school	Higher secondary	Some countries in Africa and Latin America
Middle / lower secondary	Upper secondary	Higher secondary	South Asia, Ireland, New Zealand
Lower secondary	Upper / higher secondary	Senior secondary	Ireland, New Zealand
Junior secondary	Senior / upper secondary	Sixth form	United Kingdom, anglophone Caribbean, Iraq
Intermediate school	Senior / general secondary		Middle East and North Africa, Philippines
First cycle secondary	Second cycle secondary, lycée		Francophone Africa, Ethiopia, Jamaica
General secondary	Preparatory, lyceum		Eastern Europe, Central Asia
Polymodal secondary			Mexico
Diversified secondary			Central America, Andes
Upper secondary			
Basic second stage	Basic third stage		Portugal

LEGEND

- ■ Preprimary (offered by the state)
- ■ Primary
- ▨ All secondary / secondary, first stage
- ■ Secondary, second stage
- ▨ Secondary, third stage
- [o] Compulsory grade (shading varies)
- ▨ Overlapping levels (shading varies)
- ☐ Preprimary (inconsistencies between UNESCO Statistical Yearbook 1997 and UNESCO database in SIMA query)
- * No precise data for cycle division

DEFINITION OF COMPULSORY EDUCATION FIELDS

From = Age of entry to compulsory education, being preprimary or primary level.

To = Sources vary in the way they present these data (inclusive or not). To make data comparable, here we always use a noninclusive criterion, which indicates the age of exit of last compulsory grade or the age of entry to the next grade.

Length = Number of years of duration of compulsory education.

Sub-Saharan Africa	Entrance age and duration of education by level 0 1 2 3 4 5 6 7 8 9 10 11 12 13 14 15 16 17 18 19 20	Compulsory education		
		From	To	Length
Angola		6	14	8
Benin		6	12	6
Botswana		6	16	10
Burkina Faso		6	16	10
Burundi		7	13	6
Cameroon		6	12	6
Central African Republic		6	16	10
Chad		6	12	6
Congo, Dem. Rep. of		6	12	6
Congo, Rep. of		6	16	10
Côte d'Ivoire		6	12	6
Eritrea		7	12	5
Ethiopia		6	16	10
Gabon		6	16	10
Gambia		7	16	9
Ghana		6	15	9
Guinea		7	13	6
Kenya		6	14	8
Lesotho		6	13	7
Liberia		6	16	10
Madagascar		6	11	5
Malawi		5	13	8
Mali		7	13	6
Mauritania		6	12	6
Mozambique		6	13	7
Namibia		6	16	10
Niger		6	12	6
Nigeria		6	15	9
Rwanda		7	13	6
Senegal		7	13	6
Sierra Leone		—	—	—
Somalia		6	14	8
South Africa		7	16	9
Sudan		6	14	8
Swaziland		6	13	7
Tanzania		7	14	7
Togo		6	16	10
Uganda		6	13	7
Zambia		7	16	9
Zanzibar (Tanzania)*		7	17	10
Zimbabwe		6	13	7

0 1 2 3 4 5 6 7 8 9 10 11 12 13 14 15 16 17 18 19 20

Middle East and North Africa	Entrance age and duration of education by level	Compulsory education		
	0 1 2 3 4 5 6 7 8 9 10 11 12 13 14 15 16 17 18 19 20	From	To	Length
Afghanistan		7	13	6
Algeria		6	15	9
Bahrain		—	—	—
Brunei Darussalam		5	17	12
Djibouti		6	15	9
Egypt, Arab Rep. of		6	15	9
Iran, Islamic Rep. of		6	14	8
Iraq		6	18	12
Israel		5	16	11
Jordan		6	16	10
Kuwait		6	14	8
Lebanon		6	12	6
Libya		6	15	9
Morocco		7	13	6
Oman		—	—	—
Qatar		6	12	6
Saudi Arabia		—	—	—
Syrian Arab Rep.		6	12	6
Tunisia		6	15	9
United Arab Emirates		6	12	6
West Bank and Gaza		6	17	11
Yemen, Republic of		6	15	9

0 1 2 3 4 5 6 7 8 9 10 11 12 13 14 15 16 17 18 19 20

Latin America and the Caribbean	Entrance age and duration of education by level	Compulsory education		
	0 1 2 3 4 5 6 7 8 9 10 11 12 13 14 15 16 17 18 19 20	From	To	Length
Argentina		5	15	10
Bahamas, The		5	16	11
Barbados		5	16	11
Belize		5	13	8
Bolivia		6	14	8
Brazil		7	15	8
Chile		6	18	12
Colombia		5	15	10
Costa Rica		5	14	9
Cuba		6	15	9
Dominica		5	17	12
Dominican Republic		5	14	9
Ecuador		6	15	9
El Salvador		4	15	11
Grenada*		5	14	9
Guatemala		7	13	6
Guyana		5	15	10
Haiti		6	15	9
Honduras		6	12	6
Jamaica		6	12	6
Mexico		6	16	10
Nicaragua		6	12	6
Panama		4	15	11
Paraguay		6	15	9
Peru		5	17	12
St. Kitts and Nevis		5	12	7
St. Lucia*		6	13	7
St. Vincent		5	16	11
Suriname		7	12	5
Trinidad and Tobago		5	17	12
Uruguay		5	15	10
Venezuela, R. B. de		5	17	12
	0 1 2 3 4 5 6 7 8 9 10 11 12 13 14 15 16 17 18 19 20			

Eastern Europe and Central Asia	Entrance age and duration of education by level 0 1 2 3 4 5 6 7 8 9 10 11 12 13 14 15 16 17 18 19 20	Compulsory education From	To	Length
Albania		6	14	8
Armenia		6	16	10
Azerbaijan		6	17	11
Belarus		6	15	9
Bulgaria		6	18	12
Croatia		6	14	8
Cyprus		5.5	15	9
Czech Republic		6	15	9
Estonia		7	16	9
Georgia		6	12	6
Hungary		6	18	12
Kazakhstan		6	14	8
Kyrgyz Republic		7	15	8
Latvia		7	16	9
Lithuania		6	16	10
Macedonia, FYR		7	15	8
Moldova		6	16	10
Poland		7	19	12
Romania		6	15	9
Russian Federation		7	19	12
Slovak Republic		6	15	9
Slovenia		6	15	9
Tajikistan		7	16	9
Turkey		6	14	9
Turkmenistan		7	16	8
Ukraine		6	17	11
Uzbekistan		6	18	12
Yugoslavia, Former		7	15	8

0 1 2 3 4 5 6 7 8 9 10 11 12 13 14 15 16 17 18 19 20

Western Europe and United States	Entrance age and duration of education by level 0 1 2 3 4 5 6 7 8 9 10 11 12 13 14 15 16 17 18 19 20	Compulsory education From	To	Length
Austria		6	15	9
Belgium		6	18	12
Denmark		6	16	10
Finland		7	16	9
France		6	16	10
Greece		6	15	9
Iceland		6	16	10
Ireland		6	15	9
Italy		6	14	8
Luxembourg		6	15	9
Netherlands		3	18	15
Norway		6	16	10
Portugal		6	15	9
Spain		6	16	10
Sweden		7	16	9
Switzerland		6	15	9
United Kingdom		5	16	11
United States		5	16	11

0 1 2 3 4 5 6 7 8 9 10 11 12 13 14 15 16 17 18 19 20

East Asia and the Pacific	Entrance age and duration of education by level 0 1 2 3 4 5 6 7 8 9 10 11 12 13 14 15 16 17 18 19 20	Compulsory education		
		From	To	Length
Australia		6	15	9
Cambodia		6	15	9
China		6	15	9
Fiji		6	14	8
Indonesia		7	15	8
Japan		6	15	9
Korea, Democratic People's Rep. of		5	16	11
Korea, Rep. of		6	15	9
Lao PDR		6	11	5
Malaysia		6	12	6
Mongolia		8	16	8
Myanmar		5	10	5
New Zealand		6	17	11
Papua New Guinea		6	15	9
Philippines		7	13	6
Singapore		6	16	10
Thailand		6	15	9
Vanuatu		6	16	10
Vietnam		6	11	5
	0 1 2 3 4 5 6 7 8 9 10 11 12 13 14 15 16 17 18 19 20			

South Asia	Entrance age and duration of education by level 0 1 2 3 4 5 6 7 8 9 10 11 12 13 14 15 16 17 18 19 20	Compulsory education		
		From	To	Length
Bangladesh		6	11	5
Bhutan		6	17	11
India		6	14	8
Nepal		7	16	9
Pakistan		5	15	10
Sri Lanka		5	14	9
	0 1 2 3 4 5 6 7 8 9 10 11 12 13 14 15 16 17 18 19 20			

Sources: UNESCO-IAU (http://www.unesco.org/iau/cd-data; UNESCO, *Statistical Yearbook 1999* (http://www.uis-unesco.org/en/stats/statistics/yearbook/tables/ed.htm); World Bank, *World Development Indicators 2003* (for duration of school year 1997); World Bank, Statistics Information Management System (SIMA).

Note: —, Not available.

Appendix B
Grade Completion by Income Group and Gender, Selected Countries, Various Years

Figure B.1 Grade Completion by Income Group and Gender, Arab Republic of Egypt, 1995–6

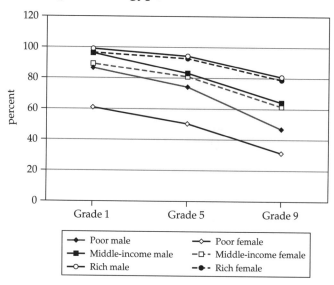

Source: Filmer 2000.

Figure B.2 Grade Completion by Income Group and Gender, Chad, 1998

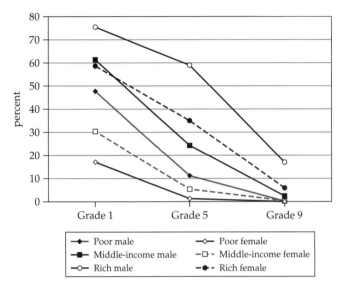

Source: Filmer 2000.

Figure B.3 Grade Completion by Income Group and Gender, Indonesia, 1997

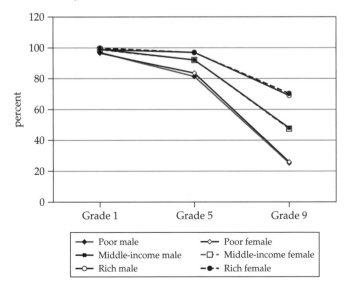

Source: Filmer 2000.

Figure B.4 Grade Completion by Income Group and Gender, India, 1996

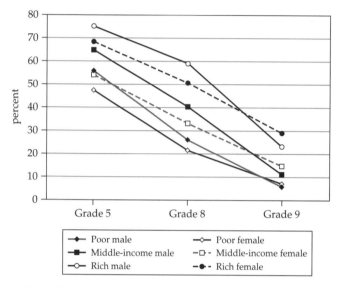

Source: Filmer 2000.

Figure B.5 Grade Completion by Income Group and Gender, Colombia, 1995

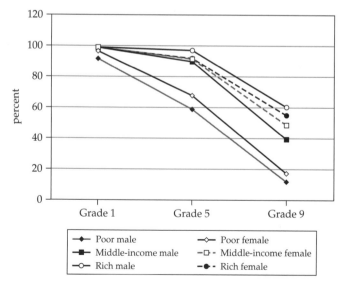

Source: Filmer 2000.

Figure B.6 Grade Completion by Income Group and Gender, Turkey, 1993

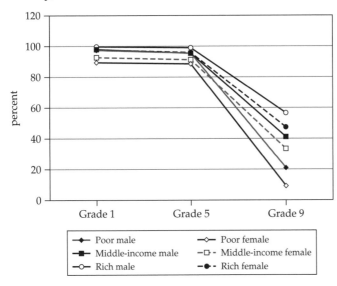

Source: Filmer 2000.

Figure B.7 Grade Completion by Income Group and Gender, Uzbekistan, 1996

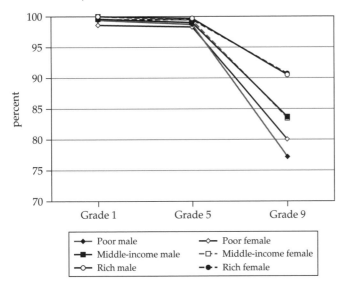

Source: Filmer 2000.

Appendix C
Educational Attainment by Income Group and Gender, Selected Countries

Table C.1 Educational Attainment of Males Age 15–19 by Income Group, Selected Countries
(percent)

Country	Completion of grade 1			Completion of grade 5			Completion of grade 9		
	Poor	Middle-income	Rich	Poor	Middle-income	Rich	Poor	Middle-income	Rich
Chad, 1998	47.7	61.4	75.5	11.2	24.3	59.0	0.2	2.4	17.0
Niger, 1997	25.0	30.4	70.1	18.8	25.1	62.5	0.7	2.1	18.7
Uganda, 1995	86.7	93.2	93.6	43.2	58.2	78.1	2.4	6.3	24.1
Indonesia, 1997	97.1	99.2	98.9	81.3	92.1	97.0	25.2	48.0	69.0
Philippines, 1998	96.3	99.8	99.1	77.1	95.8	97.5	21.0	55.9	70.5
India, 1992–93	65.0	86.8	96.6	53.4	79.3	94.6	21.6	45.6	75.1
Pakistan, 1990–91	50.8	76.6	92.4	39.6	66.1	88.3	10.9	29.0	60.5
Egypt, Arab Rep. of, 1995–96	86.5	96.2	99.0	74.2	83.1	94.3	47.0	64.2	80.7
Morocco, 1992	55.2	89.0	98.0	34.9	70.9	89.4	5.0	19.8	43.3
Brazil, 1996	89.9	97.7	99.0	40.3	75.0	87.4	5.8	23.4	32.9
Brazil (Northeast), 1996	83.3	95.1	97.1	28.6	67.2	70.0	3.0	18.2	19.0
Colombia, 1995	91.6	98.9	99.0	58.8	89.7	97.0	11.9	39.4	60.3
Turkey, 1993	97.4	97.9	99.7	95.5	95.4	99.0	20.9	41.1	56.6
Uzbekistan, 1996	99.4	99.6	100.0	98.7	99.0	99.7	77.2	83.7	90.5

Source: Filmer 2000.

Table C.2 Educational Attainment of Females Age 15–19 by Income Group, Selected Countries

Country	Completion of grade 1			Completion of grade 5			Completion of grade 9		
	Poor	Middle-income	Rich	Poor	Middle-income	Rich	Poor	Middle-income	Rich
Chad, 1998	17.1	30.4	58.7	1.3	5.4	35.0	0.0	0.4	5.9
Niger, 1997	7.2	13.5	54.9	4.5	10.2	49.5	0.1	0.5	11.5
Uganda, 1995	70.3	81.1	92.5	35.0	48.6	75.6	3.0	5.6	25.0
Indonesia, 1997	96.6	98.9	99.9	83.5	92.1	96.9	25.9	47.5	70.3
Philippines, 1998	97.6	99.6	99.1	89.5	98.0	97.7	39.4	68.3	65.8
India, 1992–93	29.3	65.1	94.3	21.7	57.2	91.8	6.1	26.7	71.0
Pakistan, 1990–91	12.2	45.4	87.0	8.3	37.5	81.9	1.5	12.5	49.4
Egypt, Arab Rep. of, 1995–96	60.9	89.3	96.5	50.4	80.9	92.7	31.3	61.5	78.8
Morocco 1992	21.1	66.2	85.4	9.5	49.3	77.6	1.1	13.0	40.7
Brazil, 1996	95.3	99.5	99.4	51.9	85.3	91.6	10.2	32.1	43.3
Brazil (Northeast), 1996	93.4	98.4	96.4	41.5	76.7	81.9	6.5	26.1	29.0
Colombia, 1995	96.5	99.0	98.7	67.7	91.4	91.8	17.3	48.7	55.0
Turkey, 1993	89.4	92.7	97.7	88.5	91.2	95.9	9.2	33.4	47.4
Uzbekistan, 1996	98.6	100.0	99.5	98.3	99.4	99.5	80.0	83.5	90.7

Source: Filmer 2000.

Appendix D
Selected Education Pyramids

See discussion in chapter 3 under the heading Secondary Education Attainment. Figure D.1 shows primary education on the bottom, secondary education in the middle, and tertiary education on top.

Figure D.1 Educational Attainment of Population Age 15 and Older

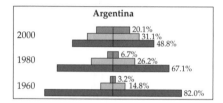

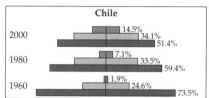

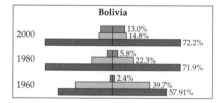

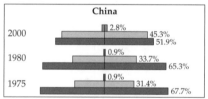

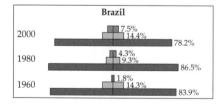

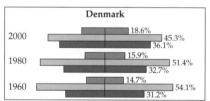

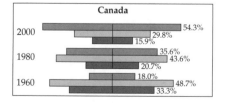

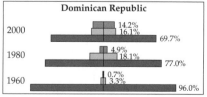

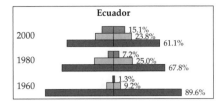

Ecuador

2000   15.1%
        23.8%
        61.1%

1980   7.2%
        25.0%
        67.8%

1960   1.3%
        9.2%
        89.6%

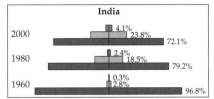

India

2000   4.1%
        23.8%
        72.1%

1980   2.4%
        18.5%
        79.2%

1960   0.3%
        2.8%
        96.8%

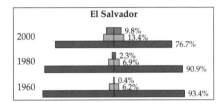

El Salvador

2000   9.8%
        13.4%
        76.7%

1980   2.3%
        6.9%
        90.9%

1960   0.4%
        6.2%
        93.4%

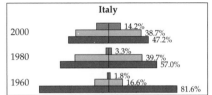

Italy

2000   14.2%
        38.7%
        47.2%

1980   3.3%
        39.7%
        57.0%

1960   1.8%
        16.6%
        81.6%

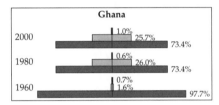

Ghana

2000   1.0%
        25.7%
        73.4%

1980   0.6%
        26.0%
        73.4%

1960   0.7%
        1.6%
        97.7%

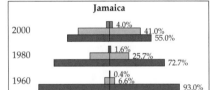

Jamaica

2000   4.0%
        41.0%
        55.0%

1980   1.6%
        25.7%
        72.7%

1960   0.4%
        6.6%
        93.0%

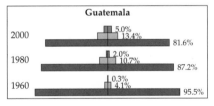

Guatemala

2000   5.0%
        13.4%
        81.6%

1980   2.0%
        10.7%
        87.2%

1960   0.3%
        4.1%
        95.5%

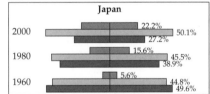

Japan

2000   22.2%
        50.1%
        27.2%

1980   15.6%
        45.5%
        38.9%

1960   5.6%
        44.8%
        49.6%

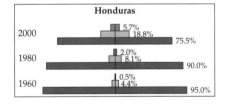

Honduras

2000   5.7%
        18.8%
        75.5%

1980   2.0%
        8.1%
        90.0%

1960   0.5%
        4.4%
        95.0%

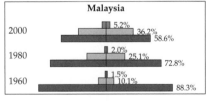

Malaysia

2000   5.2%
        36.2%
        58.6%

1980   2.0%
        25.1%
        72.8%

1960   1.5%
        10.1%
        88.3%

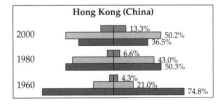

Hong Kong (China)

2000   13.3%
        50.2%
        36.5%

1980   6.6%
        43.0%
        50.3%

1960   4.3%
        21.0%
        74.8%

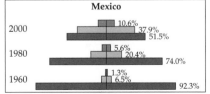

Mexico

2000   10.6%
        37.9%
        51.5%

1980   5.6%
        20.4%
        74.0%

1960   1.3%
        6.5%
        92.3%

(Continues on the following page.)

Figure D.1 Continued

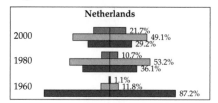

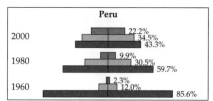

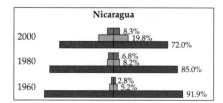

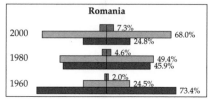

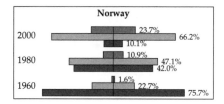

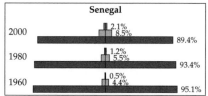

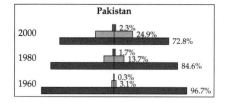

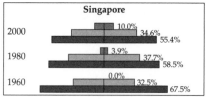

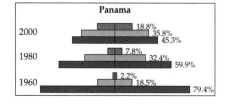

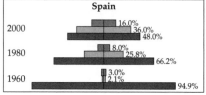

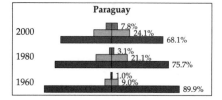

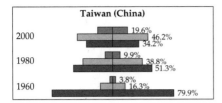

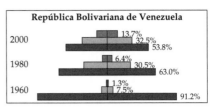

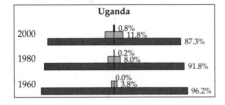

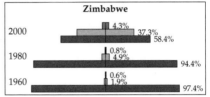

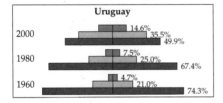

Appendix E
Gross Enrollment Rates and Educational Attainment by Income Level

Table E.1 Gross Enrollment Rates and Educational Attainment by Income Level, 2000

		GER (world weighted average = 67)			
		Low		*High*	
Educational attainment (world average = 6.5)	*Low*	**Quadrant I**		**Quadrant II**	
		♠ Guinea-Bissau	♠ Ghana		
		♠ Mali	♠ Kenya		
		♠ Niger	♠ Lesotho		
		♠ Sudan	♠ Dominican Republic		
		♠ Gambia, The	♠ Indonesia		
		♠ Benin	♠ India	■ Brazil	♠ Bolivia
		♠ Sierra Leone	♠ El Salvador	♠ Tunisia	■ Portugal
		♠ Nepal	♠ Turkey	♠ Jamaica	■ Mauritius
		♠ Senegal	♠ Zimbabwe	♠ Colombia	■ Bahrain
		♠ Rwanda	♠ Zambia	♠ Iran, Islamic Rep. of	■ South Africa
		♠ Bangladesh	♠ Syrian Arab Rep.	♠ Algeria	■ Botswana
		♠ Tanzania	♠ Swaziland	♠ Egypt, Arab Rep. of	♠ Thailand
		♠ Papua New Guinea	■ Costa Rica		
		♠ Malawi	♠ Paraguay		
		♠ Togo	■ Kuwait		
		♠ Guatemala	♠ China		
		♠ Uganda	♠ Venezuela, R. B. de		
		♠ Cameroon			
		♠ Pakistan			

Table E.1 Continued

		GER (world weighted average = 67)	
		Low	*High*

		Quadrant III	**Quadrant IV**	

Educational attainment (world average = 6.5)	*High*		■ Malaysia
			♠ Sri Lanka
			♠ Jordan
			● Italy
			■ Mexico
			● Spain
			■ Chile
			■ Uruguay
			♠ Peru
			■ Trinidad and
			  Tobago
			● France
			♠ Philippines
			● Austria
			♠ Panama
			■ Greece
			■ Barbados
			■ Argentina
			● Iceland
			■ Hungary
			■ Slovak Republic
				● Netherlands
				● United
				  Kingdom
				♠ Bulgaria
				● Japan
				■ Czech
				  Republic
				♠ Romania
				■ Israel
				● Denmark
				■ Poland
				● Finland
				● Germany
				● Switzerland
				■ Korea, Rep. of
				● Australia
				● Sweden
				● Canada
				● New Zealand
				● Norway
				● United States

♠ = Low Income   ■ = Middle Income   ● = High Income (WEF classification)

Source: Statistical Information Management and Analysis (SIMA) database, World Bank.

Note: GER, gross enrollment rate; WEF, World Economic Forum.

Appendix F
A Road Map of Teacher Competencies for a Knowledge-Based Secondary School

Martinet, Raymond, and Gauthier (2001) have developed a map of teaching competencies that can be useful as a guide to the development of teacher education programs. Their proposal has been adapted and supplemented with findings and evidence from recent research on learning to teach for purposes of this policy report.

Competencies in the Professional Domain

Acting critically as a professional, interpreting the objects of knowledge or culture in performing one's functions

- Identifying the core issues and the axes (concepts, postulates, and methods) of knowledge of the subject in order to facilitate students' meaningful learning
- Critically distancing oneself from the subject taught
- Establishing relationships between the cultural background embedded in the prescribed curriculum and that of the students
- Making the class a place open to multiple viewpoints
- Taking a critical look at one's own origins and cultural practices and at one's social role
- Establishing relationships among different fields of the subject matter knowledge

Becoming involved in an individual and collective project of professional development

- Evaluating one's own competencies and adopting the means to develop them using available resources
- Exchanging ideas with colleagues about the suitability of pedagogical and didactic options
- Reflecting on one's practice and putting the results into practice

---

Acting ethically and responsibly in the performance of functions

- Being aware of the values at stake in one's performance
- Encouraging democratic conduct in class; giving students due attention and support
- Keeping high expectations; believing that students are capable of learning and that teachers are capable of and responsible for teaching them successfully
- Explaining, for the sake of transparency and accountability, the decisions made concerning students' learning and education
- Respecting confidential aspects of the profession
- Avoiding all forms of discrimination by students, parents, and colleagues
- Making judicious use of the legal and authorized framework governing the profession

Competencies in the Teaching Domain

Designing teaching-learning situations that are appropriate to the students concerned and the subject matter with a view to developing the competencies targeted in the curriculum

- Mastering ways of representing and formulating the subject matter, with the specific purpose of making it comprehensible to others
- Understanding what makes learning specific topics easy or difficult, as well as the concepts and preconceptions that students of different ages and backgrounds bring with them to the learning of the most frequently taught topics and issues
- Analyzing students' misconceptions concerning the subject matter
- Planning sequences of teaching and evaluation, bearing in mind the logic of the content and of the learning process
- Bearing in mind students' social differences (gender, ethnic origin, socioeconomic, and cultural), needs, and special interests
- Choosing varied and appropriate didactic approaches when developing the competencies included in the curriculum
- Foreseeing learning situations that enable integration of competencies in varied contexts

Steering teaching-learning situations that are appropriate to the students concerned and the subject matter with a view to developing the competencies targeted in the curriculum

- Creating the conditions for students to become involved in situations and problems and in significant topics or projects, bearing in mind their cognitive, affective, and social characteristics

(Continued)

- Establishing a learning orientation by starting lessons and activities with advance organizers or previews
- Presenting the subject matter in networks of knowledge structured around powerful ideas
- Making available to students the resources necessary in the learning situations proposed
- Giving students the opportunity to learn, dedicating most of the available time to curriculum activities
- Questioning to engage students in sustained discourse structured around powerful ideas
- Guiding students in selecting, interpreting, and understanding the information available
- Shaping students' learning by means of frequent and pertinent strategies, steps, questions, and feedback so as to facilitate the integration and transfer of learning
- Giving the students sufficient opportunities to practice and apply what they are learning and to receive improvement-oriented feedback

Evaluating student progress in learning the subject content and mastering the required competencies

- In a learning situation, managing information so as to overcome students' problems and difficulties and modify and adapt teaching to sustain students' progress
- Monitoring students' progress using both formal tests and performance evaluations and informal assessments of students' contributions to lessons and work on assignments
- Constructing or employing instruments to enable evaluation of progress and acquisition of competencies and skills
- Communicating to students and parents, clearly and explicitly, the results achieved and the feedback concerning progress in learning and acquisition of competence
- Cooperating with the teaching staff to determine the desirable rhythm and stages of progress in the training cycle

Planning, organizing, and supervising the way the group or class works so as to facilitate students' learning and socialization

- Defining and applying an effective working system for normal class activities
- Communicating clearly to students the requirements of correct school and social behavior and ensuring that they adopt them
- Fostering students' participation—as a group and as individuals—in establishing the norms for working and living together in the classroom.
- Adopting strategies to prevent incorrect behavior from cropping up and intervening effectively if it does

Adapting teaching to student diversity

- Designing learning tasks adapted to students' potential and characteristics
- Organizing different learning rhythms according to students' capacities
- Organizing heterogeneous groups in which students work together
- Assisting the social integration of students with learning or behavioral difficulties
- Seeking pertinent information regarding students' needs
- Participating in the preparation and implementation of a plan of adapted performance

Integrating information and communication technology (ICT) into the preparation and development of teaching and learning activities, classroom management, and professional development

- Adopting a critical and well-founded attitude toward the advantages and limitations of ICT as a medium for teaching and learning and for society
- Evaluating the pedagogical potential of ICT
- Using a variety of multimedia tools for communication; using ICT effectively to investigate, interpret, and communicate information and resolve problems
- Using ICT effectively to set up exchange networks related to the subject taught and its pedagogical practice
- Helping students use ICT in their learning activities, evaluate such use, and analyze critically the data gathered by the networks

Communicating clearly and correctly, both orally and in written form, in the various contexts related to the teaching profession

- Using appropriate oral language when addressing students, parents, or colleagues
- Respecting the rules of written language in documents aimed at students, parents, and colleagues
- Knowing how to take a position, maintain one's ideas, and conduct discussions coherently, effectively, constructively, and respectfully
- Using questions to stimulate students to process and reflect on content, recognize relationships among and implications of the key ideas, think critically about the content, and use the content in problem solving, decision making, and other higher-order applications
- Communicating ideas rigorously, using precise vocabulary and correct syntax; correcting errors made by students in their oral and written work; constantly seeking to improve oral and written expression

(Continued)

Competencies in the School Domain

Cooperating with school staff, parents, and various social agents to achieve the school's educational targets

- Cooperating with other members of the school staff to define targets and in preparing and putting into effect projects on educational services
- Promoting participation and the flow of relevant information to parents
- Encouraging student participation in the management of the school and in its activities and projects

Working in cooperation with other members of the teaching staff in tasks enabling the development and evaluation of curriculum competencies, and doing so with students' needs in mind

- Knowing which are the situations requiring collaboration with other members of the pedagogical team for the design and adaptation of teaching and learning situations and the evaluation of learning
- Working to achieve the required consensus among members of the teaching staff

Appendix G
Public-Private Partnerships for Secondary Education

Broad discussions of public-private partnerships (PPPs) in the education sector treat these partnerships as a general form of collaboration between the public and private sectors. Many discussions of PPPs in education are widely available (see http://www2.ifc.org/edinvest/public.htm; Wang 2000a, 2000b). Many of these partnerships, however, could also be visualized as more conventional forms of relationship between sectors such as voucher schemes, traditional outsourcing of education inputs, and loose collaboration between the public and the private sectors in which the latter acts out of charitable or "social responsibility" motives. Some of these types of PPP can be effective, but calling them all public-private partnerships can obscure more innovative aspects that a more rigorous definition could bring out.

A more specific definition of public-private partnership is associated with a particular form of partnership that started, at least in its modern incarnation, in the United Kingdom in the 1980s and was continued by the subsequent government. In fact, more in the way of PPPs has been done in the United Kingdom under Labour than under the Conservative government. PPPs have spread fairly quickly, particularly to the English-speaking world—for example, to Australia, Canada, and Ireland. In the United States the term tends to be used in the loose sense, although PPPs in the strict sense do exist.

Among middle-income countries, South Africa has perhaps defined the approach most rigorously. According to the PPP guidelines from South Africa's National Treasury:

> A PPP is a contractual arrangement whereby a private party performs part of a department's service delivery or administrative functions and assumes the associated risks. In return, the private party receives a fee according to predefined performance criteria, which may be:
>
> - entirely from service tariffs or user charges
> - entirely from a departmental or other budget
> - a combination of the above.
>
> In addition, there must be substantial risk transferred to the private party, or else the transaction tends to be viewed as a form of borrowing.

The essential aspects of a PPP arrangement, as distinct from the direct delivery of a public service by a department, are:

- a focus on the services to be provided, not the assets to be employed
- a shift of the risks and responsibilities to a private provider for the activities associated with the provision of services.

The simplest form of a PPP is a service contract. In such contracts, a department typically awards a private party the right and obligation to perform a specific service, within well-defined specifications, for a period of perhaps one to three years. The government retains ownership and control of all facilities and capital assets and properties. A key feature of more complex PPP arrangements, such as concessions and build-operate-transfer (BOT) schemes, is the mobilization of private finance on a limited recourse basis. In the former, the concessionaire's responsibilities are expected to include maintenance, rehabilitation, upgrading, and enhancement of the facility, which may involve substantial capital investment. In the latter, the private party undertakes the financing and construction of a given infrastructure facility, as well as its operation and maintenance, for a specified period of time. Given the often substantial capital investment by the private sector under such arrangements, the contracts tend to be of long duration (25 years).

While service delivery through a PPP changes the means of delivering services, it does not change a department's accountability for ensuring that the services are delivered. The department's focus shifts from managing the inputs to managing the outcomes, i.e. becoming a contract manager rather than a resource manager.

PPPs potentially have several advantages:

- They can allow the government to create infrastructure immediately, without having to wait and without having to spend current tax revenues or borrow.
- The need to enter into a contractual relationship with entities outside the government can force the government to better specify the flow of services it wants from a facility.
- Economies of scale might be realized in large programs run by specialized private sector bodies.
- The private sector might be more efficient at construction and maintenance than the public sector, if there is competition and if reward is contractually linked to a flow of performance over many years, generating incentives for maintenance and flow of services.
- The risks associated with the facility (for example, the risk of underutilization) are more likely to be analyzed if a contractual relationship is involved. Once analyzed, they can be shared more effectively between the government and the private sector, the latter often being more capable of assuming certain risks than government is.

There are, however, disadvantages, or at least issues, to be considered:

- A mature private sector, with the access and ability to undertake long-range finance, is needed if longer-term PPPs are to succeed. The implication is that PPPs are more of an option in certain middle-income countries than in developing countries as a whole.
- The analysis of risks and the specification of contracts require a considerable degree of technical and financial sophistication.
- There may be ideological or emotional opposition to the notion of the government's paying rent or making periodic payments when it could have built the infrastructure outright.

Examples of PPPs in developed countries include the recent U.K. Building Schools for the Future (BSF) initiative. BSF is developing or improving some 200 secondary schools, using variations on the basic model in which the private sector is responsible for long-term finance, for construction, and for ensuring long-term delivery of infrastructural services from the schools, while schools as education delivery entities are managed by education authorities. In the past some 500 schools benefited from a similar approach. It was not always smooth sailing: complaints were made about inflexible execution, cost savings did not always materialize, and problems arose associated with lack of incentives for maintenance relative to construction. The more recent BSF initiative relies on a mix of procurement vehicles—not necessarily PPPs as they existed in the 1990s. Rather complex approaches such as Local Education Partnerships (LEPs) are being tested; private providers still handle the delivery of construction, but education interests are engaged in the design, and the construction aspect is set within the framework of broader education development goals.

PPPs for education in developing countries are only incipient. Thus far, they have been relatively small and in some cases of short duration. But they tend to be innovative. They do not always fulfill the rigorous definition crafted by South Africa's Treasury, but several have the virtue of actually working.

In South Africa a partnership among the Department of Water Affairs and Forestry, the Department of Education, and a private water utility has created spinning pumps, similar to traditional children's merry-go-rounds, for school playgrounds. As the children spin, water is pumped from wells into tanks, providing water for the community. The pumps also sell advertising space for spinning billboards. Free State and Mpumalanga Provinces are considering larger-scale and longer-term projects for building or improving schools. In one, a feasibility study has been done; in the other, transactions advisers have yet to be appointed. Thus far, these larger projects appear to have received considerable analytical input and consultation, but none is yet operational.

The Free State School Building PPP aims to solve infrastructure backlog problems left over from the apartheid period. Since South Africa's democratic government is fiscally cautious but needs to resolve the backlog problem, the idea is to bring in immediate financial resources from the private sector, to be paid off by the public sector over a 20-year period. Short-term public funds freed up by the infusion of private funds into construction would then be used to maintain existing assets, thus reducing deterioration. The PPP option would involve a certain degree of risk transfer to the private sector; the plan is to transfer some degree of occupancy risk (that is, the possibility that because of demographic shifts the facilities may not be needed by the time the government inherits them). How to do this is still under discussion, and the terms of the transfer have yet to be finalized. Whereas PPPs in South Africa have started in earnest in other areas (prisons, health facilities), their adoption in education has been somewhat slower.

PPPs in the traditional sense of a long-term investment might be most suitable for middle-income countries. For shorter-term needs, however, they may be suitable even in rather difficult circumstances. In Sierra Leone, a country recovering from war, PPPs in a broad sense are being used to rehabilitate schools. The private partners do not provide finance (this is done through World Bank funding), and the contracts are not as long term as in PPPs strictly defined. The PPPs are formal, contractual relationships between government and nongovernmental actors; they are intended to achieve well-specified (but sometimes multiple and comprehensive) ends; and the actors in the contractual relationship specialize in what they do best. Nongovernmental actors may include church groups and nongovernmental organizations, and there are no undue restrictions (other than capacity) on who may become a partner. Work is under way.

Colombia's capital city, Bogotá, created public-private partnerships by building schools and then letting out the management as a concession to private institutions. The contracts are long term (15 years) and specify the delivery of educational services. Private institutions are reimbursed on a fixed-cost-per-child basis. The government finances the construction; this is not a mechanism for reducing capital outlays or for expediting construction by bringing in direct public financing. As of 2003, some 277 concessions had been signed. Through concessions and subsidies, about 25 percent of publicly funded enrollment is actually in private schools. Colombia has a long history of experimentation and flexibility in these matters; as early as the 1930s voucher schemes existed whereby municipalities provided scholarships for children to attend private schools.

An example from higher education, features of which could apply to secondary education, comes from India. The state of Sikkim is one of the poorest in the country. In 1996 the state government set up Sikkim Manipal University of Health, Medical and Technological Sciences (SMU) as a public-private partnership. The objective was to set up Sikkim's first higher technical education institutions to provide new career opportunities to deserving students in the remote state. The state government, recognizing that it had limited resources and experience in running higher education institutions, entered into an agreement with the Manipal Group—one of India's leading private higher education groups—to jointly establish and manage the SMU. As an initial contribution, the state government provided the land and a multispecialty hospital, the Central Referral Hospital, to serve as an associated teaching hospital for the SMU's medical college. The Manipal Group is fully responsible for the SMU's financial and academic affairs.

Appendix H
Formula Funding in Secondary Education: Country Examples

During the 1990s and the early 21st century, many developing countries began experimenting with some kind of formula-based funding. Experience with formula funding in Chile, Nicaragua, and South Africa is reviewed here to illustrate three different approaches. Chile emphasizes funding from the national to the municipal level in a municipally decentralized situation in which public schools do not have a great deal of school autonomy but are expected to compete with private schools. Nicaragua emphasizes funding directly from national authorities to public schools under a school autonomy model. South Africa exemplifies a two-tier system of funding and provision whereby funding flows from the national level to the province via a formula and from the province to relatively autonomous schools also via a particular formula approach.

Chile

In Chile schools may be municipal (public), private unsubsidized, or private subsidized. Both municipal and private subsidized schools receive funding via a formula (or, in the case of public schools, their municipalities receive the funding). The formula is crafted by starting with a base amount, expressed in monetary units, that is subject to inflationary adjustments. The subsidies by level and type of school, as well as supplements for small rural schools, are then expressed as ratios of that base. The formula funds secondary schools at a higher ratio from the base than primary schools; the ratio is also higher for specialized secondary schools compared with general ones and for children with special needs. Small schools receive supplemental funding but only if they are rural, to avoid funding schools that have diminishing enrollments simply because they are not performing. Funding is based on measured attendance, and there are penalties for misrepresenting attendance. The total funds are thus, to simplify, the base (monetary) amount, times the ratio appropriate to the level and type of school, times the attendance.

Private subsidized and public schools at the secondary level may charge fees, within limits, and still receive subsidies, but the subsidies are reduced.

Schools charging fees must exempt a proportion of students, partly on the basis of poverty. Despite a widespread perception, Chile's system is not a true voucher system within the public sector because public schools are directly managed and provided for by municipalities; the formula does not effectively transmit powerful incentives down to the school level, and directors do not have much financial and input-purchase discretion. The Chilean system provides more resources to poor schools through special programs only, not as a regular part of the funding system.

Nicaragua

Under Nicaragua's formula-funded school autonomy model, schools have considerable managerial discretion with respect to a variety of input-purchase and management decisions. In this sense, parents at Nicaraguan autonomous schools have much more power than in the other two countries studied here and, indeed, than in most cases around the world. Nicaragua uses a system of asymmetric decentralization in granting school autonomy: not all schools are autonomous, and the granting of autonomy requires a review process. Autonomous schools are funded via a formula that takes into account school size (smaller schools receive a larger per-student subsidy) and level (secondary schools receive a higher subsidy). As in Chile, the basic drivers in the funding formula are the same for secondary schools as for primary schools; the per capita amounts are simply higher. In addition, a higher proportion of secondary schools is autonomous, and these schools charge fees to parents. Not only do more secondary schools charge fees, but at the secondary level the ratio of fee income to subsidy income from the formula is higher than at the primary level. Fees are, de facto, not exactly voluntary, but the degree of pressure seems much higher at the secondary level. There is no explicit pro-poor component in the formula, although smaller schools, which presumably cater to the poor, receive more funding because they are assumed to have a lower target student-teacher ratio and because they are provided with "equity" top-up, again on the basis of size.

South Africa

In South Africa provinces are funded via a national "equitable shares" formula. This formula does not determine the absolute amount of funding a province should receive but only its share of total expenditure allocated to the provinces. The share is determined simply by the province's relative need. The formula has several needs levers, one of which is education, with a weight of approximately 40 percent. A province's relative need in education thus contributes about 40 percent to its overall relative need. Relative education need is determined by enrollment, which is assigned a weight of one-third, and population of school age, with a weight of two-thirds. Population is weighted heavily because the formula is oriented toward need and is designed to discourage overenrollment.

Once a province receives its fiscal transfer, it does not have to spend 40 percent of it on education; the equitable shares transfer system generates only block grants. Funding of schools by provincial governments is determined by national funding norms that impose distributional requirements on each province but entail no fixed per-student mandate. The distributional requirements apply to nonpersonnel funding and to teachers. These requirements simply state that, for example, 60 percent of the funding should reach the poorest 40 percent of the children. The formula is steeply progressive, requiring that children in the poorest quintile receive 135 percent of what children in the middle quintile receive and that children in the richest quintile receive only 5 percent of what children in the middle quintile receive. Thus, the policy is explicitly stated in terms of distributional incidence and not in absolute terms. The national-to-province funding is carried out in terms of shares, not absolute amounts, and so is the province-to-school funding. As in Nicaragua, some schools are more autonomous than others; autonomy is asymmetric.

Teachers are physically provided to schools, but on a formula basis driven by numbers of students and curricular choice. A share of the total pool of teachers is, however, "top-sliced," to be allocated according to the same poverty profile as is used for nonpersonnel funding.

With respect to poverty, secondary schools are treated exactly the same as primary schools: the progressivity norms are identical. If, however, a province chooses to spend more on secondary schools on a per-learner basis, the progressivity norms are applied to this higher per capita amount.

Finally, private schools are also subsidized on a pro-poor basis in that the subsidy is reduced for schools charging higher fees. Again, the policy makes no explicit distinction between the absolute levels of per-student funding for private primary schools and private secondary schools, but the subsidy for private schools is anchored on the per-student spending in public schooling. Thus, if per-student spending on public secondary schooling is higher than spending on public primary schooling, subsidies for private secondary schooling will automatically be higher. Again, everything is expressed in ratios and shares. This procedure is meant to increase provincial autonomy, to reduce lobbying and rent-seeking, and to allow easier adjustment of spending to fiscal realities.

Source: Authors' compilation from personal communication with consultants and country officials.

Appendix I
Asymmetric Decentralization in Colombia and South Africa

Asymmetric decentralization refers to a situation in which not all decentralized units, whether provinces, states, municipalities, districts, or schools, are given the same functions, duties, and powers at the same time. Virtually every country has some form of asymmetric decentralization, either political or administrative. Colombia provides an example of asymmetric decentralization of education finances to the municipal level, and South Africa is an example of asymmetric decentralization to the school level.

It should be noted that asymmetric decentralization carries the risk of enhancing disparities, since more power is given to schools and communities that are relatively more capable. Yet it would not be reasonable to prevent schools or municipalities that clearly have the capacity for better management from managing themselves, simply for equity reasons. A middle ground would be to provide strong capacity-building assistance to the more backward schools and areas, in conjunction with decentralization to the more capable schools or areas. Stated differently, in an asymmetric model a goal of the system should be to get more and more schools into the decentralized framework. This could be done by creating a feedback loop between the measurement of capacity, using the types of checklist or certification instrument described below, and transmitting the information gathered to the unit of the ministry or other authority that carries out management training, thus ensuring that the weaker schools or municipalities receive the required training and capacity building. As part of the management training program, it is useful to have an ongoing mentoring process whereby the most advanced schools or municipalities provide on-site training to staff of the developing schools or municipalities.

Colombia

Colombia is territorially divided into departments. Within departments, municipalities are the basic entity for dealing with political and administrative matters. Each municipality has a popularly elected city council that is charged with overseeing operations and services.

Law 715 (2001) provides new regulations for key aspects of education decentralization in Colombia. The concept of asymmetry is implemented via a process of certification. Municipalities can be certified, or not certified, to perform certain functions. Certification is extended by the department (the unit above the municipality) except in the case of municipalities exceeding 100,000 in population, which before 2003 were certified by the national level according to certain criteria and are now certified simply by virtue of size. If a municipality applies for certification but the department does not grant it within six months, the municipality can appeal to the national level. Municipalities can be decertified if they fail to fulfill the requirements for certification. The national level can intervene in any municipality or level lower than the national level if the lower levels do not fulfill key obligations.

Certification has a number of implications for education:

- In noncertified municipalities, education is more of a departmental competence in general—in a sense, education is not effectively decentralized to the municipality unless the municipality is certified.
- Administrative and financial supervision of certified municipalities is carried out by the national level, but for noncertified municipalities it is left to departments. In that sense, a certified municipality has duties and powers closer to those of a department.
- Assessment of compliance with national education policies for noncertified municipalities is delegated to departments.
- Certified municipalities can manage their own education funding as received directly from the national level and can distribute school funding among the schools in the municipality. For noncertified municipalities, the main funding is distributed to schools by the department, and it is the department that receives the national funding.
- Certified municipalities can appoint teachers as long as the cost of personnel is covered by their financial allocations. Noncertified municipalities cannot appoint teachers; this is done by the department overseeing the municipality. Noncertified municipalities can, however, transfer teachers between schools.
- Certified municipalities can enter into contracts with accredited private organizations to supply education and can use their fiscal transfers to do so as long as the cost per student is not greater than the cost per student in public organizations. If the cost per student is higher, the municipality can still contract, but it has to use funds other than those coming from the fiscal transfer.

The criteria and processes for certification of municipalities with a population of less than 100,000 are under development, but they are likely to include the following:

- A development plan that is in accordance with national policy and that specifies access, quality, and efficiency goals and includes investment plans.

- A staffing and teacher allocation plan that is in accordance with national parameters; if adjustments are needed, they must be supported by a technical proposal prepared according to national guidelines. On certification, staff are formally transferred to the municipality.
- Institutional capacity to manage information systems, based on guidelines from the national level.
- A formal request to the department for technical assistance in meeting certification requirements.

South Africa

In South Africa the national government sets education policy, but at the provincial level the education budget is determined by the legislature and cabinet. The province receives a multisectoral block transfer determined by the equitable shares formula, which is largely population driven (see appendix H). There is no asymmetry in the treatment of provinces with respect to education, although the national level can generally intervene in provinces in cases of governance failure. Provinces manage schools (for example, teachers' contracts are with provinces, and provinces provide schools with teachers), but schools have considerable authority, such as the ability to charge fees, appoint extra teaching and nonteaching personnel, and influence the selection of personnel assigned to the school by the provincial government.

Asymmetries do appear at the school level; some schools are more autonomous or decentralized than others. Schools with more authority can have (or can be assigned) more duties and powers. In particular, they may

- take over the maintenance and improvement of school property
- determine the school's extramural curriculum and the choice of subject options as long as these conform to overall provincial curriculum policy
- purchase textbooks, educational materials, and equipment for the school
- pay for services to the school
- run an adult learning center out of the school, as a separate entity
- receive their nonpersonnel funding from the province as a lump sum transferred directly into the school bank account
- determine their own priorities for expenditure from their provincial lump-sum funding.

A school that has not requested these powers may nonetheless have them assigned, for the administrative convenience of the province, if the school is, in the judgment of the province, able to take on the functions. The functions can be assigned separately or as a whole. Ability to receive nonpersonnel funding on a lump-sum, block basis is determined by means of a checklist of administrative ability. The number of schools with greater autonomy is expected to grow each year as schools learn to manage their funds.

The management capacity checklists used in South Africa can vary from province to province. The checklist used in KwaZulu-Natal Province, for example, covers such topics as these:

- Is the school's governing body functioning and set up according to law, with respect to composition and procedures?
- Does the governing body function properly with regard to finances, property, curriculum, and learning materials? Do subcommittees exist for these functions, and are they headed by a governor of the school?
- Does the governing body meet the requisite number of times? Are minutes kept? How well and how often does the governing body report to all parents?
- Does the governing body follow good procedures in developing and submitting the annual budget, including consultation with a broader group of parents?
- Do extra personnel employed by the governing body have proper contracts? Is the school registered as an employer? Are proper employment records kept?
- Does the school keep proper records on students, materials inventories, and the like?
- Are there proper procedures for exempting students from fees, and are they followed?

The actual checklist is quite detailed; it includes items such as the number of signatories on the school's bank account, whether receipts are issued for all payments into the school's funds, and whether a commitment register is kept.

Appendix J
World Bank Support for Secondary Education

This appendix summarizes the World Bank's experience in supporting secondary education reforms in developing and transition countries in recent years and offers a framework for continued support of secondary education development. It draws on a portfolio review of World Bank lending for secondary education over the period 1990–2002 (World Bank 2004b) by the Bank's Operations Evaluation Department (OED).

The Operations Evaluation Department (OED) is an independent unit within the World Bank that reports directly to the Bank's Board of Executive Directors. The OED assesses what works and what does not, how a borrower plans to run and maintain a project, and what the lasting contribution of the Bank to a country's overall development has been. The goals of evaluation are to learn from experience, to provide an objective basis for assessing the results of the Bank's work, and to enable accountability in the achievement of Bank objectives. Evaluation also improves the Bank's work by identifying and disseminating the lessons learned from experience and by framing recommendations drawn from the findings.

Assessment of Recent World Bank Experience in Secondary Education, 1990–2002

World Bank lending for education began in 1963. Since then, the Bank has played a prominent role in assisting developing countries in their efforts to expand secondary education and to improve the quality of institutions and programs. New lending for secondary education grew from $148 million in 1990 to $250 million in 2004. Lending for secondary education reached a peak of $376 million in 1995. The World Bank is currently assisting secondary education development in 71 countries. (See the tables at the end of this appendix for a listing of projects by country, a synopsis of World Bank analytical work on secondary education between 2002 and 2005, and a list of World Bank publications on secondary education.)

The types of interventions and their general objectives can be summarized as follows:

In countries with high secondary education enrollments

- improving employability and productivity of school leavers through support to vocational secondary schools, especially in countries where specific shortages of vocational and technical skills have been identified
- increasing a country's competitiveness by improving the quality of general secondary education to raise the overall productivity and trainability of the labor force

In countries with low secondary education enrollments

- meeting specific shortages of educated manpower in the public and private sectors by raising secondary school completion rates
- improving the social conditions of the poor and reducing inequity by expanding access to secondary education

Until the 1980s World Bank support to secondary education had focused on the expansion of capacity and enrollments to meet manpower needs, primarily through financing school construction and equipment. A shift in Bank support followed the 1980 sector policy paper, which proposed that the Bank finance education quality and internal efficiency in those countries that had achieved adequate quality of education at acceptably low unit costs. Over the past two decades the Bank has advocated lending for secondary education mainly in countries that have already achieved universal access to primary schooling. The World Bank's 1986 policy note recommended, as a sound approach to promoting secondary education, cost recovery, accompanied by selective scholarship schemes, and the encouragement of private and community schools to improve quality and efficiency in education through competition. That position was endorsed in the 1995 strategy paper (World Bank 1995), which advocated cost-benefit analysis to determine country-specific public expenditure priorities and reinforced the priority to be given primary education, where social rates of return were estimated to be highest in most developing countries. The paper further cited higher returns to general than to specialized vocational secondary education. The focus shifted from primary to basic education, which in many cases included the lower secondary grades.

With respect to vocational versus general secondary education, the Bank has taken an increasingly clear and firm stand since the 1980s. It has discouraged support for vocational secondary schooling on the grounds of its high unit costs and mixed outcomes, which are attributed to the poor cost-effectiveness of vocational school programs and their weak linkages to employment opportunities. The Education Sector Strategy (World Bank

1999b) advocated a more holistic approach, from a sectorwide perspective: identification of context-specific reform alternatives, better monitoring and empirical research to guide reform efforts, a focus on participation and client ownership, comprehensive analysis but selectivity in supporting actions, an emphasis on quality through a continuing shift from "hardware" to "software," concentration on development and poverty impact, knowledge management, and partnerships. No specific attention was given to secondary education. Within the 1999 sector support framework, regional variations and priorities prevailed (see box J.1).

The OED review of the Bank's secondary education portfolio revealed that shifts had taken place in the balance of project objectives and components in keeping with the education sector strategy. The result was a stronger focus on educational quality, sector management, and poverty issues. Other elements of the education sector strategy, such as the promotion of private schools and cost recovery combined with scholarship schemes, did not feature prominently in the portfolio. Support for secondary education in Africa, in low-income countries, and in countries with small populations was often part of projects that included assistance for the primary or tertiary sectors.

Box J.1 Issues and Priorities in Secondary Education by Region

Sub-Saharan Africa
Distance learning; secondary mathematics and science

East Asia and the Pacific
Equity and quality; need for diversified strategies related to country conditions

Europe and Central Asia
Systemic change to allow for realignment to market demand; reform of governance; improved efficiency, equity, and sustainability

Latin America and the Caribbean
Alternative approaches to increasing access to secondary education, together with curriculum reform to improve relevance to the global economy

Middle East and North Africa
Improved relevance of secondary education, closing the gender and social gaps in participation in postcompulsory education, and vocational education to meet the requirements of a market economy

Since the mid-1990s, several factors have promoted a rapid increase in the share of lending to general secondary education. First, as primary completion rates have risen, the demand for secondary places has grown. Second, the equitable and sustainable financing and management of secondary education have become a major challenge, especially in low-income countries. Third, the role of secondary education in economic and social development is being reassessed in the context of globalization and competitiveness in the information age. Fourth, changes in secondary education are being driven by rapid transformations in technology and labor markets.

The objectives of World Bank–supported secondary education projects can be grouped into six categories: (a) expansion of secondary education, (b) poverty and equity focus, (c) gender focus, (d) qualitative improvements in secondary education, (e) rehabilitation of physical facilities, and (f) improvement of efficiency and management in secondary education.

World Bank support for secondary education since 1990 shows the following trends:

1. *Middle-income countries* with high primary enrollment rates tended to borrow for secondary education in preference to other levels. On average, countries borrowing for secondary education had higher gross enrollment rates at the primary level, stronger policy and institutional conditions, and higher per capita incomes than those borrowing to finance other levels of education. Although the effectiveness of the primary system as measured by youth literacy rates did not appear to be a constraint on providing support to the secondary subsector, countries borrowing for dedicated secondary projects had higher rates of youth literacy. Countries with higher incomes and enrollment rates but weaker policy and institutional conditions did not borrow from the Bank.
2. Country population size seemed to be another factor, with *highly populated countries* borrowing more often for secondary education projects. Countries with medium-size or smaller populations tended to combine borrowing for secondary education with assistance for other education levels.
3. In *Asia* and *Latin America* country selection for secondary education lending was also influenced by the activities of other multilateral development banks.

Secondary education projects, on average, allocated a larger share of expenditures to civil works primarily and then to equipment, and smaller shares to textbooks, training, and technical assistance than did investments in the education portfolio as a whole. During the late 1990s the focus of lending activities shifted to include more projects aimed at supporting assessment systems, management information systems, financing of reform, decentralization, school-level management, and community participation and gave more attention to labor market information and employment services. The shift was in direct response to the changing global environment, the advent of the increased use of technology in education, and the focus on knowledge, lifelong learning, and skills for the labor market.

Performance of secondary education projects. As is well known, the education sector is characterized by long gestation periods before positive outcomes are forthcoming. Concerted, continuing efforts are needed to elicit cumulative positive outcomes. Over the past two decades, country conditions were a major factor in project performance. Outcomes of secondary education projects were sensitive to country income level. World Bank project completion and evaluation reports frequently attributed good performance in project implementation to national ownership, government commitment, and improved implementation capacity. Top-down initiatives (curriculum and assessment, supply of inputs), combined with bottom-up, demand-driven interventions such as school-managed improvement funds and textbook selection, were found to be important factors in improving education quality and equity, as demonstrated by the Chile Secondary Education project.

Policy reform. Successive Bank sector strategy documents have stressed that policy reform would be possible and effective if the focus were on ensuring government commitment to equitable and sustainable financing. One approach in this direction is the promotion of private secondary schools, combined with cost recovery and selective scholarship schemes in public schools. For example, a World Bank project in Mauritius included loans and other incentives for expanding private schools. Government commitment, however, was too weak to support implementation. In China and Korea some progress was seen in cost containment, cost recovery, and increased involvement of the private sector as a result of consistent government commitment to implementing proposed reforms. Good results were realized by involving employers in the curriculum reform process at the secondary vocational level.

Increasing access. It is a fairly straightforward matter to specify and measure the number of new places created through a project or program, the quality and efficiency of construction and equipment, enrollment rates, and utilization rates. Reporting on all the measures is, however, a challenging task. Proxies such as construction and equipment of facilities in underserved areas have often been used to measure progress toward poverty and equity objectives. It can be difficult to track impacts on productivity and social indicators.

Relevance to the labor market. The quality of evidence for progress in improving the relevance of secondary schooling to labor market requirements continues to pose a major challenge. General secondary education projects that aim to meet changing labor market needs by improving access to and quality of education must focus on evidence for results beyond the education sector. Graduate employment rates and tracer studies are important instruments for studying the link between education and labor market needs. Measures to study productivity should encompass labor market–oriented macroeconomic studies. All these considerations point to longer lag times in assessing the efficacy of policy reforms in general secondary education.

Educational quality. Educational outcomes or impacts must drive the assessment of performance in the area of quality improvement objectives. Input-based measures such as numbers of teachers trained or textbooks delivered, although necessary for the short-term assessment of project or program outputs, are not adequate for analyzing the impact of the inputs on student achievement or on labor market relevance. Here again, the lag time and resources needed to conduct impact evaluation often pose a problem for full analysis of the efficacy of project or program interventions. The definition of quality objectives needs to be less vague and better linked to specific and expected benefits that can be monitored. This is especially so in the areas of proposed curriculum reforms and teacher training.

Linkage of monitoring and evaluation to institutional capacity. Proven monitoring evaluation measures include evaluation of every project or program activity during the course of implementation, facilitation of midcourse refinements, dissemination and synergies at the local or school level, and use of test results to monitor equity and target at-risk schools. The Chile Secondary Education project exemplifies such an approach. Chile's strong institutional capacity is a major enabling factor for effectively monitoring and evaluating projects and programs. Another example is Angola, where the Education I project was implemented in a context of extremely difficult institutional conditions, civil conflict, and macroeconomic instability. Monitoring and evaluation were relatively strong, with sustained commitment from the Ministry of Education. Project outcomes were measured by comparing selected project and nonproject schools on the basis of changes in transition and completion rates, the number of pupils acquiring basic literary and numeracy within four years, and the number reaching satisfactory achievement levels. In addition, a beneficiary assessment revealed perceptions about the quality of education in the project schools. These measures show that effective assessment of the efficacy of lending is indeed possible.

Financing and efficiency. Detailed analysis of subsector expenditures, unit costs, and cost-effectiveness form the bedrock for a variety of measures to increase the efficiency of the secondary education system. Internal efficiency measures such as cost recovery, double shifting, measures to reduce student dropout and repetition, school consolidation to support economies of scope and scale, reduction of the share of boarding places, and changes in teacher utilization are important. Project-financed activities and policy measures, however, should be implemented as planned, and the results should be subjected to cost analysis.

Planning and management capacity. Tracking actual versus planned implementation of proposed training, technical assistance, and studies is important, but good independent evaluation of the effectiveness of project and program activities is necessary for assessing the achievement of objectives and subobjectives related to planning and management capacity. Often, the intent is to achieve these objectives through support for management information systems, curriculum development, assessment systems, decentralization, capacity for budgeting, economic and financial analysis, planning, and policy development.

Highly satisfactory outcomes owe much to good project preparation. This can include securing approval from the national legislature (as in the case of two similar and overlapping projects in Korea) and providing timely technical assistance to prepare for the shifting of implementation responsibilities to local bodies. Lack of government or national ownership and underestimation or inadequate assessment of institutional constraints are the factors that most often make for unsatisfactory outcomes. A sensible, realistic scope for projects, relatively simple project design, anticipation of the need for legal and regulatory changes, measures to ensure adequate stakeholder assessment, and a participation strategy help improve project outcomes. A thorough assessment of the capacity of project implementation units, proactive steps to mobilize political commitment or community participation, development of capacity and procedures for procurement and financial control, and adequate study of demand-side needs, cost-effectiveness, and recurrent financing capacity help strengthen project implementation and make for positive outcomes.

Directions in General Secondary Education Development

Issues concerning the development of secondary education relate to options for structure, curriculum, financing (including recurrent cost implications and financial sustainability), and governance specific to human, social, and economic development objectives in particular county contexts. These need to be addressed in a systematic and concerted manner, accompanied by a careful assessment of the distribution and poverty impacts of Bank assistance to secondary education. It is important to strengthen the analytical basis for general support of secondary education by anchoring it in a broader analysis of country economic, financial, institutional, social, and labor market conditions.

Alternate strategies are needed to address particular challenges for the development of secondary education in low-income countries where institutional capacity is weak. The current focus on the Millennium Development Goals and on Education for All has reaffirmed the priority to be given primary education but has also increased awareness of needs at the secondary level. Furthermore, the global knowledge economy and lifelong learning goals draw the spotlight to the crucial role of secondary education as a bridge between the primary and tertiary levels and its relevance to the labor market, which rewards adaptable skills.

Future secondary education projects could rely more on deeper and broader country-level analysis; draw explicit linkages between expected project outcomes and broader development goals for economic growth, social development, and poverty reduction; monitor distributional poverty impacts even when poverty reduction is not a specific project objective; assess real constraints and opportunities; ensure that project priorities and design match locally perceived priorities and institutional capacity; focus on the analytical basis for general secondary support in a broader assessment of country economic, financial, institutional, and social conditions; and strengthen the Bank's support for secondary education through systematic prior analysis and ongoing tracking of the linkages with labor market conditions and poverty and equity impacts.

Table J.1 World Bank Support for Secondary Education Development by Objective and by Region, Fiscal 1990–2001

Objective	Sub-Saharan Africa	Eastern Europe and Central Asia	Latin America and the Caribbean	Middle East and North Africa	South Asia	East Asia and the Pacific
Expansion of secondary education	Angola Botswana Burundi Ethiopia Ghana Mauritius Tanzania	Turkey	Chile Haiti	Jordan Morocco Oman Yemen, Republic of	Maldives Pakistan	China Malaysia Papua New Guinea Solomon Islands Vanuatu
Addressing poverty reduction and equity	Ethiopia Ghana Kenya Mauritius		Chile Jamaica	Morocco Oman	Maldives Pakistan Sri Lanka	China Vanuatu
Reducing gender disparity	Tanzania			Oman	Maldives Pakistan	
Improving quality	Angola Botswana Burundi Ethiopia Kenya Mauritius Rwanda Tanzania Togo	Albania Hungary Turkey	Argentina Barbados Brazil Chile Haiti Jamaica Mexico	Jordan Morocco Oman Yemen, Republic of	Maldives Sri Lanka	China Indonesia Korea, Rep. of Malaysia Papua New Guinea Solomon Islands Vanuatu

(Continues on the following page.)

Table J.1 Continued

Objective	Sub-Saharan Africa	Eastern Europe and Central Asia	Latin America and the Caribbean	Middle East and North Africa	South Asia	East Asia and the Pacific
Rehabilitating physical facilities	Botswana Ghana Rwanda Tanzania	Hungary Turkey	Barbados Brazil Mexico	Yemen, Republic of	Maldives Sri Lanka	China Korea, Rep. of Papua New Guinea
Promoting efficiency and improving management	Angola Burundi Ghana Kenya Mauritius Rwanda Tanzania Togo	Albania Turkey	Argentina Barbados Brazil Chile Haiti Jamaica Mexico	Jordan Oman Yemen, Republic of	Maldives Pakistan Sri Lanka	China Indonesia Korea, Rep. of Malaysia Solomon Islands Vanuatu

Table J.2 Synopsis of World Bank Analytical Work on Secondary Education

Country and region	Title	Fiscal year	Output type
Africa	Secondary and Secondary Teacher Education Strategic Plan	2004	Report
Uganda (AFR)	Postprimary Education Sector Work	2003	Report
Brazil (LAC)	Brazil Northeast Education Analytical and Advisory Activities	2003	Report
Ukraine (ECA)	Education Sector Note	2003	Policy Note
Azerbaijan (ECA)	Education Sector Note	2003	Policy Note
India (SAR)	State Education Reforms	2003	Policy Note
India (SAR)	Andhra Pradesh Education Strategy	2003	Policy Note
Jordan (MNA)	Jordan Education Sector Dialogue	2003	Country Dialogue
Philippines (EAP)	Philippines Human Development Sector Study	2003	Report
Egypt, Arab Rep. of (MNA)	Egypt Education Sector Policy Dialogue	2003	Country Dialogue
Timor-Leste (EAP)	Education Sector Study	2003	Report
Brazil (LAC)	Brazil Policy Notes Education	2003	Policy Note
Philippines (EAP)	Philippines Retrospective on Policy Reform in Education	2003	Policy Note
Vietnam (EAP)	Vietnam Cost of Social Services for the Poor	2003	Policy Note
India (SAR)	Secondary Education Policy Note	2003	Policy Note
Africa (AFR)	Can Africa Reach International Targets for Human Development?	2002	Policy Note
Africa (AFR)	Community Support for Basic Education	2002	Policy Note
Slovak Republic (ECA)	Education Note	2002	Policy Note
Africa (AFR)	Skills and Literacy Training for Better Livelihoods	2002	Policy Note
Romania (ECA)	Education Policy Note	2002	Policy Note
Caribbean (LAC)	Education Achievements	2002	Policy Note
Egypt, Arab Rep. of (MNA)	Egypt Education Strategy: Progress and Prospects	2002	Policy Note

(Continues on the following page.)

Table J.2 Continued

Country and region	Title	Fiscal year	Output type
Eritrea (AFR)	Eritrea Education Sector Note	2002	Report
India (SAR)	Karnataka Education Study	2002	Report
Jordan (MNA)	Cost-Efficiency of Education Spending	2002	Policy Note
Kyrgyz Republic (ECA)	Education Sector Note and Technical Assistance	2002	Policy Note
Philippines (EAP)	Philippines Out-of-School Youth	2002	Report
Russian Federation (ECA)	Education Policy Note	2002	Policy Note
Thailand (EAP)	Thailand Secondary Education for Employment	2000	Report
Jamaica (LAC)	"Main Report," vol. 1 of "Jamaica Secondary Education: Improving Quality and Extending Access"	1999	Report

Note: AFR, Sub-Saharan Africa; EAP, East Asia and the Pacific; ECA, Europe and Central Asia; LAC, Latin America and the Caribbean; MNA, Middle East and North Africa; SAR, South Asia.

Table J.3 World Bank Publications on Secondary Education by Year of Issue

Document title	Date	Report no.
China: Challenges of Secondary Education	2001	22856
Hungary: Secondary Education and Training	2001	22855
Romania: Secondary Education and Training	2001	22857
Linking Science Education to Labor Markets: Issues and Strategies	2000	21800
Secondary Education in El Salvador: Education Reform in Progress	1999	20963
Los insumos escolares en la educación secundaria y su efecto sobre el rendimiento académico de los estudiantes: Un estudio en Colombia	1998	20934
Background Notes: El Salvador Secondary Education Project	1997	18952
Voucher Program for Secondary Schools: The Colombian Experience	1996	16232
Investing in Junior Secondary Education in Indonesia: Rationale and Public Costs	1996	18813
Public and Private Secondary Schools in Developing Countries	1994	13672
Public and Private Secondary Schools in Developing Countries: What Are the Differences and Why Do They Persist?	1994	21194
The Costs of Secondary Education Expansion	1994	17674
Environmental Issues in Secondary Education	1994	17293
Equipment for Science Education Constraints and Opportunities	1993	17346
How to Raise the Effectiveness of Secondary Schools? Universal and Locally Tailored Investment Strategies	1993	17673
Secondary Education in Developing Countries	1993	17668
Reforming Higher Secondary Education in South Asia: The Case of Nepal	1993	IDP109
Social Gains from Female Education: A Cross-National Study	1992	WPS1045
World Bank Lending for Secondary School Science: A General Operational Review	1992	11401
Secondary Education in Developing Countries: Annotated Bibliography	1992	11312

(Continues on the following page.)

Table J.3 Continued

Document title	Date	Report no.
Secondary School Science in Developing Countries: Status and Issues	1992	17347
The Empty Opportunity: Local Control of Secondary Schools and Student Achievement in the Philippines	1992	WPS825
World Bank Policy Research Bulletin (3, 1)	1992	18062
What Causes Differences in Achievement in Zimbabwe's Secondary Schools?	1991	WPS705
Vocational Secondary Schooling in Israel: A Study of Labor Market Outcomes	1989	WPS142
Student Performance and School Costs in the Philippines' High Schools	1988	WPS61
Curriculum Diversification, Cognitive Achievement and Economic Performance: Evidence from Colombia and Tanzania	1987	EDT80
The External Efficiency of Diversified Secondary Schools in Colombia	1987	EDT59
Diversified Secondary Curriculum Projects: A Review of World Bank Experience 1963–1979	1987	EDT57
Cost-Effectiveness Analysis of an In-Service Teacher Training System: Logos II in Brazil	1981	DPH8140
Why Males Earn More: Location, Job Preferences and Job Discrimination among Brazilian Schoolteachers	1981	DPH8121

Note: Documents are in English unless otherwise specified.

Bibliography

The following common abbreviations for publishing organizations are used: ADBI, Asian Development Bank Institute; IBE, International Bureau of Education; IIEP, International Institute for Educational Planning; OECD, Organisation for Economic Co-operation and Development; OREALC, Oficina Regional de Educación para América Latina y el Caribe; UNESCO, United Nations Educational, Scientific, and Cultural Organization; UNICEF, United Nations Children's Fund; USAID, U.S. Agency for International Development.

Abelmann, Charles. 2001. "Skill Competitiveness: Lessons from Leading Hotels in Asia." EASHD Paper Series, East Asia and Pacific Region, Human Development Sector Unit, World Bank, Washington, DC.

Abelmann, Charles, Lee Kian Chang, and Pinchuda Tinakorn Na Ayudhaya. 2001. "Changing Workplaces, Changing Skills: Views from the Thai Private Sector on Work-Organization, Employee Recruitment and Selection." EASHD Paper Series 1, East Asia and Pacific Region, Human Development Sector Unit, World Bank, Washington, DC.

Abu-Ghaida, Dina, and Marie Connolly. 2003. "Trends in Relative Demand of Workers with Secondary Education: A Look at Nine Countries in East Asia, Africa, and MENA." Background paper prepared for *Expanding Opportunities and Building Competencies for Young People: A New Agenda for Secondary Education,* World Bank, Washington, DC.

Acemoglu, Daron, and Joshua Angrist. 1999. "How Large Are the Social Returns to Education? Evidence from Compulsory Schooling Laws." MIT Department of Economics Working Paper 99/30, Massachusetts Institute of Technology, Cambridge, MA.

Acemoglu, Daron, and Fabrizio Zilibotti. 2001. "Productivity Differences." *Quarterly Journal of Economics* 116 (2): 563–606.

Adams, Don. 1998. "Education and National Development in Asia: Trends, Issues, Politics, and Strategies." Report prepared for Asian Development Bank, Manila.

———. 2001. "Extending the Educational Planning Discourse." *Asia Pacific Education Review* 1 (3): 31–44.

ADB (Asian Development Bank). 2000. *Promoting Good Governance: ADB's Medium-Term Agenda and Action Plan.* Manila: ADB.

ADE-KAPE. 2003. "Cambodia Secondary Education Study." Background paper for *Expanding Opportunities and Building Competencies for Young People: A New Agenda for Secondary Education,* World Bank, Washington, DC.

Ahmed, Manzoor. 2000. "Promoting Public-Private Partnership in Health and Education: The Case of Bangladesh." In *Public-Private Partnerships in the Social Sector,* ed. Y. Wang, 219–91. Tokyo: ADBI Publishing.

Aho, Erkki, and Kari Pitkänen. 2004. "Long Run of Education Policy Development in Finland: Reforms of Basic and Secondary Education since 1968." Background paper for *Expanding Opportunities and Building Competencies for Young People: A New Agenda for Secondary Education,* World Bank, Washington, DC.

Alatas, Vivi, and Deon Filmer. 2004. "Local Level Governance and Schooling in Decentralizing Indonesia." Presented at the International Conference on Governance Accountability in Social Sector Decentralization, Washington, DC, February 18. www1.worldbank.org/publicsector/decentralization/Feb2004Course/Presentations/Filmer.ppt.

Alexiadou, Nafsika, and Jenny Ozga. 2002. "Modernising Education Governance in England and Scotland: Devolution and Control." *European Educational Research Journal* 1 (4): 676–91.

Al-Samarrai, Samer, and Paul Bennell. 2003. "Where Has All the Education Gone in Africa? Employment Outcomes among Secondary School and University Leavers." Institute of Development Studies, University of Sussex, Brighton, UK.

Anglo, J., and M. Lethoko. 2001. "Curriculum Development and Education for Living Together: Conceptual and Managerial Challenges in Africa." IBE, Geneva.

Angrist, Joshua, and Victor Lavy. 2002. "New Evidence on Classroom Computers and Pupil Learning." *Economic Journal* 112: 735–65.

Association for Effective Schools, Inc. 1996. "Correlates of Effective Schools." Stuyvesant, NY. http://www.mes.org/correlates.html.

Auto, D. H., L. Katz, and A. Krueger. 1997. "Computing Inequality: Have Computers Changed the Labor Market?" Working Paper 377, Industrial Relations Section, Princeton University, Princeton, NJ.

Bacevich, Andrew. 2002. *American Empire: The Realities and Consequences of U.S. Diplomacy.* Cambridge, MA: Harvard University Press.

Bailey, Thomas, and Theo Eicher. 1995. "Education, Technological Change, and Economic Growth." In *Education, Equity and Economic Competitiveness in the Americas: An Inter-American Dialogue Project,* ed. Jeffrey M. Puryear and José Joaquín Brunner, vol. 1, 103–20. Washington, DC: Organization of American States.

Balatti, J., and I. Falk. 2002. "Socioeconomic Contributions of Adult Learning to Community: A Social Capital Perspective." *Adult Education Quarterly* 52 (4): 281–98.

Barro, Robert J. 1991. "Economic Growth in a Cross Section of Countries." *Quarterly Journal of Economics* 106 (2): 407–43.

———. 1999. "Human Capital and Growth in Cross-Country Regressions." *Swedish Economic Policy Review* 6 (2): 237–77.

———. 2002. "Education as a Determinant of Economic Growth." In *Education in the Twenty-first Century*, ed. Edward P. Lazear, 9–26. Stanford, CA: Hoover Institution Press.

Barro, Robert J., and Jong-Wha Lee. 1996. "International Measures of Schooling Years and Schooling Quality." *American Economic Review* 86 (2): 218–23.

———. 2000. "International Data on Educational Attainment: Updates and Implications." Center for International Development, Harvard University, Cambridge, MA.

Bellei, Cristián, Gonzalo Muñoz, Luz María Pérez, and Dagmar Raczynski. 2004. *Escuelas efectivas en sectores de pobres: ¿Quién dijo que no se puede?* Santiago, Chile: UNICEF and Asesorías para el Desarrollo.

Benavot, Aaron. 2004. "Comparative Analysis of Secondary Education Curricula." With the collaboration of Massimo Amadio. World Bank and IBE, Washington, DC.

Benhabib, Jess, and Mark M. Spiegel. 1994. "The Role of Human Capital in Economic Development: Evidence from Aggregate Cross-Country Data." *Journal of Monetary Economics* 34 (2): 143–73.

Bentaouet Kattan, Raja, and Nicholas Burnett. 2004. "User Fees in Primary Education." Human Development Network, World Bank, Washington, DC.

Berman, Eli, and Stephen Machin. 2000. "Skill-Biased Technology Transfer around the World." *Oxford Review of Economic Policy* 16 (3): 12–22.

Bertocchi, Graciela, and Michael Spagat. 2003. "The Evolution of Modern Educational Systems: Technical vs. General Education, Distributional Conflict, and Growth." http://www.economia.unimore.it/Bertocchi_Graziella/papers/eduweb.pdf (accessed August 18, 2003).

Bhatia, Jagdish C., and John Cleland. 1995a. "Determinants of Maternal Care in a Region of South India." *Health Transition Review* 5 (2): 127–42.

———. 1995b. "Self-Reported Symptoms of Gynecological Morbidity and Their Treatment in South India." *Studies in Family Planning* 26 (4): 203–16.

Binder, Melissa. 2004. "The Cost of Providing Universal Secondary Education in Developing Countries." Department of Economics, University of New Mexico, Albuquerque.

Birdsall, Nancy, and Juan Luis Londoño. 1997. "Asset Inequality Matters: An Assessment of the World Bank's Approach to Poverty Reduction." *American Economic Review* 87 (2): 32–37.

Bishop, John. 1998. "Do Curriculum-Based External Exit Exam Systems Enhance Student Achievement?" CPRE Research Report Series RR-40,

Consortium for Policy Research in Education (CPRE), Graduate School of Education, University of Pennsylvania, Philadelphia.

Black, Paul, and Dylan William. 1998. "Inside the Black Box: Raising Standards through Classroom Assessment." *Phi Delta Kappan* 80 (2): 139–48.

Blondal, Sveinbjorn, Simon Field, and Nathalie Girouard. 2002. "Investment in Human Capital through Upper-Secondary and Tertiary Education." OECD Economic Studies 34 2002/I, Paris.

Bloom, D. 2003. "Beyond the Basics: Patterns, Trends and Issues in Secondary Education in Developing Countries." Background paper for *Expanding Opportunities and Building Competencies for Young People: A New Agenda for Secondary Education*, World Bank, Washington, DC.

Borensztein, E., J. de Gregorio, and J. W. Lee. 1998. "How Does Foreign Direct Investment Affect Economic Growth?" *Journal of International Economics* 45 (1): 115–35.

Borman, Geoffrey D., Gina M. Hewes, Laura T. Overman, and Shelly Brown. 2002. "Comprehensive School Reform and Student Achievement: A Meta-Analysis." Report 59, Center for Research on the Education of Students Placed At Risk (CRESPAR), Baltimore, MD. http://www.csos.jhu.edu/CRESPAR/techReports/Report59.pdf.
Also published as Geoffrey D. Borman, Gina M. Hewes, and Laura T. Overman, "Comprehensive School Reform and Achievement: A Meta-Analysis," *Review of Educational Research* 73 (2) (2003): 125–230.

Bosch, Andrea, Rebecca Rhodes, and Sera Kariuki. 2002. "Interactive Radio Instruction: An Update from the Field." In *Technologies for Education: Potentials, Parameters, and Prospects*, ch. 9. Paris: UNESCO and Academy for Educational Development (AED).

Bourguignon, François, Francisco H. G. Ferreira, and Phillippe G. Leite. 2003. "Conditional Cash Transfers, Schooling, and Child Labor: Micro-Simulating Brazil's Bolsa Escola Program." In "Child Labor and Development," ed. Alan L. Winters, *World Bank Economic Review* 17 (2): 229–54.

Bowles, Samuel, and Herbert Gintis. 2002. "Social Capital and Community Governance." *Economic Journal* 112 (November): F419–F436.

Bransford, John D., Ann L. Brown, and Rodney R. Cocking, eds. 2000. *How People Learn: Brain, Mind, Experience, and School*, exp. ed. Committee on Developments in the Science of Learning and Commission on Behavioral and Social Sciences and Education, National Research Council. Washington, DC: National Academy Press.

Braslavsky, Cecilia. 1999. "The Secondary Education Curriculum in Latin America: New Tendencies and Changes." IBE–UNESCO, Geneva.

————. 2002. "New Curricula and New Demands for Teacher Training." In *The New Secondary Education: A Path toward Human Development*, 60–100. Santiago, Chile: UNESCO-OREALC.

Bray, Mark. 1996. *Counting the Full Cost: Parental and Community Financing of Education in East Asia*. Directions in Development Series. Washington, DC: World Bank.

———. 1999. *The Shadow Education System: Private Tutoring and Its Implications for Planners*. Fundamentals of Educational Planning 61. Paris: IIEP–UNESCO.

———. 2003. *Adverse Effects of Private Supplementary Tutoring: Dimensions, Implications and Government Responses*. Ethics and Corruption in Education Series. Paris: IIEP–UNESCO.

Bray, Mark, and M. V. Mukundan. 2003. "Management and Governance for EFA: Is Decentralisation Really the Answer?" Comparative Education Research Centre, Faculty of Education, University of Hong Kong. http://portal.unesco.org/education/en/ev.php-URL_ID=25755&URL_DO=DO_TOPIC&URL_SECTION=201.html.

Bregman, Jacob, and Karen Bryner. 2003. "Quality of Secondary Education in Africa (SEIA)." Paper presented at biennial meeting, Association for Development in Africa (ADEA), Mauritius, December 3–6. http://www.adeanet.org/biennial2003/papers/7A_Bregman_ENG.pdf.

Bresnahan, Timothy F., Erik Brynjolfsson, and Lorin M. Hitt. 1999. "Information Technology, Workplace Organization and the Demand for Skilled Labor: Firm-Level Evidence." NBER Working Paper Series 7136, National Bureau of Economic Research, Cambridge, MA.

British Chambers of Commerce. 1998. "Skills for Competitiveness: A Report on Skills for Business by the British Chambers of Commerce." London.

Brophy, Jere. 1999. "Teaching." Educational Practices Series 1, International Academy of Education, Brussels.

Brown, Kathleen, and Victor Anfara, Jr. 2002. *From the Desk of the Middle School Principal: Leadership Responsive to the Needs of Young Adolescents*. Lanham, MD: Scarecrow Press.

Brunner, José Joaquín. 2001. "Globalización y el futuro de la educación: Tendencias, desafíos y estrategias; Séptima reunión del Comité Regional Intergubernamental del Proyecto Principal de Educación en América Latina y el Caribe." Documento de Apoyo ED-01/PROMEDLAC VII, UNESCO, Santiago, Chile.

Bruns, Barbara, Alain Mingat, and Ramahatra Rakotomalala. 2003. *Achieving Universal Primary Education by 2015: A Chance for Every Child*. Washington, DC: World Bank.

Cabrol, Marcelo. 2002. "Los desafíos de la educación secundaria: ¿Que nos dice el análisis de flujos?" División de Programas Sociales 2, Banco Interamericano de Desarrollo, Washington, DC.

Caillods, Françoise, and María H. Maldonado-Villar. 1997. "Some Issues Relating to Secondary Education in Latin America." In "Secondary

Education: The Major Project of Education." *Bulletin* 42 (April), UNESCO–OREALC, Santiago, Chile.

Calderoni, Jose 1998. "Telesecundaria: Using TV to Bring Education to Rural Mexico." Education and Technology Technical Note Series 3 (2), World Bank, Washington, DC. http://wbln0018.worldbank.org/HDNet/HDdocs.nsf/C11FBFF6C1B77F9985256686006DC949/1635F1703FE053B385256754006D8C3F/$FILE/telesecundaria.pdf.

California State Department of Education. 1987. "Caught in the Middle: Education Reform for Young Adolescents in California Public Schools." Report of the Superintendent's Middle Grade Task Force Report, Sacramento.

Cappellari, Lorenzo. 2004. "High School Types, Academic Performance and Early Labor Market Outcomes." Dipartimento di Scienze Economiche e Metodi Quantitativi, Università del Piemonte Orientale, and IZA. Research Publication 90, National Center for the Study of Privatization in Education, Teachers College, Columbia University, New York. http://www.ncspe.org/publications_files/OP89.pdf.

Carnoy, Martin. 1999. "Globalization and Educational Reform: What Planners Need to Know." IIEP–UNESCO, Paris.

————. 2000. *Sustaining the New Economy: Work, Family and Community in the Information Age*. Cambridge, MA: Harvard University Press; New York: Russell Sage Foundation.

————. 2002. "Are Educational Reforms Working in Latin America? A New Look at Understanding Whether Education Is Getting Better." Regional Policy Dialogue, Working Paper, Education Network, Third Meeting: Secondary Education, Inter-American Development Bank, Washington, DC, April 4–5. http://www.iadb.org/int/DRP/ing/Red4/Documents/CarnoyAbril4-5-2002ing.pdf.

Caselli, Francesco, and Wilbur John Coleman II. 2001. "Cross-Country Technology Diffusion: The Case of Computers." *American Economic Review, Papers and Proceedings* 91 (2): 328–35.

Cave, P. 2001. "Educational Reform in Japan in the 1990s: 'Individuality' and Other Uncertainties." *Comparative Education* 37 (2): 173–91.

CED (Committee for Economic Development). 1998. "The Employer's Role in Linking School and Work." Policy statement by the Research and Policy Committee, CED, Washington, DC.

Checchi, Daniel. 1999. "Inequality in Income and Access to Education: A Cross Country Analysis." Working Paper 158, United Nations University, World Institute for Development Economics Research, Helsinki.

China. Various years. *National Education Finance Statistics Yearbook*. Beijing.

China, People's Congress. 1986. *Compulsory Education Law of the People's Republic of China*. Beijing.

Chua, Amy. 2002. *World on Fire: How Exporting Free Market Democracy Breeds Ethnic Hatred and Global Instability*. New York: Doubleday.

CISCO. 2004. "Cisco Systems Academy Connection." http://www.cisco. com/en/US/learning/netacad/index.html (accessed March 15, 2005).

Clark, Burton R. 1985. *The School and the University.* Berkeley: University of California Press.

Clark, Tom. 2001. "Virtual Schools: Trends and Issues; Study of Virtual Schools in the United States." DLRN/WestED and the Center for the Application of Information Technologies, Western Illinois University, Macomb, IL.

Clemens, Michael. 2004. "The Long Walk to School: International Education Goals in Historical Perspective." Center for Global Development, Washington, DC. http://econwpa.wustl.edu/eps/dev/papers/ 0403/0403007.pdf.

CNDP (Centre National de Documentation Pédagogique). 2004. "Pour la réussite de tous les élèves." Rapport Thélot, La Documentation Française, Paris.

Coetzee, J. M. 1997. *Boyhood: Scenes from Provincial Life.* New York: Viking.

Cohen, Daniel, and Marcelo Soto. 2001. *Growth and Human Capital: Good Data, Good Results.* Paris: OECD.

Colclough, Christopher. 1993. "Education and the Markets: Which Parts of the Neo-Liberal Solution are Correct?" Innocenti Occasional Papers, Economic Policy Series 37, UNICEF, Florence, Italy.

Committee on Classroom Assessment and the National Science Education Standard. 2001. "Classroom Assessment and the National Science Education Standard." National Academy of Sciences, Washington, DC.

Cothran, D. J., and C. D. Ennis. 2000. "Building Bridges to Student Engagement: Communicating Respect and Care for Students in Urban High Schools." *Journal of Research and Development in Education* 33 (2): 106–17.

Cotton, Kathleen. 1992. "School-Based Management." Topical Synthesis 6, School Improvement Research Series (SIRS), North West Regional Educational Laboratory, Portland, OR. http://www.nwrel.org/ scpd/sirs/7/topsyn6.html.

———. 2001. "New Small Learning Communities: Findings from Recent Literature." http://www.smallschoolsproject.org.

Cox, Cristian. 2004. "Policy Formation and Implementation in Secondary Education Reform: The Case of Chile in the 1990s." Background paper prepared for *Expanding Opportunities and Building Competencies for Young People: A New Agenda for Secondary Education,* World Bank, Washington, DC.

CPRE (Consortium for Policy Research in Education: Research for Action). 1998. "The Accountability System: Defining Responsibility for Student Achievement, Progress Report 1996–1997." University of Pennsylvania, Philadelphia.

Crain, R. L., A. L. Heebner, and Y. Si. 1992. "The Effectiveness of New York City Career Magnet Schools: An Evaluation of Ninth Grade Performance Using an Experimental Design." National Center for Research in Vocational Education, Berkeley, CA.

Cuban, Larry. 1986. *Teachers and Machines: The Classroom Use of Technology since 1920.* New York: Teachers College Press.

———. 2001. *Oversold and Underused: Computers in the Classroom.* Cambridge, MA: Harvard University Press.

Cummings, William K. 1997. "Patterns of Modern Education." In *International Handbook of Education and Development: Preparing Schools, Students and Nations for the Twenty-first Century,* ed. William K. Cummings and Noel F. McGinn. New York: Pergamon.

Cummings, William K., and Abby R. Riddell. 1994. "Alternative Policies for the Finance, Control and Delivery of Basic Education." *International Journal of Education Research* 21 (8): 751–76.

Curran, Chris, and Paud Murphy. 1992. "Distance Education at the Second-Level and for Teacher Education in Six African Countries." In *Distance Education in Anglophone Africa: Experience with Secondary Education and Teacher Training,* ed. Paud Murphy and Abdelwahed Zhiri, 17–40. Economic Development Institute (EDI) Development Policy Case Series, Analytical Case Studies 9. Washington, DC: World Bank.

Dager, Linda, and Rolf K. Blank. 1999. *Improving Mathematics Education Using Results from NAEP and TIMSS.* Washington, DC: Council of Chief State School Officers.

Dale, Roger. 1997. "The State and the Governance of Education: An Analysis of the Restructuring of the State-Education Relation." In *Education: Culture, Economy, and Society,* ed. A. H. Halsey, P. Brown, and A. Stuart Wells, 273–82. Oxford: Oxford University Press.

Darling-Hammond, Linda. 2000. "Teacher Quality and Student Achievement: A Review of State Policy Evidence." *Education Policy Analysis Archives* 8 (1). http://epaa.asu.edu/epaa/v8n1/.

Darling-Hammond, Linda, Ruth Chung, and Fred Frelow. 2002. "Variation in Teacher Preparation: How Well Do Different Pathways Prepare Teachers to Teach?" *Journal of Teacher Education* 53 (4): 286–302. http://jte.sagepub.com/cgi/content/abstract/53/4/286.

de Andraca, Ana María, org. 2003. "Buenas prácticas para mejorar la educación en América latina." Ed. San Marino, Santiago, Chile.

Dee, Thomas. 2003. "Are There Civic Returns to Education?" NBER Working Paper 9588, National Bureau of Economic Research, Cambridge, MA. http://www.nber.org/papers/w9588.

de Ferranti, David, Guillermo Perry, Indermit Gill, J. Luis Guasch, William Maloney, Carolina Sanchez-Paramo, and Norbert Schady. 2003. *Closing the Gap in Education and Technology.* World Bank Latin America and the Caribbean Studies. Washington, DC: World Bank.

de la Fuente, Angel, and Rafael Doménech. 2000. "Human Capital in Growth Regressions: How Much Difference Does Data Quality Make?" CEPR Discussion Paper 2466, Centre for Economic Policy Research, London.

Delannoy, Françoise. 2000. "Education Reforms in Chile, 1980–98: A Lesson in Pragmatism." Country Studies, Education Reform and Management Publication Series I(I), World Bank, Washington, DC.

Delors, Jacques. 1996. *Learning: the Treasure Within.* Paris: UNESCO.

Dessus, Sébastien. 1999. "Human Capital and Growth: The Recovered Role of Education Systems." Policy Research Working Paper 2632, Social and Economic Development Group and Social Development Group, Middle East and North Africa Region, World Bank, Washington, DC. http://econ.worldbank.org/view.php?type=5&id=2311.

de Walque, Damien. 2004. "How Does the Impact of an HIV/AIDS Information Campaign Vary with Educational Attainment? Evidence from Rural Uganda." Policy Research Working Paper 3289, Public Services, Development Research Group, World Bank, Washington, DC.

Dewees, Sarah. 1999. "The School-within-a-School Model." ERIC Identifier ED438147, ERIC Clearinghouse on Rural Education and Small Schools, Charleston, WV.

Earle, Rodney S. 2002. "The Integration of Instructional Technology into Public Education: Promises and Challenges." *Educational Technology Magazine* 42 (1): 5–13. http://bookstoread.com/etp/earle.pdf.

Easterly, William, and Ross Levine. 2002. "It's Not Factor Accumulation: Stylized Facts and Growth Models." Working Paper 164, Central Bank of Chile, Santiago.

Economist. 2003. "School Privatization." May 1.

El-Gibaly, Omaima, Barbara Ibrahim, Barbara S. Mensch, and Wesley H. Clark. 2002. "The Decline of Female Circumcision in Egypt: Evidence and Interpretation." *Social Science and Medicine* 54 (2): 205–20.

Elo, Irma T. 1992. "Utilization of Maternal Health-Care Services in Peru: The Role of Women's Education." *Health Transition Review* 2 (1): 49–69.

Evers, Williamson M., and Herbert J. Walberg, eds. 2003. *School Accountability: An Assessment by the Koret Task Force on K–12 Education.* Stanford, CA: Hoover Institution Press.

Feinstein, Leon. 2002. "Quantitative Estimates of the Social Benefits of Learning: 1 Crime." Report 5, Centre for Research on the Wider Benefits of Learning, London.

Feinstein, Leon, Cathie Hammond, Laura Woods, John Preston, and John Bynner. 2003. "The Contribution of Adult Learning to Health and Social Capital." Report 8, Centre for Research on the Wider Benefits of Learning, London.

Figueredo, Vivian, and Stephen Anzalone. 2003. "Alternative Models for Secondary Education in Developing Countries: Rationale and Realities." Paper prepared for Improving Education Quality (IEQ)

Project, American Institutes for Research, in collaboration with the Academy for Educational Development, Education Development Center, Inc., Juárez and Associates, Inc., and University of Pittsburgh. http://www.ieq.org/pdf/Alternative_Models_sec_ed.pdf.

Filmer, Deon. 2000. "The Structures of Social Disparities in Education: Gender and Wealth." Policy Research Working Paper 2268, World Bank, Washington, DC.

Filmer, Deon, and Lant Pritchett. 1999. "The Effect of Household Wealth on Educational Attainment: Evidence from 35 Countries." *Population and Development Review* 25 (1): 85–120.

Fink, Elaine, and Lauren B. Resnick. 2001. "Developing Principals as Instructional Leaders." *Phi Delta Kappan* 82 (8): 598–606.

Fiske, Edward B., and Helen F. Ladd. 2000. *When Schools Compete: A Cautionary Tale*. Washington, DC: Brookings Institution Press.

Fleming, Peter. 2000. *The Art of Middle Management in Secondary Schools: A Guide to Effective Subject and Team Leadership*. London: David Fulton.

Fretwell, D., and A. Wheeler. 2001. "Turkey: Secondary Education and Training." Secondary Education Series, Human Development Network, World Bank, Washington, DC.

Fullan, Michael. 1993. *Change Forces: Probing the Depths of Educational Reform*. Bristol, PA: Falmer.

Fylkesnes, K., R. M. Musonda, M. Sichone, Z. Ndhlovu, F. Tembo, and M. Monze. 2001. "Declining HIV Prevalence and Risk Behaviours in Zambia: Evidence from Surveillance and Population-Based Surveys." *AIDS* 15 (7): 907–16.

Gill, Indermit S., Fred Fluitman, and Amit Dar, eds. 2000. *Vocational Education and Training Reform*. New York: Oxford University Press.

Gladden, Robert. 1998. "The Small School Movement: A Review of the Literature." In *Small Schools, Big Imaginations: A Creative Look at Urban Public Schools*, ed. Michelle Fine and Janis I. Somerville. Chicago: Cross City Campaign for Urban School Reform.

Glewwe, Paul, Nauman Ilias, and Michael Kremer. 2003. "Teacher Incentives." NBER Working Paper 9671, National Bureau of Economic Research, Cambridge, MA.

Godwin, C. D. 1999. "Difficulties in Reforming Education Policy: The Hong Kong Case." *Management Learning* 30 (1): 63–81.

Goldin, Claudia. 1999. "Egalitarianism and the Returns to Education during the Great Transformation of American Education." *Journal of Political Economy* 107 (6): S65–S94.

———. 2001. "The Human Capital Century and American Leadership: Virtues of the Past." *Journal of Economic History* 61 (2): 263–92.

———. 2002. "The Human Capital Century and American Leadership: Virtues of the Past." Address delivered at the 47th annual conference series, Federal Reserve Bank of Boston, June 19.

————. 2003. "The Human Capital Century." *Education Next* 3 (Winter). http://www.educationnext.org/20031/73.html.

Gordon, E. E. 1997. "The New Knowledge Worker." *Adult Learning* 8 (4): 14–17.

Govindasamy, Pavalavalli. 2000. "Poverty, Women's Status, and Utilization of Health Services in Egypt." In *Women, Poverty, and Demographic Change,* ed. Brigida Garcia, 263–85. Oxford: Oxford University Press.

Grant Lewis, Suzanne, and Jordan Naidoo. 2004. "Whose Theory of Participation? School Governance Policy and Practice in South Africa." *Current Issues in Comparative Education* 6 (2). http://www.tc.columbia.edu/cice/articles/sgl162.htm.

Gray, John. 2004. "School Effectiveness and the 'Other Outcomes' of Secondary Schooling: A Reassessment of Three Decades of British Research." *Improving Schools* 7 (2): 185–98.

Green, Andy, Alison Wolf, and Tom Leney. 1999. "Convergence and Divergence in European Education and Training Systems." Institute of Education, University of London.

Haddad, Wadi D., and Alexandra Draxler, eds. 2002. *Technologies for Education: Potentials, Parameters and Prospects.* Paris: UNESCO and the Academy for Educational Development (AED).

Hanson, Mark. 2004. "Educational Decentralization: Issues and Challenges." Background paper for the International Conference on Governance Accountability in Social Sector Decentralization, World Bank, Washington, DC, February 18–19.

Hanushek, Eric A., and Dennis D. Kimko. 2000. "Schooling, Labor-Force Quality, and the Growth of Nations." *American Economic Review* 90 (5): 1184–1208.

Hargreaves, Andy. 2003. *Teaching in the Knowledge Society: Education in the Age of Insecurity.* New York: Teachers College Press.

Hargreaves, Andy, and Lorna Earl. 1990. "Right of Passage: A Review of Selected Research about Schooling in the Transition Years." Ontario Department of Education, Toronto.

Hargreaves, David. 2001. "A Capital Theory of School Effectiveness and Improvement." *British Educational Research Journal* 27 (4): 487–503.

————. 2003. "Education Epidemic: Transforming Secondary Schools through Innovation Networks." Advance copy. London: Demos. http://www.c2kni.org.uk/news/education_epidemic.pdf.

Harper Simpson, Ida. 1999. "Historical Patterns of Workplace Organization: From Mechanical to Electronic Control and Beyond." *Current Sociology* 47 (2): 47–75.

Hartenberger, Lisa, and Andrea Bosch. 1996. "Making IRI Even Better for Girls." ABEL2 Project, USAID, Washington, DC.

Hepp, Pedro, Enrique Hinostroza, Ernesto Laval, and Lucio Rehbein. 2004. *Technology in Schools: Education, ICT and the Knowledge Society.* Washington, DC: World Bank.

Hiebert, J., R. Gallimore, and J. Stigler. 2002. "A Knowledge Base for the Teaching Profession: What Would It Look Like and How Can We Get One?" *Educational Researcher* 31 (5): 3–15.

Hill, Paul. 2001. *High Schools and the Development of Healthy Young People.* Washington, DC: University of Washington and the Brookings Institution Brown Center on Education Policy. http://www.brookings.edu/gs/brown/HSDvlpHealthyYP.pdf.

Hirvenoja, P. 1999. "Education Policy Changes and School Choice in Europe from the Scandinavian Perspective." Paper presented at the European Conference on Educational Research, Lahti, Finland, September 22–25. http://www.leeds.ac.uk/educol/.

Hodges, Dave, and Noel Burchell. 2003. "The Industry-Education Competency Gap: New Zealand Employers' Perspectives." Faculty of Business, Unitec Institute of Technology, Auckland, New Zealand. Paper presented at the World Association of Co-operative Education conference on "Towards a Knowledge Society: Integrating Learning and Work," Rotterdam, August 26–29.

Honey, Margaret. 2001. "Technology's Effectiveness as a Teaching and Learning Tool." Testimony before the Labor, Health and Human Services, and Education Appropriations Subcommittee of the U.S. Senate. Education Development Center, Inc., Newton, MA. http://main.edc.org/spotlight/Tech/mhtestimony.htm#1.

Hoxby, C. 2000. "Peer Effects in the Classroom: Learning from Gender and Race Variation." NBER Working Paper 7867, National Bureau of Economic Research, Cambridge, MA.

Hsieh, Chang-Tai, and Miguel Urquiola. 2003. "When Schools Compete, How Do They Compete? An Assessment of Chile's Nationwide School Voucher Program." NBER Working Paper Series 10008, National Bureau of Economic Research, Cambridge, MA.

Huberman, Michael. 1995. "Professional Careers and Professional Development: Some Intersections." In *Professional Development in Education*, ed. T. Guskey and M. Huberman, 201–20. New York: Teachers College Press.

Hui, Philip K. F. 2001. "Collaboration among the Government, the Business and the Education Sectors in Promoting the Use of Information Technology in Schools: The Experience of Hong Kong." Paper presented at the seminar "Public-Private Private Partnerships in Education," Tokyo, May–June.

ILO (International Labour Organization). 1998. "Informe sobre el empleo en el mundo 1998–1999: Empleabilidad y mundialización; papel fundamental de la formación." International Labour Office, Geneva.

Ilon, Lynn. 1997. "Educational Repercussions of a Global System of Production." In *International Handbook of Education and Development: Preparing Schools, Students and Nations for the Twenty-first Century*, ed. William K. Cummings and Noel F. McGinn. New York: Pergamon.

———. 2000. "Colonial Secondary Education in a Global Age: Economic Distortions in Bangladesh." *Asia Pacific Education Review* 1 (1): 91–99.

Ireson, Judith, and Susan Hallam. 2001. *Ability Grouping in Education*. London: Sage Publications.

Irmsher, Karen. 1997. "School Size." ERIC Digest 113, Identifier ED414615, ERIC Clearinghouse on Educational Management, Eugene OR. http://eric.uoregon.edu/publications/digests/digest113.html.

Jacinto, Claudia. 2002. "Youth and Labor in Latin America: Tensions and Challenges for Secondary Education and Vocational Training." In *The New Secondary Education: A Path toward Human Development*. Santiago, Chile: UNESCO-OREALC.

James, Estelle. 1994. "The Public-Private Division of Responsibility for Education." In *The International Encyclopedia of Education*, Economics of Education section, ed. T. Husen and T. N. Postlethwaite, 2d ed. New York: Pergamon.

Kadzamir, Esme Chipo. 2003. "Where Has All the Education Gone in Malawi?" Institute of Development Studies, University of Sussex, Brighton, UK.

Kamens, D., J. Meyer, and A. Benavot. 1996. "Worldwide Patterns in Academic Secondary Education Curricula." *Comparative Education Review* 40 (2): 116–38.

Kellaghan, Thomas, and Vincent Greaney, eds. 2001. *Using Assessment to Improve the Quality of Education*. Fundamentals of Educational Planning Series 71. Paris: IIEP–UNESCO.

Kettl, Donald. 2002. *The Transformation of Governance: Public Administration for Twenty-first Century America*. Baltimore, MD: Johns Hopkins University Press.

Kim, Gwang-Jo. 2002. "Education Policies and Reform in South Korea." In "Secondary Education Africa: Strategies for Renewal," World Bank presentations at the December 2001 UNESCO/Basic Education Section: Primary Section (BREDA)–World Bank Regional Workshop in Mauritius on the Renewal of Secondary Education in Africa, Africa Region Human Development Working Paper Series, 29–40.

King, Elizabeth, Laura Rawlings, Marybell Gutierrez, Carlos Pardo, and Carlos Torres. 1997. "Colombia's Targeted Education Voucher Program: Features, Coverage, and Participation." World Bank, Washington, DC.

Kirumira, Edward, and Fred Bateganya. 2003. "Where Has All the Education Gone in Uganda? Employment Outcomes among Secondary School and University Leavers." Faculty of Social Sciences, Makerere

University, Uganda; Institute of Development Studies, University of Sussex, Brighton, UK.

Kivirauma, Joel, Risto Rinne, and Piia Seppänen. 2003. "Neo-Liberal Education Policy Approaching the Finnish Shoreline." *Journal for Critical Education Policy Studies* 1 (1): 513–31. http://www.jceps.com/?pageID=article&articleID=5.

Knapp, Michael S., Michael A. Copland, and Joan E. Talbert. 2003. "Leading for Learning: Reflective Tools for School and District Leaders." Center for the Study of Teaching and Policy, University of Washington, Seattle.

Koda, Yoshiko. 2002. "Benchmarking to International Assessments: Diagnosing Education Systems towards the Knowledge Economy." Human Development Network, Education, World Bank, Washington, DC.

Koenig, Michael A., Saifuddin Ahmed, Mian Bazle Hossain, and A. B. M. Khorshed Alam Mozumder. 2003. "Women's Status and Domestic Violence in Rural Bangladesh: Individual- and Community-Level Effects." *Demography* 40 (2): 269–88.

Krueger, Alan B., and Mikael Lindahl. 1999. "Education for Growth in Sweden and the World." NBER Working Paper 7190, National Bureau of Economic Research, Cambridge, MA.

———. 2001. "Education for Growth: Why and for Whom?" *Journal of Economic Literature* 39 (4): 1101–36.

Kurzweil, Ray. 1999. *The Age of Spiritual Machines.* New York: Viking.

Kwok, Percy. 2004. "Examination-Oriented Knowledge and Value Transformation in East Asian Cram Schools." *Asia Pacific Education Review* 5 (1): 64–75.

Lall, Sanjaya. 2001. *Competitiveness, Technology and Skills.* Cheltenham, UK: Edward Elgar.

———. 2002. "Globalization and Development: Perspectives from Emerging Nations." Prepared for the BNDES 50th anniversary seminar, Rio de Janeiro, September 12.

Lam, David, and Robert Schoeni. 1993. "Effects of Family Background on Earnings and Returns to Schooling: Evidence from Brazil." *Journal of Political Economy* 101 (4): 213–43.

Lamdin, Douglas, and Michael Mintrom. 1997. "School Choice in Theory and Practice: Taking Stock and Looking Ahead." *Education Economics* 5 (3): 211–44.

Lang, D. 2003. "A Primer on Formula Funding: A Study of Student-Focused Funding in Ontario." Report prepared for the Atkinson Foundation, "The Schools We Need" Project, University of Toronto. http://schoolsweneed.oise.utoronto.ca/funding.pdf (accessed January 2003).

Langer, Judith A. 2004. *Getting to Excellent: How to Create Better Schools.* New York: Teachers College Press.

Lanjouw, Peter, and Martin Ravallion. 1999. "Benefit Incidence, Public Spending Reforms, and the Timing of Program Capture." *World Bank Economic Review* 13 (2): 257–73.

Larach, L. 2001. "Brazil Secondary Education Profile." Secondary Education Series, Human Development Network, World Bank, Washington, DC.

Lavy, Victor. 1996. "School Supply Constraints and Children's Educational Outcomes in Rural Ghana." *Journal of Development Economics* 51 (2): 291–314.

Lee, Chong Jae. 2003. "Secondary Education in Korea." Presentation at the World Bank, Washington, DC, July 24.

Lee, Molly N. N., and Chan Lean Heng. 1999. "Skill Competitiveness: Employer Views from Malaysia." EASHD Paper Series 2, East Asia and Pacific Region, Human Development Sector Unit, World Bank, Washington, DC.

Lee, Valerie E. 2000. "School Size and the Organization of Secondary Schools." In *Handbook of the Sociology of Education*, ed. Maureen T. Hallinan. New York: Kluwer Academic/Plenum.

Le Métais, Joanna. 2002. *International Developments in Upper Secondary Education: Context, Provision and Issues.* National Foundation for Education Research and National Council for Curriculum and Assessment (NCCA), Thematic Study 8, Dublin. http://www.inca.org.uk/pdf/cav_final_report.pdf.

Levy, Frank, and Richard Murnane. 2001. "Key Competencies Critical to Economic Success." In *Defining and Selecting Key Competencies*, ed. Dominique Simone Rychen and Laura Hersh Salganik. Cambridge, MA: Hogrefe and Huber.

———. 2004. *The New Division of Labor: How Computers Are Creating the Next Job Market.* Princeton, NJ: Princeton University Press and Russell Sage Foundation.

Lewin, Keith. 2002. *Options for Post-Primary Education and Training in Uganda: Increasing Access, Equity and Efficiency.* London: U.K. Department for International Development (DfID) and Government of Uganda.

———. 2003. *Secondary Education in Africa: Issues of Cost and Finance.* Presentation to the Secondary Education in Africa (SEIA) Conference, World Bank and Association for the Development of Education in Africa (ADEA), Kampala, June.

Lewin, Keith, and Françoise Caillods. 2001. "Financing Secondary Education in Developing Countries: Strategies for Sustainable Growth." IIEP–UNESCO, Paris.

Lezotte, Lawrence W. 1991. *Correlates of Effective Schools: The First and Second Generation*. Okemos, MI: Effective Schools Products, Ltd. http://www.effectiveschools.com/Correlates.pdf.

Liang, Xiaoyan. 2002. "Uganda Post-Primary Education Sector Report." Africa Region Human Development Working Paper Series, Africa Region, World Bank, Washington, DC.

Lindblad, S., and T. S. Popkewitz, eds. 2001. "Education Governance and Social Integration and Exclusion: National Cases of Educational Systems and Recent Reforms." Uppsala Reports on Education 34, Department of Education, Uppsala University, Sweden.

Lindblad, Sverker, Jenny Ozga, and Evie Zambeta. 2002. "Changing Forms of Educational Governance in Europe." *European Educational Research Journal* 1 (4): 615–24.

Lockner, Lance, and Enrico Moretti. 2001. "The Effect of Education on Crime: Evidence from Prison Inmates, Arrests, and Self-Reports." NBER Working Paper 8605, National Bureau of Economic Research, Cambridge, MA.

Lonergan, Bernard J. F. 1983. *Insight: A Study of Human Understanding*. London: Darton, Longman and Todd.

Lundgren, Ulf P. 2001. "Governing the Education Sector: International Trends, Main Themes and Approaches." In *Governance for Quality in Education*, 25–36, conference proceedings, Budapest, April 6–9, 2000. Institute for Educational Policy, Open Society Institute, and World Bank.

———. 2002. "Political Governing: Decentralization–Evaluation. Unit for Studies in Education Policy and Education Philosophy." University of Uppsala, Sweden. http://130.238.25.247/katarinas_ILU_portal/externt/forskning/ STEP/Publications.htm.

Lundgren, Ulf P., and Henrik Román. 2003. "The Swedish Upper Secondary School System: Context, Reforms and Implementation." Background paper for *Expanding Opportunities and Building Competencies for Young People: A New Agenda for Secondary Education*, World Bank, Washington, DC.

Macedo, Beatriz, and Raquel Katzkiwicz. 2002. "Rethinking Secondary Education." In *The New Secondary Education: A Path toward Human Development*. Santiago, Chile: UNESCO–OREALC.

Mahy, Mary. 2003. "Childhood Mortality in the Developing World: A Review of Evidence from the Demographic and Health Surveys." DHS Comparative Reports 4, ORC Macro, Calverton, MD.

Malhotra, Anju, Rohini Pande, and Caren Grown. 2003. "Impact of Investments in Female Education on Gender Equality." Draft, August 27, International Center for Research on Women, Washington, DC.

Marcelo, C. 2002. "Aprender a enseñar para la sociedad del conocimiento." *Education Policy Analysis Archives* 10 (35). http://epaa.asu.edu/epaa/v10n35/.

Marsh, Julie A. 2000. "Connecting District to the Policy Dialogue." Center for the Study of Teaching and Policy, University of Washington, Seattle.

Martinet, Marielle Anne, Danielle Raymond, and Clermont Gauthier. 2001. *La formation à l'enseignement: Les orientations; Les compétences professionnelles*. Québec: Ministère de l'Education.

Mayorga Salas, Liliana. 1997. "Violence and Aggression in the Schools of Colombia, El Salvador, Guatemala, Nicaragua and Peru." In *Violence at Schools: Global Issues and Interventions*, ed. T. Ohsako, 110–27. Geneva: IBE–UNESCO.

McEwan, Patrick J. 2000a. "The Potential Impact of Large-Scale Voucher Programs." Occasional Paper 2, National Center for the Study of Privatization in Education, Teachers College, Columbia University, New York.

———. 2000b. "Private and Public Schooling in the Southern Cone: A Comparative Analysis of Argentina and Chile." Occasional Paper 11, National Center for the Study of Privatization in Education, Teachers College, Columbia University, New York.

McGinn, Noel. 2002. "Why We Should End Reforms in Education." Regional Policy Dialogue, Working Paper, Education Network, Third Meeting, Secondary Education, Inter-American Development Bank. Washington, DC, April 4–5. http://www.iadb.org/int/DRP/ing/Red4/Documents/McGinnAbril4-5-2002ing.pdf.

McGinn, Noel, and Thomas Welsh. 1999. "Decentralization of Education: Why, When and How." Fundamentals of Education Planning 64, IIEP–UNESCO, Paris.

McMahon, M. 1998. "Education and Growth in East Asia." *Economics of Education Review* 17 (2): 159–72.

McMahon, W., and Boediono. 2001. "Improving Education Funding in Indonesia." In *Improving Education Finance in Indonesia*, ed. W. McMahon, with N. Suwaryani, Boediono, and E. Appiah. Policy Research Center, Institute for Research and Development, Ministry of National Education, Indonesia; UNICEF; UNESCO.

Means, Barbara, Christine Korbak, Amy Lewis, Vera Michalchik, William Penuel, John Rollin, and Louise Yarnall. 2000. *GLOBE Year 5 Evaluation: Classroom Practices*. Menlo Park, CA: SRI International.

Mehlinger, Howard D. 1996. "School Reform in the Information Age." *Phi Delta Kappan* 77 (6): 400–7.

Middleton, John, Adrian Ziderman, and Arvil Van Adams. 1993. *Skills for Productivity: Vocational Training and Education in Developing Countries*. New York: Oxford University Press.

Milligan, Kevin, Enrico Moretti, and Philip Oreopoulos. 2003. "Does Education Improve Citizenship? Evidence from the U.S. and the U.K." NBER Working Paper 9584, National Bureau of Economic Research, Cambridge, MA. http://www.nber.org/papers/w9584.

Mingat, Alain. 2004. "Issues of Financial Sustainability in the Development of Secondary Education in Sub-Saharan African Countries." Africa Technical Department, Human Development, World Bank, Washington, DC.

Moenjak, Thammarak, and Christopher Worswick. 2002. "Vocational Education in Thailand: A Study of Choice and Returns." Economics of Education Review 22 (1): 99–107.

Moretti, Enrico. 2000. "Estimating the Social Return to Education: Evidence from Longitudinal and Repeated Cross-Sectional Data." Department of Economics, University of California at Los Angeles.

Morine-Dershimer, G., and K. Todd. 2003. "The Complex Nature and Sources of Teachers' Pedagogical Knowledge." In *Examining Pedagogical Content Knowledge: The Construct and Its Implication for Science Education*, ed. J. Gess-Newsome, 21–50. New York: Kluwer Academic.

Morley, S., and D. Coady. 2003. *From Social Assistance to Social Development: A Review of Targeted Education Subsidies in Developing Countries.* Washington, DC: Center for Global Development and International Food Policy Research Institute.

Morris, Estelle. 2001. "Schools Achieving Success." U.K. Department for Education and Science (DES), London.

Morriseau, J. J. 1975. *The Mini-School Experiment: Restructuring Your School; A Handbook.* New York: New York Urban Coalition.

Moura Castro, C., M. Carnoy, and L. Wolf. 2000. "Secondary Schools and the Transition to Work in Latin America and the Caribbean." Technical Paper Series EDU-112, Sustainable Development Department, World Bank, Washington, DC.

Mukyanuzi, Faustin, 2003. "Where Has All the Education Gone in Tanzania? Employment Outcomes among Secondary School and University Leavers." Institute of Development Studies, University of Sussex, Brighton, UK.

Mullis, Ina V. S., et al. 2001. *TIMSS: Assessment Frameworks and Specifications 2003.* Amsterdam: International Association for the Evaluation of Educational Achievement (IEA) and Boston College.

Mundle, S. 1998. "Financing Human Development: Some Lessons from Advanced Asian Countries." *World Development* 26 (4): 659–72.

Murnane, Richard, and Frank Levy. 1996. *Teaching the New Basic Skills: Principles for Educating Children to Thrive in a Changing Economy.* New York: Free Press.

Murnane, Richard, Judith Singer, John Willett, James Kemple, and Randall Olsen. 1991. *Who Will Teach? Policies That Matter.* Cambridge, MA: Harvard University Press.

Murray, D., A. Smith, and U. Birthistle. 2003. "Education in Ireland." CAIN Web Service, http://cain.ulst.ac.uk/issues/education/docs/murray1.htm.

National Center for Education Development and Research. 2003. *Green Paper on Education in China: Annual Report on Policies of China's Education.* Beijing: Education Science Publishing House.

Ncube, Mkhululi. 2003. "Where Has All the Education Gone in Zimbabwe? Employment Outcomes among Secondary School and University Leavers." Institute of Development Studies, University of Sussex, Brighton, UK.

Noah, Harold, and Max Eckstein. 2001. *Fraud and Education: The Worm in the Apple.* Oxford: Rowman and Littlefield.

Northwest Educational Technology Consortium. 2002."Virtual Schools: What Do Educational Leaders Need to Know?" Paper presented at the 2002 Northwest Council for Computer Education (NCCE) Conference, Seattle, WA, March 13.

OECD (Organisation for Economic Co-operation and Development). 1994a. "New Technologies and Its Impact on Educational Buildings." Paris.

———. 1994b. "Vocational Education and Training for the 21st Century: Opening Pathways and Strengthening Professionalism." Background paper prepared for a high-level conference, "The Changing Role of Vocational and Technical Education," Paris, November 28–30.

———. 1998. "Thematic Review on the Transition from Initial Education to Working Life: Interim Comparative Report." DEELSA/ ED(98)11, Paris. http://www.olis.oecd.org/olis/1998doc.nsf/0/ fd9a032913054bf980256754005da81e?OpenDocument.

———. 1999. *Preparing Youth for the 21st Century: The Transition from Education to the Labour Market.* Paris: OECD.

———. 2001a. *Competencies for the Knowledge Economy.* Education Policy Analysis Center for Educational Research and Innovation. Paris: OECD.

———. 2001b. *Knowledge and Skills for Life: First Results from the OECD Programme for International Student Assessment (PISA) 2000.* Paris: OECD.

———. 2001c. *New School Management Approaches: Education and Skills.* Paris: OECD.

———. 2001d. *The Well-Being of Nations. The Role of Human and Social Capital.* Education and Skills Series. Paris: OECD.

———. 2003a. *Education at a Glance.* Paris: OECD.

———. 2003b. *Learners for Life. Student Approaches to Learning. Results from PISA 2000.* Paris: OECD.

———. 2003c. *Literacy Skills for the World of Tomorrow.* Paris: OECD.

———. 2003d. *Student Engagement at School: A Sense of Belonging and Participation. Results from PISA 2000.* Paris: OECD.

———. 2004a. *Attracting, Developing and Retaining Effective Teachers.* Final Summary Report. Paris: OECD.

————. 2004b. *Completing the Foundation for Lifelong Learning: An OECD Survey of Upper Secondary Schools*. Paris: OECD.

————. 2004c. "Raising the Quality of Educational Performance at School." Education Policy Brief, Paris.

OECD and UIS (UNESCO Institute for Statistics). 2003. *Literacy Skills for the World of Tomorrow: Further Results from PISA 2000*. Paris: OECD.

OECD and UNESCO (United Nations Educational, Social, and Cultural Organization). 2001. *Teachers for Tomorrow's Schools: Analysis of the World Education Indicators 2001 Edition*. Paris: OECD.

Ohsako, Toshio, ed. 1997. *Violence at Schools: Global Issues and Interventions*. Geneva: IBE–UNESCO.

Ouchi, W., B. Cooper, and L. Segal. 2003. "The Impact of Organization on the Performance of Nine School Systems: Lessons for California." http://www.sppsr.ucla.edu/calpolicy/Ouchi1.pdf.

Pande, Rohini, and Nan Marie Astone. 2001. "Explaining Son Preference in Rural India: The Independent Role of Structural vs. Individual Factors." Paper prepared for the annual meeting of the Population Association of America, Washington, DC, March 29–31.

Patrinos, Harry A. 1994. "Notes on Education and Growth: Theory and Evidence." HRO Working Papers 39, Human Resources and Operational Policy, World Bank, Washington, DC.

Patrinos, Harry Anthony, and David Lakshmanan Ariasingam. 1997. *Decentralization of Education: Demand-Side Financing*. Directions in Development Series. Washington, DC.: World Bank.

Penrose, Perran. 1998. *Cost Sharing in Education: Public Finance, School and Household Perspectives*. Education Research Paper 27, U.K. Department for International Development (DfID), London.

Phelps, Richard P. 2001. "Benchmarking to the World's Best in Mathematics: Quality Control in Curriculum and Instruction among the Top Performers in the TIMSS." *Evaluation Review* 25 (4): 391–439.

Porter, Michael E. 1998a. "Clusters and Competition: New Agendas for Companies, Governments, and Institutions." In Michael E. Porter, *On Competition*. Boston: Harvard Business School Press.

————. 1998b *The Competitive Advantage of Nations*. New York: Free Press.

Porter, Michael E., and Scott Stern. 1999. "The New Challenge to America's Prosperity: Findings from the Innovation Index." Council on Competitiveness, Washington, DC. http://www.compete.org/pdf/innovation.pdf.

Prawda, Juan. 1992. "Educational Decentralization in Latin America: Lessons Learned." A View from LATHR 27, Human Resources Division, Technical Department, Latin America and the Caribbean, World Bank, Washington, DC.

Prime Minister Service Delivery Unit. 2001. "Better Policy Delivery and Design: A Discussion Paper." London.

Pritchett, Lant. 1996. "Where Has All the Education Gone?" Policy Research Working Paper 1581, Policy Research Department, Poverty and Human Resources Division, World Bank, Washington, DC.

Psacharopoulos, George. 1994. "Returns to Investment in Education: A Global Update." *World Development* 22 (9): 1325–43.

———. 1996. "A Reply to Bennell." *World Development* 24 (1): 201.

———. 1997. "Vocational Education and Training Today: Challenges and Responses." *Journal of Vocational Education and Training* 49 (3): 385–93.

Psacharopoulos, George, and Harry Anthony Patrinos. 2002. "Returns to Investment in Education: A Further Update." World Bank Policy Research Working Paper 2881, World Bank, Washington, DC.

Psacharopoulos, George, and Maureen Woodhall. 1984. *Education for Development: An Analysis of Investment Choices.* New York: Oxford University Press.

Psacharopoulos, George, Jee-Peng Tan, and Emmanuel Jimenez. 1986. "Financing Education in Developing Countries." Education and Training Department, World Bank, Washington, DC.

Raywid, Mary Anne. 1996. *Taking Stock: The Movement to Create Mini-Schools, Schools-Within-Schools, and Separate Small Schools.* Urban Diversity Series 108. ERIC Clearinghouse on Urban Education. Institute for Urban and Minority Education, Teachers College, Columbia University, New York.

Renchler, Ron. 2000. "Grade Span." *ERIC Research Roundup* 16 (3). http://eric.uoregon.edu/publications/roundup/S00.html.

Revenaugh, Mickey. 2004. *Virtual School Report: A Quarterly Newsletter Focused on Effective Virtual K–12 Education.* Connections Academy, Baltimore, MD.

Riel, Margaret. 1996. "Cross-Classroom Collaboration: Communication and Education." In *CSCL: Theory and Practice of an Emerging Paradigm,* ed. Timothy Koschmann, 187–207. Mahwah, NJ: L. Erlbaum Associates.

Rissman, Jeef. 2000. "Same as It Never Was: Realizing the Vision of Smaller Communities of Learners at Arlington High School." Executive summary, Arlington High School, Saint Paul, MN. Report submitted to the Bush Educators Program IV, cosponsored by the Bush Foundation and the Carlson School of Management, University of Minnesota at Minneapolis.

Robert, François, and Jean Marc Bernard. 2003. "What Middle School Model Is Appropriate for Africa in the Coming Years?" Paper presented at the First Regional Conference on Secondary Education in Africa (SEIA), Kampala, June 9–13.

Robinson-Lewis, H. 1991. "Summative Evaluation of the School-within-a-School (SWAS) Program: 1988–1989, 1989–1990, 1990–1991." Kansas City Schools, Kansas City, KS.

Rodríguez, Alberto, and Kate Hovde. 2002. "The Challenge of School Autonomy: Supporting Principals." World Bank, Washington, DC.

Romer, Paul M. 1989. "Human Capital and Growth: Theory and Evidence." NBER Working Paper 3173, National Bureau of Economic Research, Cambridge, MA.

Ross, K., and R. Levacic, eds. 1998. "Needs-Based Formula Funding of Schools." IIEP–UNESCO, Paris.

Rychen, Dominique Simone, and Laura Hersh Salganik, eds. 2001. *Defining and Selecting Key Competencies.* Cambridge, MA: Hogrefe and Huber.

————. 2003. *Key Competencies for a Successful Life and a Well-Functioning Society.* Cambridge, MA: Hogrefe and Huber.

Sala-i-Martin, Xavier, Gernot Doppelhofer, and Ronald I. Miller. 2004. "Determinants of Long-Term Growth: A Bayesian Averaging of Classical Estimates (BACE) Approach." *American Economic Review* 94 (4): 813–35.

San Juan, Ana Maria. 2001. "Las expectativas de los jóvenes y su relación con la deserción escolar." Dialogo Regional de Política, Banco Interamericano de Desarrollo, Washington, DC.

Sánchez-Paramo, Carolina, and Norbert Schady. 2003. "Off and Running? Technology, Trade, and the Rising Demand for Skilled Workers in Latin America." Policy Research Working Paper 3015, Development Research Group, Public Services, World Bank, Washington, DC. http://econ.worldbank.org/files/25491_wps3015.pdf.

Scheerens, J. 1992. "Process Indicators of School Functioning." In *The OECD International Education Indicators,* 53–76. Paris: OECD.

Schuler, Sidney R., Syed M. Hashemi, Ann P. Riley, and Shireen Akhter. 1996. "Credit Programs, Patriarchy and Men's Violence against Women in Rural Bangladesh." *Social Science and Medicine* 43 (12): 1729–42.

Schuller, Tom, Angela Brassett-Grundy, Andy Green, Cathie Hammond, and John Preston. 2002. "Learning, Continuity and Change in Adult Life." Centre for Research on the Wider Benefits of Learning, London.

Schweitzer, Maurice, Lisa Ordoñez, and Bambi Douma. 2004. "Goal Setting as a Motivator of Unethical Behavior." *Academica of Management Journal* 47 (3): 422–32.

Sharan, Shlomo, Hanna Shachar, and Tamar Levine. 1999. *The Innovative School: Organization and Instruction.* Westport, CT: Bergin and Garvey.

Shulman, L. 1998. "Theory, Practice, and the Education of Professionals." *Elementary School Journal* 98 (5): 511–26.

Sinko, Matti, and Erno Lehtinen. 1999. *The Challenges of ICT in Finnish Education.* Juva, Finland: Finnish National Fund for Research and Development.

Sirotnik, Kenneth A. 2002. "Promoting Responsible Accountability in Schools and Education." *Phi Delta Kappan* 83 (9): 662–73.

Smith, Wilma F., and Richard L. Andrews. 1989. "Instructional Leadership: How Principals Make a Difference." Association for Supervision and Curriculum Development, Alexandria, VA.

Smith, William J., Lynn Butler-Kisber, Linda LaRocque, John Portelli, Carolyn Shields, Carolyn Sturge Sparkes, and Ann Vibert. 2001. "Student Engagement in Learning and School Life: National Project Report." Ed-Lex, Faculty of Law, McGill University, Montreal.

Souza, Paulo Renato. 2003. "The Reform of Secondary Education in Brazil." Background paper for *Expanding Opportunities and Building Competencies for Young People: A New Agenda for Secondary Education,* World Bank, Washington, DC.

Spector, Michael J. 1999. "Teachers as Designers of Collaborative Distance Learning." Prepared for Society for Information Technology and Teacher Education SITE99 International Conference, San Antonio, TX, February 28–March 4.

Stasz, Cathleen. 1999. "Academic Skills at Work: Two Perspectives." National Center for Research in Vocational Education, Graduate School of Education, University of California at Berkeley. http://ncrve. berkeley.edu/AllInOne/MDS-1193.html.

Subbarao, Kalanidhi, and Laura Raney. 1992. "Social Gains from Female Education: A Cross-National Study." World Bank Policy Research Working Paper 1045, World Bank, Washington, DC.

Tawil, S. 2001. "Curriculum Change and Social Inclusion: Perspectives from the Baltic and Scandinavian Countries." IBE–UNESCO, Geneva.

Temple, Jonathan R. W. 1999. "A Positive Effect of Human Capital on Growth." *Economics Letters* 65 (1): 131–34.

————. 2001. "Generalizations That Aren't? Evidence on Education and Growth." *European Economic Review* 45 (4–6): 905–18.

Teske, Paul, and Marc Schneider. 2001. "What Research Can Tell Policy Makers about School Choice." *Journal of Policy Analysis and Management* 20 (4): 609–31.

Tompkins, J. 1988. "Dropout Prevention Program, 1987–1988." Report of Evaluation, Des Moines Public Schools, Des Moines, IA.

Torres, Rosa Maria. 1998. "Repetición escolar: ¿Falla del alumno o falla del sistema?" *Evaluación, aportes para la capacitación* 1. Buenos Aires: Novedades Educativas. http://www.fronesis.org/documentos/ torres1995repeticion.pdf (accessed June 19, 2003).

Trent, William T. 1999. "The Changing Nature of Work and Its Implications." Department of Educational Policy Studies, University of Illinois at Urbana-Champaign.

Tsang, Mun C. 1996. "Financial Reform of Basic Education in China." *Economics of Education Review* 15 (4): 423–44.

U.K. DES (Department for Education and Skills). 2004. *14–19 Curriculum and Qualifications Reform.* London: DES.

UNDP (United Nations Development Programme). 2000. *Egypt Human Development Report 1998/99.* New York.

UNESCO (United Nations Educational, Scientific, and Cultural Organization). *Statistical Yearbook 1999*. New York: UNESCO.

———. 2002. *Seminario: Hacia la construcción de un nuevo sentido para la política educativa*. Working draft, IIEP, Buenos Aires.

———. 2004a. *Changing Teaching Practices: Using Curriculum Differentiation to Respond to Students' Diversity*. Paris: UNESCO.

———. 2004b. *Global Education Digest 2004: Comparing Education Statistics across the World*. Montreal: UNESCO Institute for Statistics (UIS).

UNESCO-OREALC (Oficina Regional de Educación para América Latina y el Caribe). 2002. *The New Secondary Education: A Path toward Human Development*. Santiago, Chile: UNESCO-OREALC.

University of Pittsburgh, Office of Child Development. 1996. "The Impact of School Transition on Early Adolescents." http://www.education.pitt.edu/ocd/publications/sr1996-06.pdf (accessed March 22, 2004).

Urdan, Tim, and Steven Kelin. 1998. "Early Adolescence: A Review of the Literature." Paper prepared for the U.S. Department of Education. Office of Education Research and Improvement, for the Conference on Early Adolescence, May 7–8.

USAID (U.S. Agency for International Development) and AED (Academy for Educational Development). 2003. "Digital Opportunities for Development: A Sourcebook for Access and Applications; LearnLink Models of Use and Case Studies." LearnLink, Washington, DC.

Van de Walle, Dominique, and Kimberly Nead. 1995. *Public Spending and the Poor: Theory and Evidence*. Baltimore, MD: Johns Hopkins University Press.

Van Dusen, Lani M., and Blaine R. Worthen. 1995. "Can Integrated Instructional Technology Transform the Classroom?" *Educational Leadership* 53 (2): 28–33.

Wang, Yidan. 2000a. "Public-Private Partnerships in Health and Education: Conceptual Issues and Options." In *The New Social Policy Agenda in Asia*. Manila: Asian Development Bank (ADB) and World Bank.

———. 2000b. "Public-Private Partnerships in the Social Sector: Issues and Experiences in Asia and the Pacific." ADBI Policy Papers Series 1, ADBI, Tokyo.

———. 2004. "Governance of Basic Education: Service Provision and Quality Assurance in China." Draft, World Bank, Washington, DC.

Waterreus, J. M. 2001. "Incentives in Secondary Education: An International Comparison." Amsterdam: Max Goote Expert Center.

Watts, A. G., and D. Fretwell. 2004. "Public Policies for Career Development: Case Studies and Emerging Issues for Designing Career Information and Guidance Systems in Developing and Transition Economies." ¹⁴ Bank, Washington, DC.

Smith, William J., Lynn Butler-Kisber, Linda LaRocque, John P.
Carolyn Shields, Carolyn Sturge Sparkes, and Ann Vibert.
"Student Engagement in Learning and School Life: National Pro,
Report." Ed-Lex, Faculty of Law, McGill University, Montreal.

Souza, Paulo Renato. 2003. "The Reform of Secondary Education in
Brazil." Background paper for *Expanding Opportunities and Building
Competencies for Young People: A New Agenda for Secondary Education*,
World Bank, Washington, DC.

Spector, Michael J. 1999. "Teachers as Designers of Collaborative Distance
Learning." Prepared for Society for Information Technology and
Teacher Education SITE99 International Conference, San Antonio, TX,
February 28–March 4.

Stasz, Cathleen. 1999. "Academic Skills at Work: Two Perspectives."
National Center for Research in Vocational Education, Graduate School
of Education, University of California at Berkeley. http://ncrve.
berkeley.edu/AllInOne/MDS-1193.html.

Subbarao, Kalanidhi, and Laura Raney. 1992. "Social Gains from Female
Education: A Cross-National Study." World Bank Policy Research
Working Paper 1045, World Bank, Washington, DC.

Tawil, S. 2001. "Curriculum Change and Social Inclusion: Perspectives
from the Baltic and Scandinavian Countries." IBE–UNESCO, Geneva.

Temple, Jonathan R. W. 1999. "A Positive Effect of Human Capital on
Growth." *Economics Letters* 65 (1): 131–34.

_____. 2001. "Generalizations That Aren't? Evidence on Education and
Growth." *European Economic Review* 45 (4–6): 905–18.

Teske, Paul, and Marc Schneider. 2001. "What Research Can Tell Policy
Makers about School Choice." *Journal of Policy Analysis and Management*
20 (4): 609–31.

Tompkins, J. 1988. "Dropout Prevention Program, 1987–1988." Report of
Evaluation, Des Moines Public Schools, Des Moines, IA.

Torres, Rosa Maria. 1998. "Repetición escolar: ¿Falla del alumno o falla del
sistema?" *Evaluación, aportes para la capacitación* 1. Buenos Aires:
Novedades Educativas. http://www.fronesis.org/documentos/
torres1995repeticion.pdf (accessed June 19, 2003).

Trent, William T. 1999. "The Changing Nature of Work and Its Implications." Department of Educational Policy Studies, University of Illinois
at Urbana-Champaign.

Tsang, Mun C. 1996. "Financial Reform of Basic Education in China."
Economics of Education Review 15 (4): 423–44.

U.K. DES (Department for Education and Skills). 2004. *14–19 Curriculum
and Qualifications Reform*. London: DES.

UNDP (United Nations Development Programme). 2000. *Egypt Human
Development Report 1998/99*. New York.

————. 1994. *Governance: The World Bank's Experience.* Development in Practice Series. Washington, DC: World Bank.

————. 1995. *Priorities and Strategies for Education: A World Bank Review.* Development in Practice Series. Washington, DC: World Bank.

————. 1998. "Colombia Appraisal Report." Washington, DC.

————. 1999a. *Confronting AIDS: Public Priorities in a Global Epidemic.* World Bank Policy Research Report. New York: Oxford University Press.

————. 1999b. *Education Sector Strategy.* Washington, DC: World Bank.

————. 2000a. "A Policy Note." In "Thailand Secondary Education for Employment," vol. 1, Washington, DC.

————. 2000b. "Secondary and Secondary Teacher Education Strategic Plan—Mozambique." Washington, DC.

————. 2001a. *Engendering Development: Through Gender Equality in Rights, Resources, and Voice.* World Bank Policy Research Report. New York: Oxford University Press.

————. 2001b. "Secondary Education in Uganda: Coverage, Equity, and Efficiency." Africa Region, Technical Department, Washington, DC.

————. 2002a. "Enhancing Learning Opportunities in Africa: Distance Education and Information and Communication Technologies for Learning." Africa Region Human Development Working Paper Series, Washington, DC.

————. 2002b. "Institutional and Governance Reviews: A New Type of Economic and Sector Work." PREM Notes 75, Policy Reduction and Economic Management, Washington, DC.

————. 2002c. "Secondary Education for Africa: Strategies for Renewal." Human Development Sector, Africa Region, Washington, DC.

————. 2003a. "Closing the Gap in Education and Technology." Washington, DC.

————. 2003b. "Education Reform for Knowledge Economy Project." Project Appraisal Document, Washington, DC.

————. 2003c. *Lifelong Learning in the Global Knowledge Economy: Challenges for Developing Countries.* Directions in Development Series. Washington, DC: World Bank.

————. 2003d. "Overall Trends in Secondary Curriculum Reforms in OECD and Balkan Countries." Working Paper, Human Development Network, Washington, DC.

————. 2003e. "Reforming Public Institutions and Strengthening Governance: A World Bank Strategy Implementation Update." Report 26357. Public Sector Board, Washington, DC.

————. 2003f. *World Development Report 2004: Making Services Work for Poor People.* New York: Oxford University Press.

————. 2004a. "Learning to Teach in the Knowledge Society." Human Development Network, Washington, DC.

_____. 2004b. "Lending for Secondary Education: Review of the World Bank Portfolio, 1990–2002." By Gillian Perkins. Operations Evaluations Department, Washington, DC.

_____. 2004c. "Bangladesh: Programmatic Education Sector Development Adjustment Credit." Washington, DC.

_____. Various years. *World Development Indicators*. Washington, DC: World Bank.

Wössmann, Ludger. 2000. "Schooling Resources, Educational Institutions, and Student Performance: The International Evidence." Kiel Working Paper 983, Kiel Institute of World Economics, Kiel, Germany. http://www.uni-kiel.de/ifw/pub/kap/2000/kap983.pdf.

Wylie, C., and R. Baker. 2002. "Inquiry into Decile Funding in New Zealand Schools." A submission by the New Zealand Council for Education Research to the Education Committee of the New Zealand House of Representatives, Wellington.

Xu, Bin. 2000. "Multinational Enterprises, Technology Diffusion, and Host Country Productivity Growth." *Journal of Development Economics* 62 (2): 477–93.

Yount, Kathryn M. 2002. "Like Mother, Like Daughter? Female Genital Cutting in Minia, Egypt." *Journal of Health and Social Behavior* 43 (3): 336–58.

Zgaga, Pavel. 2002. "Capacity Building for Curriculum Specialists in East and South-East Asia." IBE–UNESCO, Geneva.

Ziderman, A. 2003. "Financing Vocational Training in Sub-Saharan Africa." Africa Region Human Development Series, World Bank, Washington, DC.

Zirkel, Sabrina. 2002. "Is There a Place for Me? Role Models and Academic Identity among White Students and Students of Color." *Teachers College Record* 104 (2): 357–76. http://www.tcrecord.org ID Number: 10832.

Index

access and quality issues in
secondary education
challenges for developed vs.
developing countries,
207–08
country-specific efforts to reduce
availability gap, 52, 53f, 55
demand-side interventions, 45
educational attainment across
countries, 50–52
education quality and relevance
by country
cognitive performance
measurement, 55–56, 57f, 58
correlation between access
and achievement, 60–62
relative performance of
high-income countries, 60
variance in student
performance within
countries, 58–59
efforts by countries to expand,
39–40, 41f
equity considerations, 40, 43
incorporation of adults, 48, 50
level of system quality needed, 39
participation rates per capita,
39, 40f
principal challenges, 62
regional and country
disparities, 44
retention and completion rates
between income levels, 45–46
participation factors, 48

between urban and rural
areas, 46–48
Africa
enrollment growth
rates, 127–28
fees or cost sharing for
education funding, 152
Asia
expansion of secondary
education, 4–5
return from general vs.
vocational education, 86
secondary curriculum
overload, 92
asymmetric decentralization
country examples, 247–50
formula funding and, 159–60
Bangladesh, 179
Brazil
access to secondary
education, 113
state vs. local decision making,
175, 177
Cambodia, 26
Chile
fees or cost sharing for
education funding, 152–53
quasi-market conditions system,
185, 188, 189
China
educational decentralization, 174
expansion policies, 49
choice models, 183